THE GHOST RUNNER

The Tragedy of the Man They Couldn't Stop

The True Story of John Tarrant

BILL JONES

MAINSTREAM
PUBLISHING

EDINBURGH AND LONDON

First published in Great Britain in 2011 by
MAINSTREAM PUBLISHING COMPANY
(EDINBURGH) LTD
7 Albany Street
Edinburgh EH1 3UG

ISBN 9781845966065

A catalogue record for this book is available
from the British Library

Printed and bound by CPI Group
(UK) Ltd, Croydon, CR0 4YY

5 7 9 10 8 6 4

For Eric and Esme

Acknowledgements

Three people above all others have made this book possible: John's son, Roger, John's widow, Edie, and John's brother, Victor. Without their memories and precious archive – without their unfailing enthusiasm and support – Tarrant's story would never have been told in this form. Almost every letter John was ever sent has been carefully stored by Edie, along with a great many others which the couple exchanged during his protracted absences. In addition, Edie has kept all her late husband's meticulously logged running diaries, newspaper cuttings and – of course – his prized cups and medals. She also kindly gave me her permission to quote from his 'deathbed memoir' (and, except where stated otherwise, direct quotations from John are taken from that work, published as *The Ghost Runner* by *Athletics Weekly* in 1979). For these, and many other kindnesses, I am indebted to the Tarrant family.

Numerous others have helped along the way. Paul Krawczynski filled me in on Lamorbey and its history. John Sherratt, Pat Grundy, Clive Somers, Tom Hockenhull, Pat Carson, Tom Nadin and Dave Allsop helped colour in Tarrant's early days in Buxton. Alice Campbell – 'the girl next door' – shed crucial light on the teenage brothers. Tarrant's half-brother and -sister, David and Elizabeth (both still in Buxton), were always welcoming and insightful, and proffered plastic bags full of memorabilia relating to their mother, Maysie, and Jack Tarrant's early life.

Remarkably, almost all of Tarrant's contemporaries on the road and track were alive, hearty and thrilled to be talking about 'the ghost runner'. Notwithstanding a few plastic knees, the years had treated most of them kindly. In the Midlands, Arthur Keily (pushing 90) came to the door of his bungalow wearing a pair of football shorts. In Leeds, Bernard Gomersall's mind was as sharp and honest as his running. In Hereford, I spoke to Derek Davies and Ken Flowers, Tarrant's companions in the TA. Ron Hill, Brian Kilby and Joe Lancaster (still smoking and living in Italy) recalled his wilful, restless years. Robbie Brightwell, Derek Ibbotson and Tom McNab added hugely to my understanding of the amateur conundrum. Almost without exception, everyone I spoke to had an opinion on Jack Crump and his successors. I have quoted from Crump's autobiography, *Running Round the World*, published by Robert Hale in 1966. Another useful background read was David Kynaston's *Austerity Britain*, published by Bloomsbury in 2008, an evocative survey of the post-war years. The quotation from *Woman's Own* in Chapter Five is taken from that book.

Other runners and friends weighed in with vital contributions: Noel Henry, Eddie Gutteridge, Phil Hampton, Ron Bentley, Peter Bennett, Alan Phillips, Tony Fern, Gordon Eadie, Colin Hunt and Lynn Hughes. Many had kept letters from John, which they kindly shared with me. Dave Bagshaw's time – after a long spell in hospital – was particularly appreciated, as were the memories of Tom Osler, the runner who'd eased Tarrant through his jet-lagged 50-miler in Poughkeepsie.

In South Africa, the kindness and hospitality of Dave and

Adrie Box will always be remembered. Bickering merrily in the front seat, the couple took me on a grand tour of Tarrant's Durban, including a memorable drive in both directions along the route of the Comrades Marathon. Dave Box's vivid descriptions and insights were priceless, as were the powerful letters from Tarrant to his friend in the fading months of his life. John's South African 'Sancho Panza' Colin Shaw was a great help, too (he now drives a taxi), as were Derek Stringer, Tony Martin, James and Gerald Delport, Jim Skevington, Billy de Swardt, Ronnie Borain, Mick Winn and (speaking from New Zealand) Dave Upfold.

A proper appreciation of John's embrace of multiracial sport was only possible thanks to Rajendra Chetty and Farook Khan. The four Indian runners who came to see me on a dark, dank Durban night were Michael Govinder, Harry Govinder, Ram Sumer and V.S. Naidoo. As I explain in the introduction, that particular brief encounter was one of the most illuminating of this entire research process.

Words of gratitude, finally, for those who fit into no convenient category. Pat Butcher, the sportswriter, who has tended Tarrant's flame carefully for many years. Mel Watman, whose tenure at *Athletics Weekly* – and sensitive editing of John's memoir – made such a difference. Christine Tomkins, John's cousin, who told me the story of how the Tarrant boys were offered the choice between Edna's family and Jack's new home in Buxton. Roger Tarrant's wife, Susan, who helped discipline the archive and whose shrewd insights were always welcome. Ian Champion, at the Road Runners Club, who told me about the colour film footage. The family of Ned Waring, who provided detail of John's tireless benefactor. Kevin Morgan at ITV and Iain MacGregor, then at Mainstream, who got this project launched. Claire Rose, my editor, whose attention to detail far exceeds my own. And, last but also longest, my wife, Kay, who has heard me recap this story so many times she knows it as well as I. At times I'm sure she thought I was malingering in bed, but while she worked her day job, her constant support and patience have got me to the end, and her careful, honest scrutiny of the manuscript has made it a much better thing by far.

Contents

'And the street is singing with my feet . . .'
'Mirrorball', Elbow

Introduction

John Tarrant had been dead for nine years when I first heard his name. The man has been haunting me ever since. At the time, I was a researcher at Granada Television in Manchester, working on a documentary marking the centenary of the Salford Harriers. Running as an activity had never interested me, but the runners were fascinating, and this unfashionably working-class outfit linked arms with a fast-waning industrial age. It was 1984 in Margaret Thatcher's Britain, and every factory closure was taking a club like this down with it. Miraculously, the Harriers had somehow clung on. Although its members were mostly still drawn from Lancashire's imperilled blue-collar army, they'd wisely kept their overheads low. After 100 years, they still had no clubhouse, preferring instead to change in the back room of an immense Victorian alehouse before training in the leafy dell of Boggart Hole Clough, a nearby public park.

Over the decades, the Harriers had produced few stars, and most of those were forgotten: local heroes from a golden, prelapsarian age between the wars when thousands crammed athletics stadiums to watch Manchester's undernourished amateurs take on the world. During months of research, I'd met many of them, all well into their 80s, eking out their lives on memories and a state pension. Of them all, Eddie Hughes had been my favourite. In pictures taken during the 1920s, he always seemed to be shivering, fixing the trackside photographer with unsettling, ravenous eyes. But in his pomp he could run like a mustang, and no matter which Oxbridge superstar they shipped north to humiliate him, Eddie had usually prevailed. Now here he was – teary-eyed and pitifully thin – welcoming me into his Eccles council house.

We talked for hours. He made me tea and sandwiches, and he rolled out stories which could have been plundered from an Alf Tupper comic strip. In every one, he started as the underdog, and in every one he emerged as the victorious hero. 'There was one race where they brought an American and two Oxford runners just to make a fool of me,' he told me. 'I was 33–1 in the betting and the *Sporting Chronicle* said I hadn't a chance. But I told my father-in-law they'd have to have wings to beat me that day, and I told my best mate Harold Doggett to empty his pockets on me at those odds.' Had he won? 'Oh yes, I beat 'em. I beat 'em all by a yard and 'alf.'

When I got back to the Granada studios – just fifteen minutes away – there were two police officers in a panda car waiting for me. Eddie had dialled 999 after I'd left, saying some of his winner's medals were missing and that 'a television researcher called Bill' must have stolen them when his back was turned. I offered to return with the officers to Eddie's house, where I was met at the door by a weeping 83-year-old man. The medals had turned up down the back of his sofa, and he was beside himself with distress. How could he make it up to me? Did I want him to write a letter to my boss? No making up or apology was required.

'Those medals must mean a lot to you,' I said.

'I've got nothing else,' he replied. 'They're everything. They're all I have left. In my day, I knew blokes who'd pawn them for food, but I allus kept mine. I never got no money outta running. Not a single, solitary halfpenny.'

By the time we finished filming, I'd met many like Eddie Hughes – men who seemed entirely at odds with what was happening around me. Since the beginning of the 1980s, the last rites had been read over amateurism in sport. Big names were starting to tuck big sums away in their trust funds, and the age when a working man had run for the top prize of a wedding ring – as Eddie Hughes had once done – seemed improbably distant, and also very sad. Over pints of Robinsons bitter after the last night's shoot (a training run in Boggart Hole Clough), many in the Salford Harriers agreed, and as we drifted into the Moston night one of them thrust a disintegrating paperback into my hand. 'It's a shame you weren't here when John Tarrant was alive,' he said. 'You might want to have a look at this some time.'

Weeks, possibly months, passed before I took up his invitation. The book didn't seem especially seductive ('An *Athletics Weekly* publication', long out of print), and we had a film to edit and transmit. 'John Tarrant's Own Story', as the book was subtitled, might have been appealing if you'd heard of John Tarrant, but I hadn't, and around Granada Television, nor had anyone else. The title, however, kept catching my eye. Like this book, it was called simply *The Ghost Runner*, and reading the back-cover blurb I saw that the esteemed runner turned writer Christopher Brasher had billed it as 'a classic of sporting literature'. Flipping it over again, I looked closely at the face of the man on the cover. There was something odd about it.

Captured mid-stride, against the startling back-light of an autumn day, the runner I took to be Tarrant appears to have no eyes. With his head down, and his mouth sucking air, he shows us only empty black sockets. No hint of the man behind flickers in or out of them. All we are offered is a frowning bubble of concentration driving in our direction, all personality temporarily masked and all light in his eyes withdrawn. It is the photograph of a mystery.

'As a moving testimony to the power of the human spirit,' promised the back cover, 'John Tarrant's story will be of inspiration to all.' It was also only 110 pages long, and I was now sufficiently curious to pass beyond the cover.

Within a few hours, I had finished it. Rarely had I read a book that was so poorly written and yet so unutterably powerful and moving. Never had I come across a life quite so mystically fused with persistent tragedy and infrequent fulfilment as John Tarrant's. All my life, I had been in the thrall of adventure stories, knowing sections of Captain Scott's diaries by heart and able to quote verbatim from Mallory's Everest letters to anyone foolish enough to test me on them. By the 110th page, it seemed clear to me that Tarrant's story should be considered in the same breath as theirs – and that it was somehow remarkable that it wasn't.

Just like Scott's, Tarrant's autobiographical memoir had been penned in the knowledge of his imminent death. And just like Mallory, Tarrant had been consumed, and ultimately destroyed, by seemingly ludicrous goals. But unlike either of those men, Tarrant lacked literary flair, and neither the source of his fame (running) nor the nature of his dying (cancer) could compete with heroic failures of such magnitude. If his story was to persist, he needed a champion, and I rapidly became a master of the dinner-table precis of his life.

Born in London in 1932, he'd been sent to a brutal children's home in Kent in 1940 and languished there with his beloved younger brother for seven hateful years. By the time his father turned up in 1947, Tarrant's mother had died of TB, and a new stepmother was in place, together with a new life in Buxton, in the Peak District of Derbyshire. To stave off post-war teenage boredom, Tarrant had taken up amateur boxing, competing in a handful of fights – earning £17 'expenses' – before quitting for the sake of his health at the age of 19. From now on, he decided, running would be his sport. Naturally fit, and instinctively solitary, he took easily to the self-imposed disciplines of long-distance, but in the 1950s, when he tried to join a proper running club – the Salford Harriers – he made a naive, and fateful, mistake.

Deeming honesty to be the policy of gentlemen, Tarrant formally declared his £17 to the athletics authorities, who responded with a lifetime ban from all competition in Britain and overseas. As far as the sport's law enforcers were concerned, Tarrant had sullied the amateur codes by taking cash for sport. Barring a miracle, he was urged to find another way of blowing off steam. Tarrant wasn't the first to fall foul of the prevailing Corinthian purism. Others had been kicked into the sporting wilderness for lesser transgressions and never returned. But Tarrant was made of sterner stuff.

To fight back, he became what the tabloid press later dubbed 'the ghost runner'. Turning up in disguise at major long-distance events around the UK, he would wait until the starting pistol was fired before leaping in amongst the other runners. The more the stewards wailed, and gave chase, the more the general public took this 'man with no number' to their hearts. As official determination to stop him grew ever more desperate, Tarrant's subterfuge and cunning developed to match it. Arriving on the back of his brother's motorcycle, he would inch up to the race start, his running kit concealed under a long coat and his face hidden by a flat cap pulled down low to fox officials already armed with his photograph. Where necessary, once races had started, his brother would simply run protesting stewards off the road.

In the terrible years of frustration which followed, Tarrant never once gave up on the fight against his ban. Even when he finished in the top three, knowing his result would never be recorded, he kept going. Everyone knew he was world class, but Olympics after Olympics slipped by and he was never permitted to run for his country. Instead, he set world records at inhuman distances such as 40 miles and 100 miles. He travelled to the United States and lived alone in South Africa, defying the fury of international officials, to make his case and show the world that he was as good as – and invariably better than – the runners who didn't labour under the same teenage curse, the same ludicrous stigma of professionalism.

Supported only by his wife and family, he battled on, the bane of establishment luminaries like Harold Abrahams and the darling of left-oriented newspapers like the *Daily Mirror*, for whom his story epitomised the kind of vile snobbery and institutionalised bullying which should have been swept away with Churchill. For more than a decade, he'd been a cult hero – a niche sporting legend – and then as suddenly as he'd arrived he was gone, dead of stomach cancer in 1975.

From the moment I read it, the book became one of my most precious objects. Very few copies had ever been sold, and I knew it would not be easy to replace. Whenever an office move was looming, I always made sure Tarrant's memoir moved in my briefcase, and, 25 years after the book had been given to me, when Granada Television and I grew weary of each other, it was safely stored in my threadbare box of parting possessions. With time on my hands, I read it again properly for the first time in years, and if anything – in an age of Premier League venality – the potency of the story seemed even greater than before. To have been deprived of so much for so little seemed obscene.

And yet, sadly, on more attentive reading, the gaps in the story struck me more forcefully than ever. The mystery posed by the eyeless man on the cover seemed no closer to an answer. Whatever was going on behind those black sockets had not been addressed by this simple and affecting memoir. Beyond its impersonal, periodically bitter, narrative – with its dreary litany of race results – the three-dimensional John Tarrant lay unrevealed. Who truly was the man beneath the coat and cap? What was the truth of his story? And why was he still haunting me so many years after poor Eddie Hughes and his 'stolen' medals?

I've looked in a lot of places for the answers. I've met a lot of people, many of whom – oddly – seemed to have been expecting me, or someone like me, to turn up one day; they were happy, relieved and not remotely surprised that this man's life was finally being explored at last. Tarrant's indomitable widow, Edie, and his wonderful brother, Victor, have been principal among those helpers, and without them – and their mounds of letters, cuttings and diaries – this task would have been impossible. Alongside them, John's son, Roger, has been a good friend and shoulder, too. But one encounter above all others made me realise that however well – or badly – I set down this story I should never underestimate just how remarkable John Tarrant was.

After more than a year's research, I had travelled to Durban in South Africa to try to understand the final, troubling phase of Tarrant's life. The man himself had come this way 40 years before, driven – like Mallory – by an obsession which devoured and distorted him. His quest was not to scale a mountain but to win a race: the Comrades Marathon – the ultimate test for a long-distance athlete – 56 killing miles across the orange hilltops of the Zulu homelands. Like me, he had travelled to Durban alone. Unlike me, Tarrant had stayed, finding work on the city's hectic docks and a lonely bed in a workers' hostel at the stinking perimeter of a railway siding.

It is hard for a non-runner to understand his sacrifice, or the sacrifice he had enforced on his family. In Durban, the white South African officials loathed him, even more than their London counterparts. Tarrant was an outsider, a gatecrasher and a troublemaker whose illegal participation in South African races brought unwanted attention to a political system that was already reviled throughout the world. And yet the harder they tried to drive him out, the tighter Tarrant clung on. Not until the final night of my trip did I begin to make any sense of it.

All day, the skies had hung over the Indian Ocean, heavy with unseasonal rain. After dark – as usual – no one and nothing was stirring out in the white suburbs where I was staying. Huge dogs bristled behind towering security gates. Land Cruisers with blacked-out windows stalked silent avenues. With little to do but pack, I dozed lazily, only to be roused by a voice outside my hotel door telling me that I had four visitors. Did I want to see them? I was curious. My lodgings were remote. No visitors were expected, and on a foul autumnal night like this, I couldn't imagine why anyone would have travelled. I asked the manager to show them up, and I was astonished when he led four elderly Indian gentlemen, dripping with rain, into my presence. 'Are you the man writing about John Tarrant?' they asked.

They had come to tell me that Tarrant had been their hero; that during his stay in South Africa he had been the *only* white man who had ever dared to run with them; that he had defied vague police threats to join the first-ever non-racial road race; that he had treated them, and every other black, coloured or Indian runner, as a friend and equal; and that after he had gone they had established a marathon, and awarded a trophy, in his memory. From a plastic bag, one of them produced the now-tarnished silver cup. 'He left it for us before he went home,'

20

they said. 'That man knew no barriers.' Tarrant's name had been etched into its side.

It was a moving and unexpected encounter. In South Africa, Tarrant had found unconditional love from people who, like him, had been codified and condemned. It didn't explain everything, but it made sense of the happiness he'd found here. It made the portrait necessarily softer and much more complete.

It hasn't always been easy to like this man. At times – I'll admit it – I've loathed him. Self-centred, destructive and lacking emotional intelligence, he steered his adult life around the things he wanted, regardless of the impact on those closest to him. But hadn't that been true of my other childhood heroes? Force of will – is that what I admired? Like Scott and Mallory, Tarrant so often substituted courage for judgement. Utterly fearless on the track and equally unafraid of so-called grander men cast in gilded moulds, Tarrant had fought class bigotry and prejudice alone for so long – and had endured a childhood so bereft of tenderness – he no longer knew or cared what people said or felt about him.

Experience had made him impervious to opinion, indifferent to the creeping luxury of post-war Britain, unconcerned by money and his constant lack of it. Tarrant was ascetic, angry and – where work was concerned – incorrigibly lazy. Anything, and anyone, that ever stood in his way had to step aside until the great wrong was righted – which it never truly was. Even as he lay dying in a Birmingham hospital, the old amateur credo was limping shamefully away, but the change would come far too late to save John Tarrant, ever the outsider, even where history was concerned.

John Tarrant had been dead for almost a decade when I first heard his name. I had never seen him run and had obviously never heard his voice. Two years into the work for this book, one of those regrets was magically rectified. Word had reached me that a large collection of colour film had been lodged with Birmingham University, featuring road races from right across Tarrant's great era. Suddenly, there he was. Striding out under the Kodak sunshine on the Isle of Wight, his hair shaved up to his ears, and not a man on the road to touch him. Raising his arm powerfully in victory, he slumps alone into a deckchair and gratefully accepts a cup of tea.

At that moment, a smile splits his face, and those deep, hooded eyes come out from their hiding place. I had seen the ghost at last.

Prologue

They were looking for him. He could tell. But then, these days, they always were. The race stewards with their clipboards and clipped accents, their stopwatches and black ties and their humourless faces. He could see them now, probing every pair of eyes in the growing, muttering crowd. But not his. Not yet anyway. Standing back and alone, he'd become a master of invisibility: a grubby cup pulled down low over the dark hollow of his eyes; a long, hastily buttoned overcoat . . . and then the giveaway he prayed no one would see . . . the lean, protruding bare legs . . . and two feet laced into worn black track shoes.

Only minutes to go now – the stewards were retreating – and as the runners stretched out across the start, stinging the spring air with the tang of liniment, he felt the familiar sharp spike of envy and anger. How many times had he done this now? How many more times would it take?

Out on the street, the athletes stretched and limbered like horses in a paddock, the printed numbers on each man's vest, front and back, straining at their safety pins. All he wanted was a number. Christ, he was as good as they were. Better than most. Race after furtive race, he'd shown that. From Windsor to bloody Liverpool and God knows where else. There wasn't one he couldn't beat. All he wanted was a number. A lousy number on a lousy vest.

Every eye was on the tape now. He could look up safely. A portly steward propping up a crumpled trilby was readying the field for the gun. On your marks. Get set. Twenty-six miles. Twenty-six glorious miles. He stiffened. The voice, as always – to his ears – sounded regal and remote. Posh. Proper. Not like him. Not like him at all. More like the bloody Queen on the radio at Christmas. How many times? As many times as it bloody well takes, he thought. Until the end. Until I've won. Until it's decided.

The pistol cracked. The runners surged. And now he was running too, his coat and cap gone, sidestepping through the querulous, clamouring crowd. 'It's him! It's him!' But he was away now, gathering pace and closing in fast on the swarm of athletes ahead of him. The stewards couldn't catch him – not now, not ever – and tomorrow he'd be headline news again. The ghost runner. That's me. John Tarrant. Ghost runner.

This was what he did. This was what he was. All he ever was. All he ever wanted to be.

Chapter One

This Is What I Am

1940 – A Prelude

On a pleasant, warm morning in an already strange wartime spring, the hourly train to Sidcup was making its stop–start way out of central London. Looking down over the grey rooftops, passengers could work out the hidden lines of streets from the high-standing canopies of roadside trees, now coming fast into leaf. At the end of almost every terrace, rain-washed cricket stumps and goalposts had been chalked unevenly onto walls. But in the avenues and parks, along the pavements and back alleys, it seemed – to the eight-year-old boy drawing figures on the grimy carriage window – as if nothing was moving, as if the entire world had given up and fled.

Months before, there'd been other trains – hundreds of trains – trains draining every British city of its young, but the boy, who was called John, had not been among them. Now, finally, it was his turn for a ride on a train, not quite alone and not with the guilty thrill of evacuation, either. John's company, as the train shuffled ever deeper into the suburbs, was the only three other people he'd ever really known: his mother and father and his impassive younger brother, Victor, each one falling further into silence as the steam swept behind them and as John's fragile mother turned a face shining with tears towards the sunlight.

As Sidcup station drew nearer, the family ran out of things to say. John's parents could find no fresh words of encouragement. Every expression of hope had been exhausted. Everything would soon be back to normal, they promised. John's mother would be well again. The war would be over and won, in weeks, not even months, if the papers were to be believed. John shouldn't worry, and Victor, thankfully, would have an older brother to look out for him. We'll come and see you just as often as Hitler allows. We'll write and send you pocket money. We won't leave you forever. We love you. Don't cry.

Just a few strides from the station and there it was. Not the warm evacuee's embrace of a welcoming surrogate family or the wartime sanctuary of a hilltop farm. Instead, the brothers were entering a children's home in Kent, the Lamorbey Children's Home, so perfectly framed by its enormous circular park of arching deciduous trees that for a moment even John's downcast heart must have soared after the family's gloomy walk to its gates.

For a few hours – days at best – the boys would be buoyed by the promises of their departing parents. But what was to follow in the dreadful, lonely months and years ahead would extinguish any first-felt sense of hope and expectation. At just eight years of age, John's childhood was over. What he would subsequently brand a 'living hell' had begun.

John's new companions were not gleeful evacuees but the detritus of London's slums. Kids in care. Kids who spoke with their fists. Tribal urchins who coagulated naturally into feral gangs and who bullied outsiders and loners without mercy. To prevent anarchy, the staff at John and Victor's new 'home' perpetuated an ethos in which beatings were the norm and ritual humiliation often seemed the sole guiding principle. A boy who pissed in his bed, for instance, would have to stand on public display with the urine-soaked sheet draped over his head.

For almost seven years, this was to be John's home. He'd be a teenager before he was free of it, if indeed he was ever truly free of it. To the few who really knew John Tarrant, this was where he had been made. Every truculent, bitter outburst; every draining and debilitating race; every hard-fought stubborn mile of his extraordinary world records; every bloody snarl at authority: everything would somehow find its way back to what had happened at Lamorbey in Kent.

Not until 1947 – two interminable years into the peace – were he and Victor collected and returned to a normal family life. Except by then it was anything but normal. When the brothers were finally 'rescued', their mother was long dead, their father was remarried to a stranger and their new life was set to start again not in London but in the cold, unfamiliar embrace of the Pennines.

No matter how far or how hard John Tarrant ran in his life, he would never quite get away from its terrible start.

Eight years earlier

In later years, John Tarrant would usually cut a distant, remote figure, at his happiest when alone, with nothing to threaten him but the open road and a stopwatch. As a child, his world had been very different. It had been the crush and grime of the London which spills southwards from the Thames in a welter of bus routes and council blocks, with an alehouse seemingly on every corner and a decrepit snooker hall not far behind. It was then, and still is, a grainy, gritty unloved part of the city.

Ancient villages fused into an unfashionable urban melt. Walworth. Peckham. Brixton. Places, like Camberwell Green, where the strangled remnants of a rural yesteryear linger only in street names very much at odds with the concrete and the clamour. Here, ten minutes past the Elephant and Castle, at the point where the Peckham Road collides with Camberwell New Road, where the pound shops and pawnbrokers still turn a tidy profit, is Warner Road and the squat, prison-like block of flats opposite the bus depot which was to be John Tarrant's first family home.

He'd been born north of the river on 4 February 1932, at Queen Charlotte's Hospital, Shepherd's Bush, the first son of John and Edna Lilian Tarrant, a couple who'd married two years before in south Lambeth and whose life, to this point, had been distinguished only by the sort of anonymous poverty which would later characterise the desultory working years of their firstborn, now christened John Edward Tarrant, and happily kicking his strong legs in the family's airless top-floor flat.

The baby's father had been christened John, too, but to the world he was simply Jack, a name which perfectly suited the raffishly eccentric persona he'd cultivated, and which he would never quite let go. Even in his 70s, it was not unusual for Jack Tarrant to enter a bar wearing a full-length herringbone coat and a monocle, drop to his knees and sing a song before passing around his hat for beer money. His lifelong catchphrase – affected in an eye-rolling toff's accent – was 'I don't suppose you can lend me a dollar', and, although in later years the dollar became 'a fiver', it remained a slogan uttered as much in need as it was in jest.

Money was tight for the newly-weds. Jack had been working as a hotel porter when he'd married Edna Sorrell in 1930 on a warm Midsummer's Day in Lambeth, and now, two years later, he was still scraping the same living, supplementing a bellboy's wage with the tips he won around the lobbies and restaurants of hotels like the Regent Palace, tucked darkly behind Piccadilly. This was the young Jack Tarrant's manor; the world where he could duck and dive, smarm and smile, and lavish his roguish charm on wealthy guests struggling through rotating doors with their matching leather valises and hatboxes.

Everyone knew Jack Tarrant. Jack Tarrant was an operator, a charmer, a chancer, and even if he didn't have a bean in his pocket – even if the veneer was thin – he'd make sure people remembered him. A meticulously concocted look would take care of that. Silk scarves. Fedoras. Neat double-breasted suits and immaculately knotted ties. A constant rose in his lapel and a mat of dark hair slicked down with margarine and salt. Even the moustache was fastidiously precise, pared right down to the finest of lines along the width of his top lip (and in later life darkened with an eyebrow pencil).

But Jack was more than just a stereotypical wartime spiv. Unlike his son John – who would easily be browbeaten by men of rank – his father knew how to speak to and manipulate these people. He knew how to work them and work the scams. It was in his nature; it was in his blood. Jack's grandfather James had been a stagecoach driver. James's son Charles Tarrant had maintained the stables of Duntisbourne House – 70 acres of rolling Cotswolds seclusion – presiding over two grooms and ensuring that the horses were constantly ready for a spot of hunting or an excursion to the spa at Cheltenham.

Jack understood class but didn't want a country life. His father, Charles, might have been happy breeding horses for the gentry, but it wasn't for him. Jack had been born and raised around Cirencester, but before he was 20 he'd decamped to London to experience the thrilling rush of a city prising its way out of a depression. By 1930, he was living in Miles Street, Lambeth, spending his days, and much of the nights, trolleying suitcases, ever ready with a quip and a needy, dog-eyed pause before guests, luggage and gratuity disappeared forever behind the rattling cage gates of a hotel lift. By then, Jack had more than his own survival to worry about. Early that year, he'd met and proposed to a parlour-maid called Edna Lilian Sorrell. Less than 12 months later, she was pregnant for the first time.

Very few photographs of Edna survive, and those that do have a sorrowful air. In one – taken when she was just eighteen – she peers sadly off camera through watery eyes ringed with tiredness. Her stockings have wrinkled around the back of her ankles. Her lips are thin and pale and turned down at the corners. Wearing a drab suit and a hat pulled down over her dark eyebrows, she looks, for a teenager, to be desperately sad. Details of her early years, or of her courtship with Jack Tarrant, are as elusive as the photographs. Until his own death, almost 50 years later, Jack would always carry a small picture of Edna in his wallet, but no letters have survived, and she was to die long before her children were able, or sufficiently interested, to find out.

Born in Middlesbrough in 1908 – the daughter of a 'motor engineer' – she had, like countless teenage girls in Edwardian England, chosen a life in service, a choice which drew her south to London and eventually into the seductive orbit of the wisecracking valet-porter Jack Tarrant.

However they'd met, the couple now had a life together – and by February 1932 they had their first child, John Edward, a responsibility which stretched chronically limited resources. Paid badly for only eight hours, Jack was forced to stitch four extra, unpaid hours onto his daily shift, relying on his charm and chutzpah to tempt tips out of weary travellers thankful for his muscle. For Edna, these were long and lonely days. The fifth-floor rooms of their flat were small, and cold in the winter, and the building had been designed in 1915 by architects with little awareness of the needs of a young mother.

There was no lift, and the folding buggy was half a century away. On warm days, Edna would walk the pram to the main road and slalom between honking London buses before passing away an hour on Camberwell Green, once the centre of village life, now filmed permanently with the fine black soot of the city. As the traffic thumped by, she had a great deal on her mind. Climbing up and down the half-lit stairs of their block was proving more of an effort than it should have done for a young woman in her mid-20s. Even with the baby and the shopping, she surely shouldn't be as breathless as this. Perhaps it was only her hormones. Less than a year after the birth of her first child, Edna was pregnant again, and in May 1933 John was joined by a brother, Victor Arnold. They would very soon become inseparable, and nothing, until John's death in 1975, would break that bond.

Unexpectedly, the arrival of this second child was to ease the growing Tarrant family's problems rather than worsen them. Even the hard-pressed local council could see that a top-floor flat was unsuitable for raising two very young children, and a move was arranged to new accommodation in Tooting. It wasn't far away – half an hour by bus, south through Clapham and down the Balham High Road – and yet, in every respect, it was a joy-filled switch for Edna, who'd grown crushed and weary in Camberwell, and whose health was now causing significant concern. A new home might be a happy, restorative distraction. A proper house, too – at 241 Cowick Road, a fine pre-First World War red-brick terrace on a quiet, airy, neighbourly street, with a small garden at the back and an even smaller one at the front guarded by a gate and a thickly rambling privet.

Today the house and the street have changed very little, even if the neighbourliness – or some of it – has gone. Almost every door sports the same sticker: 'no uninvited callers'. The occasional car streaks past too fast spilling rap from open windows. And yet, for all this, there's still a pleasing calm about the place that Edna and her sons must have loved. A few hundred yards away on Upper Tooting Road, things are very different. Every square inch of the pavement seems measled with black dots of hardened gum. There's a shop called Dreamland boarding up its windows, permanently. Nearby, in another shopfront, Punjabi suits sparkle and shine across from Dado's Indian English Afro Grocery, promising pure basmati to the rain-dodging shoppers otherwise torn between the Polish deli, the halal food emporium and TK Maxx. If it was round here that Jack Tarrant once went looking for an anaemic pre-war pint of flat London bitter, pulled amidst the Woodbines and mirrors of a street-corner pub, then he'd struggle today. The Upper Tooting Road has moved on, and Cowick Road's former council houses sell for £265,000 and more.

In 1938, for the young John Tarrant, the few months he spent in Tooting were beyond mere value. They were priceless. 'To this day I can remember the joy of my mum and dad,' he recalled – a thrill which was amplified when Edna discovered Tooting Bec Common. Turn left out of the front door, then left again, and there it was. Enormous. A revelation. A woody oasis of sycamore and oak, rowan and ash, criss-crossed by looping secret paths and switchbacking tracks hardened by the passage of kids' bicycles. On top of the freedom of a front and back garden, John and Victor had an entire park to explore – and a black and white terrier called Dixie to explore it with. In December 1938, the brothers had been given the dog as a Christmas gift, and if Jack wasn't portering and the sun shone, the entire family would make their way to the rustling green respite of the common.

Notwithstanding the sooty fogs which could still reduce London's buses to a crawl, the Tooting air would have done Edna good, but it was still not enough to put a brake on the accelerating decline in her health. By 1939, she had almost certainly been diagnosed with a complex cocktail of illnesses which included sugar diabetes and that curse of pre-war inner-city dwellers, tuberculosis. On its own, TB – or consumption as the Victorians preferred to label it – would have presented Edna's doctors with a significant challenge. Despite decades of research, it was still a disease which perplexed and mystified scientists. For its sufferers, however, there was no mystery. Edna's symptoms would have been horrifying. Coughing blood, night fevers and weight loss led to exhaustion and often death. In severe cases, the infection could even move from the patient's lungs into the lymph glands and spine, and around 100 million people were to die of it in the twentieth century alone.

By 1946 there would be a vaccine, but it had come too late for Edna. Before then, there was no agreed effective treatment. Worse still, it was a disease which continued to evoke a sort of superstition one would associate with the Dark Ages. Within living memory of Edna's infection, there were still people who believed it to be caused by excessive masturbation. What was indisputable was that when combined with diabetes, tuberculosis was extremely hard to treat. And what made matters even worse for Edna Tarrant and her family – and just about everyone else – was that Britain had just declared war on Germany.

It was a moment John would remember with pinpoint clarity for the rest of his life. On a warm September afternoon, less than one blissful year after moving to Cowick Road, Edna called the children in from the front garden to listen to the radio. The Prime Minister was making his national call to arms, and as the radio orchestra hit the last note of 'God Save the King', Britain's Second World War began to the sound of an air-raid siren droning fretfully over the Tooting skies. For the first time, the Tarrants scrambled out of the kitchen door and down into the corrugated-iron Anderson shelter Jack had assembled in the back garden. Over the coming months, like millions of Londoners, the four of them would become familiar with the dark, dripping damp and the chilly metallic tang of their refuge.

By day, Edna strove to personalise it, softening its bleak interior fittings with familiar items from the house. By night, she could do nothing to ease the terror of her two young boys, and although no bombs fell until the following year, the constant false alarms ate steadily at her family's nerves. 'It worried me a great deal and poor mum's health began to get worse,' wrote John many years later.

They were not alone in their state of panic and confusion. As war was declared on Hitler's Germany, gloomy pundits were predicting four million civilian casualties in London. During those first four fevered days of September 1939, in what was billed as Operation Pied Piper, around three million city-dwellers were evacuated from Britain's urban target zones, most of them young children, and many of them singing excitedly as they embarked on their great adventure.

Within one week, every fourth Briton would have a new address, but none of the Tarrant family was among them. Whilst the image of a child-free London read well in the newspapers, it was simply not true. Only half of Britain's school-aged children ever boarded those trains for the countryside, and most of them would be dragged back by Christmas when the Luftwaffe failed to show.

For the remainder, there were too many complications.

Parents who couldn't, or wouldn't, let their children go. Parents with very young children – brothers and sisters – who simply couldn't, or wouldn't, be separated. Parents who were unwell, and whose circumstances were already compromised by ill health. For some or possibly all of these reasons, the Tarrants clung together in Cowick Road through the 'phoney war' of that winter, choosing the false alarms and bitter nights in the Anderson Shelter over the separation of evacuation.

John and Victor were now just seven and five years old. Jack and Edna were 32 and 31. If, in the privacy of their thoughts, they imagined the New Year would bring an early end to the nightmare, they were wrong. There was a new complication on the horizon, one that would terminate the happy family life they'd constructed in Tooting. In the autumn of 1939, every fit male between the ages of 18 and 41 had been put on notice of conscription. The armed forces urgently needed men to fight, and only those employed in vital work would be exempt – a category that wasn't likely to include the duties of a London hotel porter, even one as adroit and amenable as Jack Tarrant. To begin with, only those able-bodied men aged between 20 and 23 would be called to arms, but it wouldn't be long before the older ones joined them. Unless Hitler lost his nerve, the clock was ticking towards the start of Jack's war, and behind their blackout curtains, after John and Victor were asleep, Jack and Edna argued deep into the night over what they should do for the best.

By May 1940, it was a decision which could no longer be deferred. Edna's condition was worsening, and against the growing threat of a German bombing campaign, Jack had been called up to man the anti-aircraft batteries being deployed in and around the capital. It was an impossible situation with a terrible outcome. John and Victor would be put immediately into the care of London County Council. 'There was no alternative but for the family to break up,' John remembered later, in characteristically neutral tones which entirely masked the trauma and sense of frantic despair they must all have felt.

The Tarrants' tearful train journey down to Sidcup marked the end of their time together as a family. The four of them would never again live under the same roof. The two boys would be left at the gates of the Lamorbey Children's Home; Edna would be taken to a sanatorium, where she would spend most of the next two years; and Jack would march off to be measured up for his uniform.

No one would ever know John Tarrant quite like Victor did. And in later years, when he was quizzed about his intriguing brother, Victor would always insist that the answers could be found in one place. It was in the harsh dog pit of the Lamorbey Children's Home, he would say, that Tarrant's persona began to take shape. Ascetic, tough and anti-authoritarian. Self-sufficient and solitary. A loveless boy, indifferent to material possessions, with a ferociously sensitive radar for perceived injustices. A boy who does not give in or squeal out in pain. A child of spartan qualities, whose closeness to his younger brother quickly became the key to each sibling's survival and would prove crucial to John's subsequent emergence as one of the most controversial figures in post-war British sport.

Victor may have been right. Hundreds of children were to have their lives retooled by Lamorbey. Opened in 1902 by the Poor Law Union of Deptford and Greenwich, it ran – latterly as the Hollies Children's Home – until its eventual closure in 1998, and for its surviving alumni the experience still casts a compelling shadow. On a fast-growing website, you can scroll through their memories – many of them happy ones of days evoked with fondness or wistful regret. Not every member of staff, it seems, was a bad apple. Not every regime was rotten.

Other messages on the website tell a very different story. At the end of their time at the home, the Tarrant boys would leave together. In the home's early days, others were not so lucky. Upon arrival, brothers were often separated from brothers, sisters kept apart from sisters. In some rare cases, siblings lost each other forever. Others, for whatever reason, simply never saw their parents again. Among the notices left in recent years on the website, one plaintive message reads simply: 'I am looking for any information about my family as I have just found out my parents were not killed during the 2nd World War as I originally thought. I was only about 3/4 years old when I left The Hollies . . .'

In the spring of 1940, the Tarrants felt certain that Lamorbey would not be for long. Edna would improve and the war would end. In the meantime, John and Victor felt encouraged by the woody splendour they had discovered behind the gates. To this day, in its new guise as an upmarket housing estate, it's still a calming retreat from the noise of nearby Sidcup, where black-blazered schoolchildren pour clumsily from their morning trains sporting the motto 'Strive to Succeed' on their breast pockets. A few yards from where the kids now line up at bus stops are the same imposing buildings which the Tarrants came to loathe so ferociously, standing in the same benign circle of parkland and (rather frustratingly) exuding not one scintilla of menace.

Just like Cowick Road, the fabric of John Tarrant's former world has changed very little while its monetary value has been transformed. The formerly ice-cold pool block, where children once turned blue in the freezing water, is now a country club. 'Beauty room by appointment.' 'No card, no entry.' The architect Thomas Dinwiddy's iconic clock-faced water tower has been converted into flats. The huge dormitory blocks have been recast as luxury apartments, and at night their wheelie bins are filleted by foxes whose ancestors no doubt knew thinner pickings before the children moved away.

Around the edges of the park, indifferent new builds have filled older gaps, but it's still the enormous Edwardian buildings of this former campus for London's washed-up problem kids which catch the eye, many of them still carrying the names they were given by the good men of Greenwich and Deptford over a century before. The Beeches. The Firs. The Oaks. Red-brick fortresses rising four floors from their gardens. Among them is The Limes – its exterior absolutely unchanged – the same vast dormitory where John Edward Tarrant first unrolled his blanket in the spring of 1940, fully expecting to be back with his parents within a matter of months, not knowing he would still be sleeping there seven years later.

John and Victor were now in care. Responsibility for their well-being and for every second of their waking day had been transferred. However long the pair of them stared ruefully at the gates, Jack and Edna were not coming back, and, if they were to survive, there were some quick adjustments to be made. Not all of the 600 children crowded into the home's dormitories had been reared with the same care that Edna had lavished on her boys. Many of them were hard, street-fighting kids, East End boys, unwanted waifs with nothing to go back to and even less to fear. Victor would later liken them to 'packs of wolves', kept in check, night and day, by a 60-strong staff for whom routine and discipline were the twin tenets of an unforgiving faith.

John and Victor would get a taste of both those things almost immediately. Clutching each other tightly, they were frogmarched to a matron who inspected them for lice and then hit both boys with a stick for holding hands. 'We're not having that,' she said, before separating the brothers and assigning them to the dormitories where they would live, Victor to Birch House, John to Lime House. That night, for the first time ever, they would not be sharing a bedroom. Very rarely were siblings allowed to stay together, and Victor and John would see each other only at church and on the short walk to and from the nearby school.

Next, the brothers were introduced to their new 'parents'. In a grotesque parody of home life, each dormitory block had its own 'mother' and 'father' – members of staff – whom the children were encouraged to address as 'Mum' and 'Dad'. Like every fresh arrival, John and Victor were given a number, which they found already stitched into the second-hand clothing left in a box at the end of their new beds. Unlike names, number tags didn't need to be removed when the clothes were outgrown and handed to a new arrival. Victor was No. 17 and John was No. 8. Each wore a uniform of threadbare, grey short trousers, patched grey pullover, grey socks and studded black boots, enhanced for schooldays with a blue and white tie, a black raincoat and a cap. There was also a tiepin, which John was soon beaten for losing. If they were unlucky enough to be at Lamorbey when they reached 14, they'd be allowed to wear long trousers.

Lights out was at 7.30 p.m. (even on Christmas Day), but what little sleep the pair got on that first night must have been challenged by wretched dreams. Around them were dozens of other dislocated children, and the sound of nightly weeping was to become as familiar to the Tarrants as the air-raid sirens. Invisible behind the veil of darkness, it seemed that even the pack leaders of Lamorbey's 'wolves' wished they were somewhere else.

The next day – like every day – began at 7 a.m. with a dormitory inspection, during which any tear-streaked child who'd wet his bed would be caned, deprived of breakfast and ordered to stand with the yellow-stained sheet over his head. Passing boys were given dispensation to punch the bed-wetter, who was then dispatched to the laundry room with the sheet still draped across him. At night, according to John, the punishment continued. Bed-wetters were made to stand bare-footed in their nightshirts on cold concrete until the house father was ready for sleep. Few crimes generated more paranoia or rumour. It was whispered that some children tied string around their penises at night to stop themselves soiling their sheets. It was even claimed that one staff member attached car batteries to the rubber sheets, a mild electric shock being his chosen way of tackling the endemic nightly leakages. No one seemed entirely sure if any of it was true, but no one was ready to completely discount the stories, either.

Those boys who'd got through the night unscathed would join the queue for the outside toilet and wash house. Bare-chested, they'd ablute in cold water, dress and then make their way to the canteen for 7.30 a.m. Wartime shortages ensured that breakfast, like all the meals, was served in tiny quantities – a problem for Victor, who in adult life would work as a chef, and who invariably felt hungry. After a year at the home, he was assigned the daily task of lighting the staffroom fires in his dormitory block, a duty he enjoyed and for which a kindly house officer rewarded him with the welcome crusts from her morning toast.

When he was caught eating them by another staff member, Victor refused to reveal where they had come from and was birched for his silence. 'They put a piece of rubber in my mouth, stripped me naked and laid me over a card table with the whole block watching,' he remembers. The old hands had told him to count down – six, five, four, three, two, one – so he'd know when it was nearly over, but in Vic's memory, the beating didn't stop when he reached one and he fainted. Three weeks later, what with the rubber sheets and the raggedy school shirts, the wounds still hadn't healed. During a ball game – 'skins and vests' – in the home's gymnasium, his PE teacher spotted the sores on Victor's back and legs and took him to the headmaster for an explanation. After that, Victor was never beaten again. 'Maybe it was a coincidence . . . Maybe it's because I was eight years old at the time.'

After breakfast came the daily pre-school parade, during which the home's superintendent strode darkly between the motley ranks of trembling children, summoning overnight reports on their behaviour from each dormitory's 'mum and dad'. Miscreants would be caned six times across the hand, but it was always the hypocrisy – not the actual beatings – which festered the longest in the young John Tarrant's head. 'On a cold day the superintendent wore woollen lined gloves up to his elbows . . . lecturing us how to keep our hands warmed by rubbing them towards the flow of blood to the heart.' Bitterly he noted every double standard. 'Although there was rationing due to the war,' he noted wryly in his memoir, 'the House Father and Mother appeared to go short of nothing at meal times.'

For the children, having already run the gauntlet of wet beds and canings, their daily schooling came as something of a relief. At 8.30 a.m., strung out in a seemingly endless file, the entire population of Lamorbey would snake silently through the grounds, past the two murky ponds and out between the wrought-iron gates, heading either to Burnt Oak Primary School or Black Fenn Boys' School. For these few minutes, it was possible to locate your brother or your sister, and every weekday John would seek out Victor before the school gates closed and the three Rs began. It was here that John perfected the laboured, left-handed writing that became familiar to those on the receiving end of his campaigning correspondence, every word placed perfectly between the lines with what sometimes feels like an immense effort of concentration.

Today, Black Fenn is gone, but Burnt Oak – just 100 yards from the old home's gates – is much as it always was. Built in 1903, it has fairly recently acquired a new neighbour across the street, Bexley Youth Centre ('putting young people first'), and its catchment no longer includes the dislodged juveniles of London's inner suburbs. Today's intake get whisked home in cars by waiting mums to watch cartoons or log on to Facebook. In 1940, for Lamorbey's displaced strays, the school bell at 3.45 p.m. meant a reverse march around the corner to their dormitories, where the early evening was spent polishing shoes or darning holes in their clothing, a skill which never deserted John, and which ensured that even when his battered running shoes were held together by sticking tape his socks, at least, were entirely free of holes.

On weekdays, no free time was allowed, and every dormitory block was alive with activity – none of it unsupervised. Bucketloads of soil-black potatoes were scrubbed and peeled. Two boys from each floor would polish their section of the mahogany banister which snaked and gleamed down to a hallway where more boys worked up a lethal shine on the parquet floor. There were toilets to clean, coal buckets to fill and house officers' fires to rekindle.

Unsurprisingly, the children were constantly hungry, wolfing down the nightly white bread and tea – and even eating their apple cores – to stave off the pangs. But sometimes even hunger couldn't force them to eat the food on offer. Victor Tarrant had never seen tripe before, let alone tasted it, and baulked when it appeared one evening on his plate. The next day, at breakfast, dinner and tea, the same uneaten frill of tripe was placed in front of him. And so it went for the next three days until 'I finally had no choice but to stand on a bench and eat it . . . It had gone green, but I still swallowed it down.'

In the few precious minutes the children found for themselves, frustration and resentment sometimes boiled over into mischief. A regular evening dare for new boys required them to sneak downstairs into the house mother's sitting room and open the curtains to prove that they'd been there. When John Tarrant's turn came – according to Victor – he was apprehended by a master 'waving a rubber baton up and down'. In the beating that followed, ten-year-old John almost passed out. 'He knocked him down the stairs, then hit him over the head, across the face, then he picked John up and lashed into him again.'

Bedtime, and lights out couldn't come soon enough, for everyone, children and staff. In the five blocks housing the boys, and the twenty smaller cottages housing the girls, the uniquely deep silence of the blackout would fall briefly over the entire Lamorbey complex. For a precious few minutes, there'd be only the whispering of the trees or the barking of a fox. But it wouldn't last long. Soon the whispers and the coughing would begin, followed inevitably by the sound of muffled sobbing. And once the coast was clear – and the house officers were away warming their hands over their blazing coal fires – you'd hear the sound of a window being gingerly opened, and very soon after the glassy sound of piss splashing in the grave-dark gardens far below.

Everyone had heard dark stories about Lamorbey. Children were said to have vanished into the night, desperate to get back to their parents. There were even rumours of suicides – of children hanging themselves from the banisters – but, like those of the rubber sheets and the car batteries, it was never clear whether the stories started in fact or in febrile, whispered schoolboy chatter. No regime which functions without love or affection can get by without casualties, and, in that respect, Lamorbey would be no different. 'Those years were a living hell . . .' insisted John, 'The place was worse than any borstal and yet none of us were criminals.'

Despite loathing every brick of Lamorbey, the brothers never once shared their unhappiness with their parents. Indeed, 30 years would pass before Victor told his father that 'we never told you for we knew how much you loved us and worried about us'. Instead, the two boys waited patiently for the news that they would be going back home. All over Britain, thousands of evacuees already were. They'd been retrieved from their country homes and reunited with their familiar beds and toys. Meanwhile, for John and Victor, weekly letters from Edna were a solace, and the sixpence she enclosed for weekend sweets at the Sidcup tuck shop was a joy. But her visits had become more infrequent as the war, and tuberculosis, took hold. Just when they wanted their mother to be strong and to rescue them, it must have been shockingly clear to both boys just how steep her physical decline had become.

In a remarkable handful of photographs of those rare visits which have survived, it's possible to sense the despair in their faces. In one, John's lifeless eyes peer sadly into the lens, his knees dirty, one sock rolled half down and both hands resting wearily on his waist. In another, he and Victor are standing back to back, indifferently clutching new toys. Victor has a wooden train but stares emptily into the distance. John appears to have a sailor's cap. In the background, the ancient oaks of Lamorbey are in full leaf. It must be early summer 1941. In less than a year, Edna would be dead.

It wasn't easy for their father either. Since his call-up, Jack had been attached to the Royal Artillery as an anti-aircraft gunner, stationed in London in preparation for the Luftwaffe bombers which everyone fully expected to come. In his official army photograph, he looks uncomfortable and impatient, his eyes narrowed beneath the trademark dark Tarrant brow, a man with a lot on his mind and very little of it the German war machine. The staff at Lamorbey, on the other hand, were thinking of little else.

During the long, warm August of 1940, the Battle of Britain was fought out in the languid blue skies above them. The children had seen dogfights between German Messerschmitts and the RAF's nimble Hurricanes. Victor and John had stared in open-mouthed fascination as at least one plane plunged into the golden fields beyond their horizon. At the local school, as summer ebbed away, the teachers held regular air-raid drills, instructing tittering children to lie face down on the ground, hands over heads, should they be caught outside in the middle of an attack. So far, the air-raid sirens had been only drills, or false alarms, but on 7 September 1940, the laughing stopped and the terror began. That afternoon, escorted by more than 500 fighters, 364 German bombers attacked strategic targets around the Port of London. The same night, another 133 bombers crossed the English Channel, and by daybreak on the 8th more than 400 Londoners were dead and another 1,600 injured.

When the Poor Law Union of Deptford and Greenwich had built Lamorbey, they had chosen their site well, but even they could not have anticipated a war of terror from the air which put 600 children directly under the flight path of the biggest aerial armada ever seen. Almost every night for eight months, John and Victor cowered in the home's massive subterranean shelters as the bombers flew towards the city. At its worst, they were kept underground for three days and three nights, the demoralising endless drone of the planes clearly audible, along with the dull distant thump of impact and detonation.

For once, the staff didn't need a cane to maintain silence.

Almost everyone had someone back up there under the bombs. Somewhere in that burning city, John and Victor's mother was helplessly ill in a hospital. Somewhere on a rooftop, their father was manning an anti-aircraft battery, firing hopelessly at planes which could drop their bombs from much higher than Jack's shells could reach. As day followed night – as the fires hissed and the hosepipes spewed water on the ruins – he'd join teams of soldiers and civilians looking for survivors, pulling away at the rubble with his bare hands. Back at Lamorbey, as the all-clear rang out, his two sons would risk beatings to scour the grounds for shrapnel, crowing loudly when they found any – and recoiling in shock when some of it was still warm to the touch.

For 57 consecutive nights, the bombs fell on London, and with familiarity came complacency. Once it had become clear that the home was not a prime German target, the boys were not always herded into the shelters. Occasionally, the rulebook was relaxed. A contemporary of the Tarrant brothers remembers the dormitory lights even being left on – behind tightly drawn curtains – because so many children were plainly terrified by the grim nightly call and response of modern war, with its overture of approaching planes followed by the responding bass crump of the anti-aircraft guns. The brave ones would watch the glowing skies through a chink in the curtains. The bed-wetters would wait anxiously for the all-clear, and even the fiercest of Lamorbey's 'wolves' would lie quietly until Göring's Junkers and Dornier bombers had returned to refuel and reload.

And then, suddenly, on 11 May 1941, it was over. That night there was no assault on London's docks, and for the first time in two months the guns of Jack Tarrant and his exhausted fellow soldiers stayed silent. Routine re-entered people's lives. The living buried their dead – those that they could find – and reconnected with their surviving families and friends. Jack put on his uniform, and Edna wore her favourite white floral-print dress, with straw hat, and together they caught the train down to Sidcup, relieved to find their boys in good heart, wrestling with each other in the sunshine, John's socks rolled down and his school cap angled untidily across his right ear.

As always, Jack and Edna had taken their Box Brownie camera. With the family sharing so little time together, the photographs, for Edna especially, were precious. Propped up in her hospital bed, she would gaze at them for hours, trying hard to ignore the sadness they had captured: Victor willing himself to disappear into her embrace; John's eyes non-committal and downcast; her own heavy with the secrets of her situation.

Edna Tarrant had survived the Luftwaffe, but she would not live to see the peace. Although tuberculosis was in decline by the 1940s, it was still a terrible disease. Left untreated, it would almost certainly lead to death, and those who survived it did so with scarred and damaged lungs. Edna had never been a strong woman. There were complications – she also had diabetes – and she died on 16 May 1942, at St John's Hospital in Battersea. She was 31 years old. John was ten and Victor was just eight. At the Lamorbey home, both boys were given the news in their separate blocks in front of other children. Victor would never forget how he was told. 'The woman in charge said, "I've got some news for you, and don't you go scriking about it all over the place."'

A week or two later, taking compassionate leave from his unit, the boy's father caught the dismally familiar train from Cannon Street to Sidcup, walked through the gates and embraced his two sons. Two years in Lamorbey had already thickened their skin, but not enough to hold back the tears. John's memory of his mother was unequivocal: 'We could not have been better cared for or had a better mother. She was a kind, considerate, loving person who would sacrifice anything for the benefit of her family.'

For her funeral at Streatham Cemetery on 21 May, a small notelet was printed for mourners, bearing the well-chosen words: 'We saw her fading like a flower, but could not make her stay.' Out of the family's tragedy, however, would come an entirely unexpected form of salvation.

Tuberculosis was highly infectious, spread in the tiny droplets of a sneeze – or by a mother's kiss. Since it was also thought that a child could inherit a predisposition for the illness, the decision was taken to remove John and Victor from Lamorbey rather than risk their spreading TB through 600 children. No one could be sure if they carried the deadly bacillus, but no one was taking any chances, either.

Shortly after Edna's death – still under the care of the London County Council – they were removed to the Burrow Hill Sanatorium Colony at Frimley, established after the Great War as an isolation centre for up to '80 colonists or tuberculous boys'. For the first time in two years, John and Victor would be sleeping under the same roof – in an airy single-storey wood cabin with stable doors opening onto a hundred-acre summertime jungle of flowers, vegetables and fruit trees. 'Utopia. A heaven,' Vic calls it, remembering 'beans on toast for tea'. Because food was thought to stave off TB, the inmates were assured of good meals in satisfying quantities, and although the brothers were quickly given the all-clear, it didn't seem to matter. Despite a chronic wartime shortage of trained staff – and the perpetual threat of closure – the secret paradise of Frimley folded happily around them.

By day, according to a contemporary article on the home, they were given 'instruction on gardening and clerical work, also English, History, Arithmetic and Economic Geography'. Between lessons, John learned how to repair shoes, and by night they slept year-round behind permanently open windows in sometimes bitterly cold single dormitories without heating. Fresh air was seen as the key to managing TB, and at least one medical expert proffered the opinion that an abundance of it was 'instrumental in building up resistance . . . to the strains of adolescence and puberty at a later date'.

For the Tarrant brothers, this meant a relaxed open-air existence in absolute contrast to the mean-spirited claustrophobia of Lamorbey. Those who stayed there as children recall lashings of cocoa, thick slices of bread and pork dripping, regular medical check-ups and night-time high jinks illuminated by torches in and around their quarters. For two blissful years, John and Victor were able to enjoy this alfresco Frimley lifestyle, untroubled by one single symptom of tuberculosis. Every day there was counted as a blessing, and every day they lived in dread of being rumbled. Either they'd been forgotten or they simply looked too sickly to be moved. But then, just as the hostilities reached a climax in northern Europe, came what John called 'a sad day for us both'. He and Victor were ordered back to Lamorbey.

John, even more than Victor, must have been crestfallen at the news. Although he'd made no fuss, the older brother had been the target of persistent bullying during his first spell at the home. There was something about this shy, self-contained, scrawny young boy that drew him into fights in which he was always outnumbered and invariably badly beaten. With their father absent, John had also taken over the day-to-day job of protecting his younger brother. To their peers, they had become known as 'Big Tarrant' and 'Little Tarrant'. 'He was stubborn. I've never known anyone so stubborn,' remembers Victor. 'The more you knocked him back, the quicker he'd get up and the more determined he'd get up, too. He was quite placid until you riled him.'

In their early teens, both Big and Little Tarrant had clearly settled into the character traits which would define them as adults. Desensitised by their years at Lamorbey – and by the early loss of their mother – both were naturally introverted and quiet. They were also extraordinarily close and had developed a secret language in which they could communicate privately – if necessary, even in the company of others – long after their years in a home were over. But where Victor could apply guile and diplomacy to a difficult situation, John could often respond only with candour and force. Like anyone who has been institutionalised, he could be spiky and suspicious, with a damagingly knee-jerk mistrust of authority which he could never shake off.

Years later, one of his fellow athletes would describe Tarrant as 'an invariably taciturn character who repelled approach'. It was hardly surprising. He hadn't known a normal family childhood and found it difficult to mix naturally. When cornered, Victor could deploy his easy-going sophistication and natural charm to ease his way out of a tight spot, whereas John – who was easily tongue-tied – would resort more naturally to his fists. Confronted by a problem, or a physical challenge, the teenage John Tarrant preferred to walk straight into it, regardless of the consequences. Act now, think later. 'If I was a willow, my brother was an oak,' says Victor. For the home's tribal ringleaders, it made him a fascinating target, even if it meant they'd pick up a few bruises along the way.

It didn't help matters when, for a brief period after the war, John seemed to show genuine signs of intellectual promise. A visiting US Army officer conducted IQ tests at the home, and John's score was sufficiently high to merit a trial at the local grammar school. As if being a 'swot' wasn't bad enough, John found himself walking to school in a uniform which was different from those of almost all of Lamorbey's other children, some of whom assaulted John so thoroughly that he promptly handed his blazer back and resumed his place in his former class.

It had been a sign, at least, that things were changing. The war in Europe had ended in May 1945, and in July the British electorate had kicked out Winston Churchill, giving a decisive mandate for modernisation and reform to Clement Attlee's Labour Party. People wanted something better for their country and their children – even those forgotten ones at Sidcup, where there were swift and entirely unexpected improvements. Weekly pocket money was increased to one shilling (five pence) a week, rising to one shilling and sixpence (seven and a half pence) for anyone over fourteen. Out went the old paper-thin grey uniforms, with their stitched in numbers; in came more personalised outfits chosen from the tailor's shop, along with new overcoats and woollen gloves. Health inspectors began to make more regular visits, and in tune with the push for revitalisation came new football and cricket pitches to supplement the barbaric chill of the home's unheated indoor swimming pool.

Not that John had any interest in – or the necessary talent for – team games. Football and rugby really didn't appeal to his instinctively solipsistic nature. For John Tarrant, there would have to be something less complex than those convoluted sports involving mud-caked boys in pursuit of a misshaped ball, chased by a fat man with a whistle. Something more tangible and intimate and explosive was required. Something that he found on a hot July day in 1946 at Black Fenn School's annual sports day.

According to family mythology, this was the summer when John not only discovered the thrill of competitive running but, in the process, managed to silence forever the Lamorbey thug who had been the most persistent thorn in his side. Eight children toed the whitewashed line on the grass that July afternoon; ahead of them, four laps around the school field. And while bored children squabbled and plucked petals off the daisies, the untested Tarrant brothers lined up fretfully alongside John's nemesis: the same youth – his name forever lost – who had won this half-mile race unchallenged for as many years as anyone cared to remember.

From the start, John streaked into the lead, only to enter the final lap with his legs leaden and his adolescent puff all but gone. It would become the story of his life. 'Seldom have I experienced such pain and suffering,' he wrote, recalling with pride how he had still somehow found the energy to drive past the leaders, taking first place by little more than an inch. It was an outcome which surprised nobody more than the 14-year-old John Tarrant himself. At no point in his life had he ever pushed himself forward like this. In his own words, his victory was the school's 'most unexpected success' of that summer and – despite the vicious beating he took from the loser – he was back the following year to hold onto his title of champion half-miler, this time by a much wider margin.

Something, as yet undefined, was stirring in Big Tarrant. The mouse had roared. Despite the subsequent thumping, he had thoroughly enjoyed crushing his rival, and the quivering thrill of victory was a feeling he wouldn't quickly forget. To make it even more satisfying, he had done it in front of his brother. Towards the end of his life, John would say that he 'never quite equalled that feeling of elation at winning my first race'. But that wasn't true. Moments of supremely intense euphoria lay ahead of him. What was true was that few races would ever again be so joyously free of anxiety and complications – or so ridiculously short.

It was now the summer of 1947, and John couldn't help his mind turning constantly to his future. There was going to be no return to Cowick Road in Tooting. He knew that. The family which had flowered there was no more, and a world war had been fought and won in the seven years since that awful parting at Lamorbey's gates. At 15, John had reached the age when the home moved its teenagers on to men's hostels where they could begin their adult working lives. Unlike many of the children there, however, the two brothers were not orphans, and John had no intention of leaving Victor behind on his own.

Although Edna had been dead for five years, they did – supposedly – still have a father. Jack Tarrant – the chirpy porter turned wartime gunner – had survived the Luftwaffe's worst and was somewhere out there enjoying a Britain at peace. Knowing that, it must have been hard for the brothers not to stare at the calendar and wonder where he was. If the war had ended two years ago, why were they still in a home? Why were they still in care? Where exactly was their home now? And, more to the point, where exactly was Jack Tarrant?

Other people had been pondering the same questions. Sometime after VE Day – shocked by the boys' continuing presence at the home – a small delegation of Edna's relatives had travelled from Yorkshire to Lamorbey with a life-changing proposal for their nephews: leave the home now and travel to northern England to live with your mother's family. It was a tantalising moment. Were the Sorrells acting alone, or had they received Jack's blessing? Either way, John and Victor politely rejected the offer and chose to stay where they were. Their father would surely come for them eventually.

Chapter Two

'An Honest Endeavour'

1947

Even if Victor and John had screamed for him from the top of Lamorbey's tallest oak, it's unlikely their father would have heard. Jack Tarrant hadn't only lost his wife, his home, his job and his children during his London war, he'd also lost a significant part of his hearing, worn away by the shock waves which slammed through his head every time his ack-ack gun had tossed a shell into the clouds. For the rest of his life, there'd be a brown cable leading to a large earpiece from a battery pack in his breast pocket. And whilst it didn't quite gel with the comedy monocle or the white rose in his buttonhole, at least Jack Tarrant didn't have to pay for it. Britain had a National Health Service on the way. Free care for everyone, regardless of age, class or creed. A modern, egalitarian society was dawning in which – according to the script – young men like John and Victor would feel embraced, and where they would flourish. Assuming, that is, their father could find anywhere for them to live.

Jack Tarrant's war had already been a strange one. Watching his young wife die slowly in a sanatorium had upended all his expectations. Surely it was supposed to be the women who mourned lost heroes, not broken-hearted husbands hastily burying their brides in a lull between air-raid sirens. With the boys still in care, Edna's death had also spelled the end for 241 Cowick Road. Proper families needed bigger homes, and the council had moved swiftly to install new tenants. If Jack was discomfited, it wasn't for long. At heart, he was a pragmatist, and his infatuation with a tuberculous parlour-maid had always been a risk. Even in her teens, Edna had seemed too frail for life. Carrying on without her would be painful, but he'd survive. For the time being, the kids were where they had to be. It was London – in wartime – and people needed people like Jack Tarrant.

By the time Edna's death was registered, he had already fallen back on his feet. With the Blitz over – and with all German eyes fixed on Russia – the gun batteries had been scaled down. Noting his previous occupation of valet-porter, someone appears to have recommended Jack to an army captain in need of a batman. It was a match made in military heaven. No one knew his cufflinks or regimental ties or mess-room etiquette quite like Gunner Tarrant. No one knew better when to be seen and when not to be seen – or what to be wearing when one was seen. According to Edna's death certificate, he now resided behind the nineteenth-century facade of 25 Wilton Crescent, Knightsbridge – a hugely desirable corner of Belgrave Square, haunt of gamblers, inebriate poets, recalcitrant lords, diplomats and army officers. Described today as one of the best addresses in central London, its former residents include Swinburne, Mountbatten and a two-times President of Colombia. No mention these days – in the gushing blurbs of Belgravia's upmarket estate agents – of a one-time hotel bellboy with a pencil moustache.

For the next three years, Jack worked hard as Captain D. Robertshaw's shadow, and when the war ended in 1945, it did so with a resounding endorsement. In the opinion of his good captain, Jack Tarrant was 'an honest, reliable, trustworthy, pleasant personality with exceedingly good manners . . . all factors which are beneficial to a good valet'. Obsequiousness – or the pretence of it – had always come easy to John and Victor's father. It was ironic that, in the testing years to come, his first-born son would find deference the hardest thing of all.

By the close of hostilities, Jack had also found another female companion for his bed. Maysie Seddon was ten years his junior, but in every other way his equal for attitude and savvy. Like some 65,000 other women, she'd joined the Auxiliary Territorial Service at the outbreak of war, finding her way to London – from Cheshire – to do whatever was required for victory. Trained as a chiropodist, she'd tended parade-weary feet before working up to the rank of corporal in the Military Police, but it was most likely during an attachment to one of the city's anti-aircraft batteries that she first met Jack Tarrant.

In many ways, he couldn't have found a woman less like his first wife. John's mother had been brittle and unworldly, with a mournful dark-haired beauty. Maysie was earthy and streetwise, with a long, wide face, thin lips and darting, curious eyes. If there was a sting of guilt in the batman's heart, it soon passed. Unlike his sons, Jack wasn't comfortable in his own company, and he'd learned that no one mourns for long in wartime. There was fun on offer with this feisty girl from the north country, with her snappy tongue and ever present fag, and so Jack dived in head first. Before long, she was sitting with Jack – both in their military uniforms – on the dreaded slow train to Sidcup, ahead of them their first meeting with Edna's other two young men.

If John and Victor had expected news on their own future, they were to be disappointed. Much as Maysie had relished the independence and thrill of her London adventure, she had absolutely no intention of staying in the South once it was over. And until she and Jack had a home, there was no prospect of his sons joining them. Throughout 1945, she had begun to make plans for a permanent return home to the green fields and hills of north-west England. If Jack Tarrant, the one-time prince of London's hotel lobbies, wanted their relationship to last, he'd have to turn his back on his beloved West End.

But it wasn't merely homesickness which was calling Maysie away from the capital. Although she never revealed it to John and Victor, her own family narrative had been as damaged as their own. Her birth mother had been an unmarried parlour-maid working in the service of a childless Cheshire spinster called Elizabeth Seddon. In an act of self-motivated philanthropy, Elizabeth adopted her servant's illegitimate baby girl, and it was to her surrogate mother – 'Ninna' Seddon – that Maysie felt compelled to return. Given what had happened, it wasn't surprising that the two women were close. Many years later, Maysie would even move Ninna into a bungalow near the Tarrants' new Derbyshire home; by this time, she was a lonely, rheumatic, bath-chair-bound woman, wheeled out on sunny days by the illegitimate child who had taken her name.

Whatever Jack Tarrant felt about leaving London, the trauma which bound Maysie to northern England simply could not be denied. After she received her discharge papers, the two of them travelled immediately to Cheshire, where they were married on New Year's Day 1946. As with all weddings, there were undercurrents. Privately, Ninna – who was clearly something of a snob – felt that Maysie was marrying beneath her. Jack's beery repartee might have made them laugh the froth off their pints around Camberwell, but it did nothing for Elizabeth Seddon. Outwardly, however, she smiled icily as the couple took their vows at Hazel Grove Congregational Church before a restrained but happy reception at her home on West

Park Road, Bramhall. Butter was still rationed and the wedding cake was of modest proportions. Guests from the Tarrant side of the new family were also in short supply. Jack's two sons – Maysie's two new stepchildren – had been unable to travel up from Kent, and another eighteen dreary months would pass before they too made the trip north to the hills.

As they were for everyone, the first years of the peace for Jack and Maysie were a strange mix of the thrilling and the unnerving. Encouraged by a Labour government promising radical change, expectations everywhere were sky high, and yet the realities of ordinary life rarely seemed to match them. After six years of war, people's stoicism had worn thin. Everyone understood that rebuilding would take time, but no one had expected the discomfort that went with it. In the summer of 1946, Jack Tarrant was finally released from the army, his record carefully noting that he had been a 'trustworthy, sober and industrious' soldier. Nothing he had encountered during his relatively risk-free war would have prepared him for the civilian challenge which now lay ahead.

Within weeks of their wedding, Maysie had discovered she was pregnant, and in August the couple – both now demobbed – moved into temporary prefab accommodation on the outskirts of Buxton. As the birth date loomed, and the nights closed in, condensation streamed down the walls of their bungalow and collected in pools on the lino. At night, it was only slightly warmer on the inside than it was out on the street. Secretly, Maysie Seddon had probably always harboured anxieties about taking on Jack's teenage boys, but, as the baby fidgeted inside her – and as winter's first chill rolled off the fells – those doubts multiplied. Until things were settled, John and Victor would have to stay a little longer in Sidcup.

By Christmas 1946, the situation was starting to improve.

The couple's new son, David, was safely delivered, and Jack was picking up work, initially as a labourer at one of the many limestone quarries which pockmark the Peak District hills, and then later at a Buxton firm fabricating brake linings. The jobs were gruelling, filthy and lung-choking, not at all what Jack was used to. When a softer vacancy came up, with the local council, he leapt at it. For the rest of his working life, Jack Tarrant would earn his crust as one of Derbyshire's more colourful dustmen. A few years later, while Jack was patrolling the streets in his refuse wagon, an intense-faced young athlete drew level with and then quickly passed his moving vehicle. With pride, Jack would turn to his cabful of cheering colleagues and tell them that they had just been overtaken by his son, the famous ghost runner.

South of the town, the housing situation was improving, too. Set on a pleasant, south-facing slope – with fine views towards tree-crested hills – a new council estate was nearing completion, and the three-strong Tarrant family was high on its waiting list. In the summer of 1947, they were given the keys to 90 Sherwood Grove, a pebble-dashed end house in a short terrace, with clear views to the rear over a shallow ravine, and, on good days, the prospect of all-day sunshine falling on a large and private rear garden. The snootier end of Buxton referred to the estate as 'Chinatown', but Maysie and Jack didn't care. Finally, they had a house, and, to their credit, they moved swiftly to unite the entire brood under one roof for the first time.

Once again, the boys' father caught the train south to the Sidcup children's home where John and Victor had waited patiently for more than seven years – and where they now stood, bags packed, ready to take their chances with Maysie and their infant brother. As it was August, the buildings of Lamorbey sweltered under a rich, green, deciduous canopy. Children were racing back for their lunch from Burnt Oak

School in an endless chattering crocodile. The mood had mellowed at the home since their own brutal indoctrination – 'an absolute transformation', John said – and in thanks for that post-war blessing, he would put his X next to the Labour candidate in every election that followed.

Walking in silence against the tide of hungry children, John, Victor and their father reached the brick-pillared gates for the last time, each lost in his own secret welter of thoughts and possibilities. For Jack, who barely knew these slender, silent, dark-haired teenage men, there was the daunting challenge of somehow bringing his new family of strangers together. For John and Victor, there were simply too many unknowns to count and too many heartbreaking memories to be rid of. Without a backward glance, the trio turned right, then left again and walked the 100 yards to the railway station. Not one of them would ever come this way again.

By the time John Tarrant left Buxton, he would know every inch of its roads and fells, and his story would have been told by every newspaper in Britain, but that summer of 1947, the Derbyshire town was as unknown to him as he was to the world. In London, the brothers had grown up assuming that the background groan of city traffic was a universal constant. Now, as their final connecting train rolled south from Manchester – through Chapel-en-le-Frith and then Dove Holes – they were looking out on a slatey Northern landscape which must have seemed entirely alien. Houses made of stone not brick. Uneven walls of bleached limestone running steeply up to boggy moorlands out of thickly wooded valley bottoms, between fields peppered with sheep. Nothing seemed to be straight or flat, either. Not like the Tooting Road at all. Here, the valleys twisted and dipped, as Manchester's own thick forest of suburbs gave way to smaller villages and the railway made its final dip down into the place the Romans had called Aquae Arnemetiae.

Apart from a V2 bomb which had exploded apologetically in a nearby field, the war – like most things – had largely passed Buxton by, and even today there's something out of time and endearingly unfashionable about the place. Like Bath, it had built its name on the geothermal waters which rise from the earth at a constantly soothing 28°C, imbued with such healing powers that ailing rheumatics have flocked there for centuries. And like Bath, the town sprouted a mass of distinguished buildings to amuse and to house its miracle-seekers when not 'taking the waters'. Today, most of this classical Georgian and Victorian fabric is as well maintained as it was 200 years ago. Apart from the sadly decaying eighteenth-century Buxton Crescent, there's the Pump House, and the perennially popular Buxton Opera House (home of the annual International Gilbert and Sullivan Festival). There's also the soporific charm of the Pavilion Gardens, and a few timeless shopping arcades to stroll in. But then, as now, Buxton is a spot which favours mostly senior pursuits. Nothing too energetic. A slow foxtrot at the Tuesday tea dance at best. Not a town over-endowed with testosterone, and an interesting conundrum for two teenagers who'd been incarcerated in a home since they were in short trousers.

For the time being, however, the challenges of John and Victor's social life would have to wait. At 90 Sherwood Road, the newly expanded family was encountering some teething problems – and they weren't just baby David's. It was hard enough being an overnight stepmother, but, at 27, Maysie was only 12 years older than John and carried no natural authority into the relationship. She was also far less tidy than her stepson, whose years in a regimented home – with its inspections and beatings – had made him fastidious and precise, his life uncomplicated by possessions. Back at Lamorbey, the brothers had each been assigned a locker for their personal treasures. Victor's concealed his precious stamp album. John's was permanently empty.

The constant clutter and the serried rows of drying nappies were not easy for him to take. Worse still, both Maysie and Jack were heavy smokers, something to which John – whose monastic streak had combined with the memories of his mother's lung disease – was ill equipped to adjust. For years, John and Victor had known only fresh air and open windows. Now, in Buxton, despite the proximity of pristine moorland ozone, they were unwillingly recycling their parents' Players untipped fags. On a typical day, Maysie could puff her way through up to 100 cigarettes, and when rations ran low – or when the local newsagents turned her away – she'd pop a few tea leaves in a pipe and smoke them instead. Or so people said.

Respect for their father – and the lingering subservience learned at Lamorbey – meant that little was ever said to break the superficial calm of the household. If necessary, the brothers would retreat into the secret slang they'd learned at the home, but their stepmother was no fool and quickly worked out what they were saying. What she couldn't do, however, was provide the tactile mothering which the brothers had never really had. One neighbour would say later that it looked like the boys were 'being kept under . . . as if their parents might not have been doing their best for them'. But it was far more complicated than that. To survive for so long in the home, the brothers had made themselves emotionally self-sufficient. They had learned, in effect, to live without anyone's love but each other's.

From across the street – in the house where she still lived 60 years later – an attractive 14-year-old called Alice Campbell was intrigued by these new arrivals. Kittenishly, she would always make sure she was out on the street in the warm summer evenings which followed the brothers' arrival in Buxton. There was something about their closeness and intensity which excited her. Both had their charms, and 'at various times' she fell for both of them, but it was Victor who'd been the most blessed by good looks, and it was Victor who blossomed the most naturally in the company of a girl.

'John was fascinating but withdrawn and kept himself to himself,' she recalls. 'Victor was a little reclusive, too, and although they both found it hard to make friends, Vic was also much more handsome and had coped better with leaving the home than John had . . . Maysie did her best, but John needed someone softer and kinder, a mother. He'd never had softness and kindness and so he didn't know how to give any out.'

With hindsight, even Victor can see how different they were: 'We'd been compressed by that home. Being older, John had suffered more than me. He didn't know how to express himself. He didn't have the knack of living normally or socialising. Later, yes, when he ran, I think he found that means of expression.'

It was around this time that John and Vic were Brylcreemed and besuited and packed off to the studios of Boards of Buxton for a family photograph, one that precisely captured the characters of the two young men Alice was getting to know. Although little more than a year separates them – John is 17 and Victor is 15 – the gap appears far wider. Victor smiles effortlessly, almost sensuously; his body is relaxed and his blue eyes are warm and alive beneath the dense black thicket of his eyebrows. Next to him, John is striking, too, with the same vertiginous family brow hiding deep-set eyes. But in John the nose and lips are fuller, and his posture exudes impatience and seniority. Looking at them, it's no surprise that it would be Vic who finally took Alice's hand, leading her for midsummer walks, and juvenile kisses, in the swirling pollen-dusted meadows just beyond the estate, or that for John there would be merely the consolation prize. After work, up and down Sherwood Road, the coquettish Alice Campbell graciously allowed him to teach her how to ride a bicycle.

Such adolescent yearnings as John Tarrant had were, in any case, now being sublimated through full-time employment. Victor still had some schooling to be done and was enrolled at Kent's Bank around the corner. John, meanwhile, had been taken on as an apprentice by the local council and placed under the wing of local plumber Stan Carson. It was to be the first of a lamentable lifelong string of unsatisfactory, badly paid jobs. Although for the next few years he'd dutifully lug baths and cisterns up and down stairs and repair the frost-shattered pipes of Buxton's fast-expanding council estates, there was always an indolent streak – a half-hearted indifference – about John's approach to work. At lunchtimes, the two men would nip back to Stan's house for a sandwich and a brew. Pat Carson, Stan's wife, remembers an intensely quiet 'raw-boned' boy who never spoke about his family. 'They existed, him and his brother, just about. We knew Maysie and she was a bit rough. I don't think John knew family life like we knew it, but he never seemed to complain.'

In the afternoons, when they weren't installing boilers, John and Stan would be called into Buxton to work underneath the town's disintegrating thermal baths, lagging the pipes alongside curious rats. Afterwards, John would cycle briskly back to join Vic and Alice outside their houses on Sherwood Road. Made tired by hot work and the August sun, John would lie back to stare at the clouds, half-heartedly cleaning his tools. 'He was always pretty lazy,' says Alice. 'It seemed to fit that he'd polish his tools in a horizontal position.' Just occasionally, he'd stir himself enough to push Alice on her bicycle, but more often, as the chatter wore thin, he'd watch resignedly as Victor and she pedalled off, giggling, into the twilight.

It wasn't much of a social life, but for anyone their age Buxton had very little else to offer, and the brothers' initial relief at being out of Lamorbey had quickly given way to the frustrations of living in a retirement town where it always seemed to rain. By the middle of 1950, although both were working and earning – Victor rising daily at 5 a.m. to make bread at a local baker's – Buxton continued to disappoint them. Like everyone else of their age in Britain, they had a craving for escapism which the local cinema's endless diet of cowboy films simply couldn't satisfy.

Although John was now 18, the town's pubs were not an attractive option, either. He didn't like beer, and they were mostly full of older men reminiscing about Winston Churchill and the war, through the same stinky cloud of tobacco he'd left at home. It didn't help that identical frustrations were afflicting every other city, town or suburb in so-called austerity Britain. That was somewhere else and this was Buxton. Like his entire generation, Tarrant was restless, twitchy and bored. For some, the answer would be Bill Haley, all-night dancing and rock and roll. For John Tarrant, the solution would take the unlikely shape of a boxing promoter called Tommy Burton – an association which was to shape almost every single moment of the teenager's subsequent troubled life.

Long before reality television, it was boxing which held out the hope of salvation and wealth to the young working-class men of post-war Britain. Football was still the big crowd puller, but it would be another ten years before the cap on players' wages was removed. Even England's biggest star, Tom Finney – like John Tarrant, a Northern plumber – earned barely £14 a week, a lot more than the council was paying to fix leaks but still not enough for one of those new Triumph Mayflowers everyone was talking about. Compared to boxing, football also seemed deeply unglamorous; its heroes were lumpen and pedestrian, the kind of plodding men you'd not look at twice in the Buxton high street, with their centre partings and wholesome, toothy grins.

Boxers, on the other hand, appeared to inhabit a world marked by a dangerous swirl of excitement and scented permanently by violence. For every flat-nosed, punch-drunk loser who'd tell you about the downside, there seemed to be a champion whose fingers sprouted diamonds and whose girls wore furs. You couldn't pick up a newspaper without reading what these legends earned, and the frantic commentaries on their fights drew rapt listeners to the radio like filings around a magnet. In 1951, for example, millions listened agog as Sugar Ray Robinson took a purse of £28,000, expecting to thrash Britain's Randolph Turpin, only to come unstuck against an opponent who had travelled to the bout on the Underground. In the same year, Joe Louis, washed up and under investigation by the US Internal Revenue Service, dragged himself back into the ring for $300,000 only to be pulped by Rocky Marciano. And it was in this year, 1951, that boxing truly arrived in Buxton.

'Joe Louis was our idol,' remembers Tom Hockenhull, whose father sold antiques and owned only the second-ever television in Buxton, a tiny Bush with a nine-inch black and white screen It was Tom's dad, Ted, who first encouraged his son and a group of friends to set up a punchball and a makeshift ring in a back room at his house. 'It was either that or run the streets. None of us was big on pubs or girls back then.' Twice a week, for an hour or so, they'd jab, skip and clinch and dab their bloodied noses before clustering around the Bush to watch whatever they could make out between blizzards of electrical snow, the result – it was later announced by television engineers rushed up from London – of 'interference caused by rheumatic treatment equipment at the thermal baths'.

Sometime in late 1949, probably through the influence of Vic – who'd recently taken up cycling in a serious way – John found himself drawn into this fraternity of aspiring pugilists. In his own words, he 'drifted' into it, just as Vic drifted out. But unlike his brother, John quickly discerned something about this intensely confrontational sport which stirred him. For some time, he'd been popping into Ben Simpson's seedy first-floor gym down on Buxton's Torr Street, stepping around the threadbare mats, to shin up the ropes or flex his pectorals on the parallel bars. Even by John's solitary standards, the sessions had been aimless and unfocused, but pulling on worn gloves in Ted Hockenhull's back room on Macclesfield Road rekindled the forgotten feeling he'd enjoyed winning the Black Fenn half-mile, and although in later years he would constantly downplay his exploits in the ring, there's no doubt he now set himself to succeed.

Buxton itself was waking up, too, albeit reluctantly. For the first time ever, news stories shared space with advertising on the front page of the local *Advertiser*. Alongside ads extolling the benefits of bile beans crept in racy reports headlined 'Scouts Camped in the Rain' or 'Money Stolen from Shop' and just occasionally stories which hinted that Buxton – like everywhere else – wasn't all afternoon teas and hot baths: 'Man Who Hit Taxi Driver Is Gaoled for a Month'. Generally, however, excitement – like coal – was in gloomily short supply, and there was precious little evidence to change Vic's view that Buxton was 'dead'.

To keep people's minds off the food rations and the threat of power cuts, there were concerts at the Pavilion Gardens by the Buxton Winter Orchestra, with special guest turns by Felix

Mendelssohn and his Hawaiian Serenaders; at the Playhouse Theatre (cheap seats 1s 6d), you could swoon to the Modernaires and buy tickets for the following week's production of *Macbeth* by the Adelphi Guild Theatre. For anyone under the age of 25 and unmarried, it spelled misery. Little wonder the local electrical retailers were insisting that television was here to stay, or that Tommy Burton's big idea caused such a sensation in this sleepy little town.

As Buxton preened itself for the last Christmas of the 1940s, attentive readers of the *Advertiser* would have noticed the advance ripples of this new phenomenon, hidden away on the back page between the hunt reports and the table tennis scores. After an interval of three years, 'fight nights' were to be reintroduced at the Town Hall, promoted by an ex-RAF boxer turned local get-fit club entrepreneur called Tommy Burton. By promising to showcase up-and-coming local boxers, alongside so-called top Northern hard cases like 'Sheffield's coloured craftsman Lionel Binney' and 'Stockport's very own "Nipper" Harvey', Burton clearly reckoned he'd found the formula to get the townsfolk away from *Dick Barton: Special Agent* on their Bakelite radios. If he was right, then, for one night of the week at least, it seemed as if Buxton's very own Felix Mendelssohn would be getting some serious competition.

It was a prospect which had a great many in Buxton spluttering into their sherry. For the town's elderly residents, the very idea that clots of gore would soon be spraying around its fine buildings was final proof that the world under Labour had been detached permanently from its senses. For the rest, it was a welcome sign that things were finally perking up after the deprivations of war. 'We'd had nothing like it before,' says Pat Carson, who, with husband Stan, would be standing enthusiastically in the queue for tickets to see whether John Tarrant could handle the ferocity of the ring. Alongside them, on that bitter-cold evening early in 1950, were the several hundred other curious Buxtonians who'd turned up at the Town Hall in their caps and scarves to watch twelve boxers batter each other senseless in six gruelling fights.

As a runner, Tarrant would never quite master the stage fright and the debilitating anxiety which devoured him before, and often during, almost every major race. Now, for the first time in his sporting life, his skin prickled with dread. Scheduled to fight last, John listened to the waves of cheering and jeering through the bare walls of his changing-room but was too paralysed by nausea to bring himself to watch. As each pair of fighters shuffled out shivering under the spotlights, he'd hear the bell ringing to announce the rounds, followed by the stifled thud of punches to unguarded midriffs and the harder, bonier snap of a fist cracking into a face.

As each pair returned, swimming in adrenalin and blood, Tarrant's anxiety mounted. Had he been fighting a stranger, it might have been easier, but he wasn't. Tommy Burton had recruited this first roster of raw fighters locally, and John's middleweight opponent was an 18-year-old sparring partner called Neil Somers – also a member of Ted Hockenhull's makeshift back-room boxing club. According to Alice Campbell, Neil was tall, thin and dark-haired, a keen sportsman, 'very lively, outgoing but a bit mouthy'. According to Neil's brother Clive, he was also one of John's better friends. 'They used to train at Tommy Burton's club in Cavendish School gym. They cycled together, too. But although my Neil was much more serious about it than John, they were always very evenly matched when they fought each other.'

To huge cheers from the partisan Buxton crowd, John and Neil finally pulled aside the ropes and stepped onto the blood-speckled canvas, where – after a knowing touch of each other's gloves – they stood toe to toe and started trying to knock each other out. Looking on, first proud and then no doubt horrified, were Jack, Maysie and Victor, averting his eyes every time Neil's be-leathered fist clubbed into the face of his brother. At Lamorbey, he'd already seen John take enough unsolicited beatings from other boys. Watching it through the ropes of a boxing ring didn't make it any easier. But at least here John was giving as good as he got, and after four two-minute rounds, with both still standing, the bout was declared a draw. 'A fair decision,' wrote John, adding casually that 'for our efforts we were paid the sum of £1 each'. A piffling sum with catastrophic consequences.

Although the Town Hall stank of liniment for days afterwards, everyone had good reason to be pleased by Buxton's inaugural boxing extravaganza. The 650 fans who had streamed happily out into the night had been shaken from their winter torpor and could talk of little else for weeks. Tommy Burton had trousered a respectable lump of cash and wasted no time planning a sequel for the following month. The triumphant winners were already dreaming of securing titles in front of 45,000-strong crowds at White City, and even the losers, packing ice on their bruises, could reflect on a memorable night. But few of them are likely to have been charged by the evening's events quite like John Tarrant.

As he rushed home to Sherwood Road on his bicycle, he felt both electrified and bewildered by the whole experience. In the ring, he'd been powerful, fearless and strong. Manual labour had thickened him up. At 5 ft 11 in., he weighed in at a muscular 11 stone, and had a prodigiously broad and barrel-like chest. It hadn't been stylish, and he'd fought like an idiot, but no one could deny him his brute courage and, apart from Victor, everyone had been stunned by the bloody-minded, gladiatorial edge he'd displayed. 'He'd learned how to handle himself at the home,' says his brother. 'I knew that very well.' John had been hit – often and hard – but for eight incredible minutes the

71

pain simply hadn't registered, and, as he irritably wafted away Maysie's cigarette smoke, he couldn't wait to get back in and do it again. Vic could stuff his cycling. John would be a warrior and, in these hard times, maybe earn a handy few bob into the bargain.

A few days later, he had yet another reason to be satisfied with his night's work. Under the headline 'Packed House at the Town Hall', John made his first-ever appearance in a newspaper photograph, frozen by the *Buxton Advertiser*'s flashbulb as a bloodied Neil Somers landed a thrashing right-handed haymaker to the side of his unprotected face. Out of nowhere, Buxton's quietly spoken apprentice plumber had found himself centre stage in a town where everybody knew everybody else. It was early days, but John liked how this felt. His challenge now was to get known as a winner and not just as a plucky makeweight. It would become one of the themes of his short sporting life. Simply taking part would never be enough.

In the years which followed the war, it wasn't hard for a would-be boxer to find cheap advice. Dismal gyms run by cauliflower-eared ex-squaddies were popping up everywhere. Punch-drunk former professionals fallen on hard times were two a penny, and around Buxton a diminutive, Dickensian ex-fighter called Bert Webb could frequently be seen shadow-boxing invisible foes as he mooched around the streets. Bert had notched up 40 fights, but his twisted-nosed brother Freddie had fought in 100 more – could even have been a contender, some said – and together they tried to inject some boxing discipline into the pale-skinned youths hanging around to decipher the fuzz on Ted Hockenhull's temperamental nine-inch television set. 'We had one or two trainers,' deadpans Ted's son Tom, 'but they couldn't always be relied on . . . one of them was sometimes in prison.'

For some of the town's residents, this insalubrious lust for boxing, with its unappetising hangers-on, was all getting a little out of hand. There was now even talk of it spreading from the Town Hall to the sanctum of the Pavilion Gardens. Where next? The Opera House? The very idea of it. Ridiculous. Something had to be done, and in March 1951 the council staged an impassioned debate which considered terminating the Town Hall's use as a venue for any more nights of braying crowds and uncouth thuggery.

Under a typically risqué headline – 'Fears for The Town Hall's Paint' – the *Advertiser* revealed how some locals even feared 'activities of this kind' might somehow damage the building's recently restored interior. To the huge relief of Tommy Burton and his roster of fighters, the progressives won the argument. The boxing would continue and the wheezing conservatism of Buxton's elderly establishment had been temporarily beaten on points. 'It would be a poor show,' proffered one councillor (his name presumably withheld for his own protection), 'if a bit of sport was outlawed for the sake of a lick of paint.' Fight nights were in Buxton to stay until people got bored with them, and in the spring of 1951 there was precious little sign of that.

If anything, the spat over the Town Hall's decor had made people even more curious, and, despite seats trading at 2s 6d each, some 1,000 of them poured into the Pavilion Gardens to see the first of that year's promotions in its new and classier venue. According to the local paper, 'many local fight fans seeking cheaper seats were unable to get in', and even the mournful *Advertiser* was forced to concede – albeit in articles probably penned by Tommy Burton himself – that the fights 'were the most successful held in Buxton since before the war'. Successful, that is, for almost everyone apart from John Tarrant.

Although that week's rag would later describe his catchweight bout with Roy Simpson as a 'fight packed with honest endeavour', the reality had been somewhat less appealing. Bellowed on by a crowd hidden somewhere out there beyond the murky wreaths of spotlit cigarette smoke, the two lads had sucked in the rank air of spilled beer and sweat and had battered punches into each other's faces for four merciless rounds. After eight minutes, with both fighters drenched in blood, the final bell had sounded and it was over. As always, Tarrant had battled indomitably, but it hadn't been enough. Roy Simpson was declared the winner on points after 'a punch and punch again match . . . which ended with both sides looking like Red Indians', or so acting referee Tommy Burton told the *Advertiser*.

Burton was onto a winner. This first night, before costs, had taken around £250, and for most of that year – always on the last Wednesday of the month – his money-spinning jamborees at the Pavilion Gardens continued to pull in the crowds. Even in the green warmth of summer, despite elegant competition from Garth Gainsford and the Buxton Spa Orchestra, there was no let-up in either the public's interest or John Tarrant's determination to make something of himself in the ring. In September 1951, his photograph appeared again in the *Buxton Advertiser*, where he was described as 'the head boy of the Buxton Amateur Boxing Club' and seen receiving a £10 donation towards club equipment from the legendary Garth Gainsford himself.

In a separate picture, the very broken-nosed Freddie Webb is seen 'demonstrating a body blow to club member Tom Hockenhull'. But whatever ring craft the Webb brothers were imparting, it was clearly not enough for John. He may have lacked motivation as a council plumber, but where boxing and later running were concerned, no exertion was too much. Bert and Freddie Webb were an improvement on his DIY training regime, but Tarrant was in desperate need of proper advice.

That summer, he'd fought once more on a Burton promotion, knocking his opponent out in two rounds and earning a win bonus which boosted his purse for the night to thirty shillings. Two months later, he'd been hammered in 58 seconds when a Macclesfield teenager called Johnny Hough 'rattled home a series of blows to Tarrant's face with machine-like rapidity'. In his four previous fights, said the *Advertiser*, Tarrant had recorded two knockouts, one draw and one loss. To see him so easily crushed by Hough was a 'great disappointment for local boxing patrons' and drew the following prophetic comment from the vanquished teenager: 'There has been a lot of preparation . . . I'll be back.' A great many others would hear that phrase – or one very like it – from John Tarrant in the years ahead.

It was now exactly one year since his first drawn fight with his friend Neil Somers, and although the two of them sometimes featured on the same bill, they were never to fight each other again in the ring. They did, however, have one brutal fight which never appeared in an official programme. Witnesses remember it kicking off in a changing-room when John insisted he had become a better fighter than Neil, and when Neil, unsurprisingly, asserted that the reverse was true.

With bare fists, and with no one making any attempt to stop them, the two had a 'blood and guts' fight which some declared a second draw, and which Tom Hockenhull remembered as a narrow triumph for Neil. Whoever won, the fight did not result in lasting animosity, and it concluded with a friendly shaking of hands. For John, it was a lesson: either get better or get out. 'I had begun to take my boxing very seriously,' he noted. Four times a week, from the autumn of 1951, he had started making a forty-mile round bus trip to train in a converted attic above a Stockport pub.

His new mentor was Ted Douglas – in John's view, 'a totally

honest man' – who'd been scratching out a living from boxing since the 1920s. In his loft gymnasium, lit dimly by leaking skylights, sagging punchbags swung in the gloom around the square of canvas and rope where Ted's roster of hopefuls bobbed and weaved and bled, to the constant barking of instructions from the side. Epic fights at Belle Vue Stadium in Manchester were remembered on the peeling posters which lined the walls. Johnny Curley and Billy Hindley in 1929. 'Kid' Lewis and Len Johnson in 1925. Legend had it that Johnson had won £1,000 for that fight and that 6,000 had poured into the King's Hall to watch.

Suddenly, on the threshold of Ted Douglas's gym, listening to the squeaking of boxing shoes across the canvas, Tarrant sensed the thrilling weight of these possibilities. It didn't matter that the odds were stacked against him or that the sport was riddled with corruption and backhanders. It didn't matter that for every winner with bad debts and a goodtime girl on his arm there were a hundred gap-toothed losers. For the first time in his life, John could feel some fire and purpose in his belly. In his heart, he knew he was no plumber, and every punch he landed took him further from the black hole of Lamorbey.

The species of boxing which found its habitat over inner-city hostelries, however, rarely came without complications. For the previous 12 months, John had turned out in his kit at Buxton Town Hall as an unlicensed boxer. It wasn't illegal. It simply meant that Tommy Burton's monthly promotions sat outside the British Boxing Board of Control. Just occasionally, a dodgy licensed boxer might show up at Buxton fighting for a few quid under a false name, but for the most part they were evenings which gave aspiring amateurs their first chance of glory under the lights. Anyone yearning for adulation at Belle Vue or White City would need to get a licence, and it was for that reason that Tarrant was now catching the infuriatingly slow bus through the hills to Stockport four times a week.

Unfortunately for John, Ted Douglas was not impressed by what he saw. With 35 years' experience in the fight game, Douglas knew a promising fighter when he saw one, and in John Tarrant he didn't see one. After just one workout and a little gentle sparring, Ted told Tarrant bluntly that he simply wasn't good enough to join his roster of licensed boxers. If he wanted to stick around for a trial period of six months, that was entirely up to him. But if John hadn't improved when that was over, he could save himself the bus fares to and from Buxton.

Throughout that winter of 1951 and deep into the following year, Tarrant strove desperately to prove Ted Douglas wrong. The bashful teenager who'd taught Alice Campbell how to ride a bicycle was now so consumed by his ambition that his friends and family barely recognised him. At home, Maysie's calorie-swamped packed lunches were waved away in favour of healthier food, which John prepared carefully for himself. On the nights he wasn't heading up to Stockport, he'd be up at Ben Simpson's gym or pounding the streets of Buxton in his plimsolls. When the fights came, he simply couldn't get into the ring fast enough, but, whilst the regular punters still cheered, Tarrant's results were inconclusive.

In February, he'd 'recovered well after a slow start,' the *Advertiser* noted, 'to earn a points victory over Les Mitchell of Sheffield'. In April, he'd been hammered conclusively for a second time by his ferocious Macclesfield nemesis, Johnny Hough. Finally, in October, despite 'showing improvement' and finishing with 'fierce attacks', Tarrant was outpointed in a welterweight scrap against Manchester's Cliff Roberts. Waiting for him after the fight was over, John's half-brother David registered his first and only memory of Tarrant's fighting days: 'He was cross because he'd been beaten. I remember him saying, "Let's get my money and bugger off."'

It hurt like hell, but Tarrant was washed up as a boxer. It wasn't courage he lacked – and his pain threshold seemed to know no ceiling – but his all-action style was too predictable, and he was taking too many dangerous punches in the face. No matter how many times Ted told him not to, John couldn't help wading in, fists windmilling, from the first bell. The shrewd fighters – the ones who'd done their homework – simply waited for their opening and then picked him off. Bang. Down. Fight over. 'Not much of a boxer. All arms,' is how one Buxton contemporary remembers him.

At his Stockport gymnasium, Ted Douglas stuck to his word and told a crestfallen Tarrant that his six months were up and that he should find another sport. According to John's memoir, Douglas added the prescient caveat 'that if fitness was all that mattered in boxing, John Tarrant would be a world champion'. Most people, at this disheartening juncture in their lives, would have slipped quietly downstairs for a few consoling pints of Robinsons bitter. But John didn't drink, and there was a bus to catch back to Buxton. Tarrant never fought again.

Less than two years had elapsed since he'd first boxed on a Tommy Burton promotion inside the freshly painted Buxton Town Hall, during which time he'd fought just eight times, pocketing a grand total of seventeen pounds. By his own admission, his biggest purse had been four pounds, and of those eight brief, murderous fights, just five had ended with John Tarrant's weary arm raised in victory; the others he preferred not to talk about. In the bitter decades ahead, much would be made of John's so-called violation of amateur codes, and many things would be claimed about his status as a professional boxer. But under even the most fleetingly focused microscope, John's misdemeanour – if it ever truly was one – appears to disintegrate. His tragedy would be that no one who could have helped ever chose to look.

It was true that Tommy Burton had slipped him a few quid now and then, but John had never secured a professional licence and Tommy's informal recompense fell way short of the costs Tarrant was incurring simply to get to Stockport and back four times a week. It was pocket money and nothing more, a bit of rent and housekeeping for Maysie. Nobody was getting rich, and by the time he quit, according to Victor, John's boxing had already cost him far more than he'd ever earned from it.

On top of this, despite being described as 'head boy of the Buxton Amateur Boxing Club', Tarrant had never been formally affiliated as an amateur either. The real truth was that, in terms of precise sporting definitions or organisations, John Tarrant simply didn't exist and had therefore broken no rules. He'd arrived in that grey town from nowhere and been drawn into boxing – like Buxton itself – on a teenage surge of spontaneous exuberance. Suddenly, in this flat and elderly post-war town, there was something he could do, something which would be his, something which would get him out from under Jack and Maysie's feet, and which, to everyone's surprise (no less John's), unlocked sides to a personality which had been dulled in those empty years at the children's home in Sidcup.

If it was a crime to have thrown himself into it without qualification, then he was guilty. But that was just John's way. He had merely wanted desperately to succeed and found himself opposed to mere half-measures. No one had ever stopped to check the rules. No one was thinking much beyond the weekend, anyway. And even if Tommy Burton made a tidy sum out of his monthly promotions, his boxers never did. Mostly they were young kids like John, fighting because they'd nothing better to do, in a town which – if you were under 20 – had nothing better to offer.

But John was no longer a teenager and had – so far as he knew – turned his back on boxing for good. It had been barnstorming and brilliant, but it was over. He didn't yet know it would haunt him forever, like a witch's curse. There were other things on his mind now, and as he threw his gloves into the corner of his Sherwood Road bedroom for the last time, John pondered the recent changes in his circumstances. Victor was gone, away on National Service, and they had a new baby sister crying in the room next door. And if that wasn't enough, it looked as if he'd found himself a girlfriend. Rolling over in bed to avoid aggravating the bruises around his right eye, John checked the wake-up time on the luminous face of his clockwork alarm. Bright and early again tomorrow. Ten miles' running before breakfast.

Chapter Three

'Torrance of Buxton'

1952

Although for a teenager the joyless spa-town weekends might
have dragged, there was nothing remotely flat about Buxton as
a location. Almost every route out of the place rises sharply
across the flanks of the voluptuous Pennine hills which embrace
it. During the winter, when the snows come hard and the winds
drive choking drifts across the withering moorland passes, the
town can be cut off in an instant. Come summer, with the
curlews piping high above the moors and lapwings zagging
nervously around their nests, Buxton seems to simmer within
that same amphitheatre of hills, now green, and alive with the
rustling of new leaf and the chuckle of spring water breaking
free of its deep limestone prison.

To a city boy arriving from a children's home in 1947, it had
seemed a foreign, and entirely pointless, landscape. Five years
later, with a pack of ice pressed to his swollen face for the last
time, those same fells had become the key to John Tarrant's
entire future. As much as boxing had stirred him, there was
still something about the sport which had left him unsatisfied.
He still prickled with unspent adolescent energy. As endorphin
hits went, it was far too mild a rush for John Tarrant. His

physical chemistry demanded more than six minutes of adrenalin and two black eyes every few months. He'd had his fill of playing the human punchbag for Buxton's blood-hungry punters. The gloves could go back in the wardrobe, but he'd hang on to the shorts and the black boxing pumps.

Ever since he'd first turned up at Ted Hockenhull's place on Macclesfield Road, John had been a glutton for the necessary masochism of weekly training. One or two of the lads could skip longer or punch the bag harder, but no one – absolutely no one – could touch John Edward Tarrant when they got out on the streets for a lung-burning burst of road work. 'We'd started off on a circuit round the houses, walking 300 yards then sprinting 300 yards,' remembers Ted's son Tom. 'But after a couple of weeks John could run it all and lap us twice into the bargain.'

It wasn't pretty. Out on the road, John was as awkward and angular as he'd been in the ring. The stride, like the punches, never quite flowed. There was no elegance or physical poetry about his movement. But even in his rawness – as he flew effortlessly along the steep lanes around Buxton – John's legs seemed tireless and his immense barrel-like chest seemed to shelter a heart capable of perpetual rhythmic motion.

At Lamorbey, he'd learned how to stifle pain and keep going, never showing or sharing what he was feeling, an emotional blank moulded by a childhood of solitary disappointments. He didn't particularly care – or really notice – if people found him remote and unapproachable. That was their problem, not his. What mattered was that he – and Vic – had survived this far and that now, suddenly, he could launder a lifetime of frustrations through an activity which electrified him, and in which, in some mistily untutored way, he already knew he could excel.

Years later, John would keep a meticulous log, detailing every training run – and every competitive race – of his extraordinary, blighted career. Sadly, there is very little evidence to show just how far and how fast his new obsession was moving at this early stage. However, from the late summer of 1952, it's clear that John had begun to take it very seriously indeed. Running was what he would call his 'first love', and he conducted this early phase of the relationship with all the blind ferocity of an affair.

Five days a week, alone and untutored, in sunshine or snow, he would grind up and down the Pennine gradients, incrementally building up the dogged strength which would become his lifetime trademark. From the beginning, as it almost always would be, the open road was John's track. Not for him the slithering cross-country helter-skelter of the fields and fells or the blistering speeds of middle distance. Up in the shadow of Combs Moss and Axe Edge Moor, there were days when he never even felt tired, when he felt he could run forever, never happier than when climbing steeply, his mind at war with every sinew until the slope eased and he could allow himself one glance across the hilltops back towards Buxton, his thoughts a whirr of self-imposed times and challenges, the landscape a succession of gateposts, junctions and landmarks which he reached faster, and with less effort, every time he wrenched on his pumps and braved the hilly air.

There were other reasons why John was suddenly finding the solitary catharsis of running to be so necessary and so intoxicating. Life in the family's Sherwood Road council house had never been easy. Lately, it was becoming intolerable. In the summer of 1950, Jack had fathered his second child with Maysie, obliging John to share the chaotic domestic crush with a baby sister, Elizabeth. With Victor at his side, the fag ash and the fractious siblings had been bearable, but by 1951 Victor was gone, quitting his job at the Buxton bakery to do his National Service in the kitchens of the RAF.

At the children's home, although they had been separated, the pair had never been more than a few hundred yards from each other. In Buxton, they'd shared adjacent bedrooms. Now, for the first time in their lives, the two young men were truly living apart. There were no tears and no sorrowful goodbyes, but Tarrant's running had helped fill the gap. Pounding the hills, he'd found purpose and distraction. Victor would be back to play his part. Of that he was certain. Just as Victor was certain that his older brother would thrive without him. 'Me leaving made no difference to John whatsoever,' he says. 'He was so independent. He didn't rely on anyone else. We didn't even run together. At the time, I didn't know what he saw in it. It didn't make any sense.'

Others were leaving Buxton, too. The Pied Piper of National Service was calling the town's teenage boxers away to do their duty. But there would be no call-up letter for John. For years, poor diet and malnutrition had been linked to a rare but chronic and life-threatening infection of the mastoid bone in children's ears. At some time in the money-starved months before they moved to Tooting, Jack and Edna Tarrant must have become aware that John's health was failing. On top of the virulent infection filling his nose and ears with pus, they'd have noticed anaemia, sleeplessness, poor digestion and a worrying loss of appetite. As the world crashed into war, surgeons performed emergency mastoid surgery on both of the boy's ears. Twelve years later, it would ensure that John was ineligible for National Service and could not follow his brother and his friends into uniform. 'He had a hole behind each ear,' recalls Victor, 'but it was OK. He'd been lucky and could hear as good as anything, although I was always apprehensive while he was boxing. I always worried something would happen to him.'

Within four years, John Tarrant would become Buxton's most

celebrated sportsman, but in 1952, as the town was drained of his contemporaries, there was another man living quietly in this genteel market town who could already lay claim to that title. Like John, he was a passionate runner, although his best and most illustrious achievements were long behind him. His name was George Bailey. He was in his 47th year, and whilst his path would cross John Tarrant's only briefly, it would do so with regrettable consequences for the younger man.

Everyone in Buxton knew 'Bulldog' Bailey, and his story – just as John's would shortly be – was the stuff of legend. Born locally in 1906, Bailey was the son of one of the stonemasons who built the web-like lattice of Derbyshire's dry limestone walls. Like Tarrant, George had dabbled in boxing as a teenager, before switching to hill running in a bid to get fit after falling out with cigarettes. He took a job in the local limestone quarries – as John later would – running the 20-mile round trip to work in a pair of heavy leather boots. Naturally agile and fearsomely strong, his success in umpteen Pennine village races brought him to the attention of the illustrious Salford Harriers, and, beyond that, into a thrilling world of which John Tarrant had known absolutely nothing until they met.

Despite their nearly 30-year age difference, their similar backgrounds ensured a powerful connection. It was uncanny how much they already shared: the impecunious parents; the adolescent boxing; the solitary running; the hard physical graft of their daily jobs. But it was what George Bailey had done when he'd reached John's age which most fascinated Tarrant, and it was to hear those stories – again and again – that he called regularly for the older man, ringing his doorbell, jogging on the spot outside in the cold, until they were both ready for a gentle circuit of the roads above Buxton. They talked as they ran, with Tarrant forever squeezing more detail out of Bailey's inspirational yarns.

In 1930, at the age of twenty-four – four years older than Tarrant was now – George had won a gold medal, running in a British vest, at the steeplechase in the inaugural Empire Games in Canada. Two years later, he'd narrowly missed another medal at the Los Angeles Olympics, controversially denied because the entire field had accidentally run one too many laps. In the heady years that followed, he'd run for England many times in the International Cross Country Championships, finally retiring from front line competition, aged just 32, with a sackful of stories and the medals to back them up – medals which now glowed brightly in the trophy cabinet presented to him by Buxton's proud burghers, and which Tarrant would admire over a post-training cup of tea.

To the younger runner, Bailey's life seemed impossibly exotic, packed with experiences which made Tarrant drool. Such as the weekend he'd won a grandfather clock in a race in Scotland and walked home from the station with the clock strapped to his back. Or the sea voyage to the Los Angeles Olympics, when the Varsity runners such as Lord Burghley had sailed in first class, while those from the Northern clubs had been crammed into steerage. Or the time George had been suspended for three months by the unforgivingly stringent Amateur Athletic Association after someone had belatedly reported him for taking part in an 'unregistered' village sports event.

Tarrant already knew that he could run, but there were only so many times you could go on beating yourself. Hearing what George Bailey had achieved changed everything. With an almost messianic certainty, Tarrant realised that the competition he craved must be at the highest possible level. Not an impossible task, surely. George Bailey had gone from a Pennine quarry to a glitzy art deco stadium in Los Angeles (albeit in steerage). Why shouldn't a Buxton plumber who'd survived a world war and the icy purgatory of a children's home do the same? By the end of 1952, Tarrant had formulated a vague plan. Running alone – or in Sunday fun runs – was getting him nowhere. To follow Bailey, he would have to join a proper running club. After that, the rest would surely follow.

Like his mentor, Tarrant had set his heart on joining the Salford Harriers. Formed in 1884, it was a road-running club which, in many ways, seemed to be the perfect fit. Proudly working class, and rooted defiantly in north Manchester, the Harriers had been – in their glorious 1920s heyday – the glamour club of Northern athletics, aggressively recruiting brilliant raw talent from the factories to run in meetings which attracted fiercely partisan crowds, often many thousands strong.

So staunchly proletarian were the Harriers that for decades they ran the club from the back snug of an Edwardian pub. John felt certain that under their wing he would quickly make an impact and start winning races. But before he could even contemplate an application, there was a problem to deal with: a £17 problem – the cash he'd pocketed at Tommy Burton's boxing promotions. The money had once seemed so trivial, inadequate and hard-won, but it now presented John with a horribly vexing dilemma, one which gnawed at the very core of his persona.

It had probably never been in his nature to be dishonest. Edna Tarrant had always drummed into both boys the merits of truthfulness, lessons which sat well with John, who, by nature, was transparent and direct, lacking the necessary intellectual sharpness for deception or evasion. The conundrum he now faced, however, put this natural inclination for honesty into direct conflict with his newly clarified aspirations. Sport had not yet entered the professional era, and the so-called purity of amateurism – where honour and participation were deemed their own rewards – was often enforced by administrators with a rigour which bordered on the terrifying. Money, in athletics, was still a dirty and very dangerous word.

In seeking to join the Salford Harriers, John would be asked if he'd ever earned money from sport. Should he 'forget' the £17, there was a very strong chance that his deception would never be discovered and that all would be well. Equally, there was no reason to be certain that someone wouldn't eventually shine a light on Tarrant's secret. It had been an anonymous snitch who had shopped George Bailey, and Bailey had been banned for a minor infraction which had happened years before he was famous. And what if Tarrant *did* formally declare the winnings? It would be impossible to predict how the authorities would react. George had escaped with a three-month ban, but by that time he was already an international athlete. Would they be so lenient with an unknown council plumber from Buxton?

John's conclusion, after much agonising – and advice from George Bailey – was that forgiveness would prevail, and that the reward for his truthfulness would be fairness and compassion. In a civilised world, run by reasonable – albeit faceless – men, it seemed entirely sensible to expect such an outcome. A slap on the wrist – a fine, or maybe a brief suspension at worst. It was only £17, and, as Victor kept saying, the whole lamentable fiasco had cost him significantly more than that in bus fares. Setting out the precise details of his boxing 'career', and enclosing a five-shilling (twenty-five pence) fee, John wrote to the Derbyshire Amateur Athletic Association seeking the formal recognition as an amateur he needed before he could join the Salford Harriers. It was done.

Tucking the letter into his running shorts, he trotted down Sherwood Road towards the postbox. Just enough time to jog up to Wye Dale and back home before dark. Nothing too

demanding tonight. He was out again later – around at Edie's
– and she liked him smart and washed, with a jacket and tie
and his hair swept back. Life was on the up, he thought. Life
felt good. He checked his watch and quickened his stride. As
always at this time of night, the roads were alive with dust-
whitened lorries, each one complaining loudly under the
weight of its limestone cargo. Above the din, John was sure he
could hear the roar of the crowd already, and behind it the first
stirring bars of the national anthem. The letter was on its way.
Soon he would be a proper runner. And just maybe he'd have
a wife.

Although Victor was now stationed in West Kirkby, serving up
porridge in an RAF canteen, John was not entirely stuck with a
47-year-old former Olympian for company. For two years, he'd
been quietly courting a girl from his estate, confessing shyly to
Victor that he had been 'smitten' by the first and only close
female companion he would ever have. It wouldn't be Alice
Campbell, the girl he'd once taught to ride a bicycle. She was
not to be the one. The stuttering teenage fire she'd kindled for
Victor had been snuffed out by his National Service, and
although John intrigued her, the chemistry was missing. 'It was
hard to imagine him with girls,' she reflects. 'He just didn't
have the necessary social skills.'

In the corners of her heart, Edith Light would probably have
agreed. The young man who called from the council to fix her
father's burst pipes had been so painfully withdrawn it was
almost impossible to talk to him. He wasn't a terribly good
plumber, either – invariably melting pipes with his blowtorch
before mending them. After Alice Campbell had met him for
the first time, she'd concluded that John needed someone
'softer and kinder, a mother'. The teenage Edith – or Edie, as
she preferred to be known – had seen exactly the same thing: a

haunted-looking young man who'd lost his mother far too young.

In a small town like Buxton, the Lights were a hard family to ignore. Everyone eventually found their way into Potters, the town's esteemed outfitters (established 1860), and when they did so, they'd most likely have their goods wrapped in brown paper and string by Edie's father, Harold, the store's punctilious odd job and delivery man, a character who was as much a part of the legendary Potters ambience as the outsize Y-fronts and 'cross your heart' bras in the windows.

Altogether, there were eight Light children, whom Harold and his wife, Ellen, had produced and raised in their council house on Grove Lane, just around the corner, as it happened, from where Jack and Maysie Tarrant were struggling with a complex new family of their own. Unlike Jack and Maysie, however, Harold Light liked his domestic space to be tidy and his gleaming horse brasses to be spirit-level straight, a fastidiousness which he was delighted to see emerging in his daughter Edie, and which now ensured her revulsion at the shambolic situation which prevailed inside her boyfriend's family home. It was hardly surprising that when John finally asked Edie out – having somehow patched up her father's burst pipes – she insisted their courting take place at her house and not his. Or that, just this once – mindful of the overflowing Sherwood Road ashtrays – John was happy to do as he was told.

In every other respect, Edie would quickly discover, John invariably did only what he liked, and what he liked, to the exclusion of any other activity, was running. By his later epic standards, the distances were still derisory, but Tarrant's mileage was climbing, and with it his stamina. He now thought nothing of 60, 70 or 80 weekly miles, leaving little time for a relationship from which romance seems to have been completely absent. 'It's true. He wasn't romantic,' Edie admits. 'We didn't go to dances – he wasn't a dancer. We didn't go to the cinema – he didn't like the cinema. Sometimes we'd go for a day out and he'd take his running kit. I couldn't get away from it. Looking back, we didn't do much together at all . . . I used to say to him sometimes, "Can we go somewhere?" But we never did.'

To Alice Campbell, it was a puzzling relationship: 'It was as if Edie had decided early on to marry John, and that was that.' Where Alice was inquisitive and self-sufficient, Edie was unquestioning and fiercely traditional. If she harboured any misgivings, she kept them to herself. John was a good-hearted, honest and kind man. He wasn't the type to be looking at other women, and he'd a steady job with the council. In Buxton, she could do a lot worse. When the question came (which it would), she would say yes. And maybe, eventually, just like the boxing she'd loathed, he'd grow out of the running as well. But there was something else – something they never really talked about – which made them very close.

Edie had also recently lost her own mother – a victim of leukaemia – and understood perfectly how John felt and what he needed. A traditional girl lacking grand dreams of her own, she harboured no discomfort about the notion of being a traditional wife, one who backed her husband's dreams without question, however much personal sacrifice might be entailed. When it was required, her dedication would be unconditional, and without her John would never have achieved a fraction of what he did. Sadly for Edie, the price was to be a terribly high one, measured in many long years of penny-pinching loneliness spent in a town miles away from the beloved Peak District of her childhood.

On 12 September 1953 – after a respectable courtship of almost three years – John and Edie were married at Buxton's London

Road Methodist Church. The bride carried pink carnations and 'wore a dress of blue satin covered with fine net'. The groom – described in the *Advertiser*'s report as a 'well-known boxer and runner' – wore a light-grey double-breasted suit (quite probably from Potters) and a toothy, bashful smile. In the wedding photographs, Edie's arm is looped tenderly through John's left elbow, and from John's generous cuff an immense fist emerges, looking as unsure what to do with itself as Tarrant seems, his shyness all too apparent amidst the alien formalities of a wedding which, of their parents, only the couple's fathers had survived to see.

On the left of the group stands Harold Light, chest puffed forward, hands clasped smartly behind his back, his face wearing a warm smile beneath a crop of greying hair. To the right is Jack Tarrant, his shoulders slumped and his left arm hanging loosely at his side. For a wartime valet, the bearing is scarcely military; the suit seems too small, and Jack's centre-parted hair already sports the suspiciously flawless gleam of a mane which, in later years, retained its colour thanks to the contents of a bottle. Both men beam proudly into the lens of the camera, but, tellingly, Edie's head is tilted towards John – and her father. Behind the scenes, an important decision had been reached in Harold Light's favour.

There'd been little resistance from John, but when the honeymoon was over the couple would be setting up home in Grove Lane, and not at Sherwood Road with Jack and Maysie. Privately, John's father almost certainly breathed a deep sigh of relief. It wasn't that he didn't love John or like Edie. It's just that they were so intense about everything – and without John around, he could enjoy his guilty pleasures without the guilt. In every way, it was the best solution. His son could still come round and romp on the rug with David and Elizabeth; he and Maysie and the children could relax as a family again. Perfect.

As the beer flowed at the wedding reception – and as the newly-weds headed for their honeymoon in Blackpool – Jack lit a Woodbine and quietly toasted the fortuitous change in his circumstances. With John living round the corner, there was something new he might be able to do. For some time, he'd been thinking about breeding rats. It was only a thought, but there was no way he'd have done that with Edie in the house.

Fifty miles away, John and Edie were looking out of their train window as the Tower loomed into view, and with it their one-week honeymoon at a Blackpool boarding house. As John only had one suit, he'd travelled in the same cavernous jacket and tent-like trousers he'd worn for the ceremony. Edie, meanwhile, had switched into a dark suit, with a calf-length skirt and trim five-button jacket, which suited her petite hourglass figure. At the Sunny Snaps studio on Central Beach, they posed side by side next to an open-top MG sports car for a souvenir photograph.

In the picture, John has slipped his arm protectively around Edie's waist, but his face is a comical study in nervous wedding-night anxiety, and it is she who looks the more relaxed. Perhaps by now they've unpacked their bags at their bed and breakfast and John has had to explain the presence of his running kit. Perhaps by now he's already asked if she'd mind if he went for a quick jog along the beach. Just a few miles of light running before their fish-and-chip supper after a long and trying day.

He'd have told her it was important, and she would have known, by this time, just how important it was. It wasn't her place to make a scene. Not even on this night. Not even though for the rest of her life she would remember the running before she remembered anything else about her honeymoon. 'He ran on the beach every day,' she says, 'just to keep active.' Allowing him to run along the beach at Blackpool – or anywhere he chose – was the least she could do. By this time, she (and only she) knew the full extent of the terrible nightmare in which her husband was tangled up. Without the discipline of his solitary training – even on their wedding day – she'd have forgiven him for going insane.

Tarrant had sent his letter to the Derbyshire Amateur Athletic Association expecting fairness and compassion. What he'd got back was a formal rejection and a full reimbursement of his five-shilling application fee. Furthermore, in the accompanying letter from the AAA's official, he was advised, bizarrely, that reinstatement by the Amateur Boxing Association (ABA) would be necessary before his application to compete as an amateur athlete could be reconsidered. The two organisations, it seemed, had a reciprocal agreement, each respecting the 'decisions, suspensions, disqualifications and re-qualifications' of the other. If John could demonstrate that he was an amateur in the eyes of the boxing authorities, then he'd be accepted as an amateur by everyone else.

For even a trained lawyer, let alone an unqualified plumber, this would have been a perplexingly surreal and troubling development. So far as John knew, he'd never been affiliated to the ABA. How then could they reinstate him if they had no record of him on their books? It was like something out of *Alice in Wonderland*, or worse. Tommy Burton's fight nights had been ad hoc small-town affairs which largely set their own rules. To the best of his knowledge, he'd never belonged to any sporting organisation, let alone the Amateur Boxing Association, but if this was what the AAA required, then he had no choice other than to give it a try. It seemed cockeyed, but to become an accredited runner he must first be accepted as an amateur by the authorities in a sport he'd turned his back on, a sport which had never formally known of his existence in the first place.

Once more enclosing five shillings, he wrote to the Midland

Counties ABA, outlining his crimes and misdemeanours and asking that they accept him into their ranks. A week or two later, they too refused to accept him, and, after six months of writing and hoping, Tarrant was right back where he'd started. Two things had changed, however, and they would be important. First, the secret was out about his £17 prize money, and even if he regretted his candour there was no turning back that clock. Second, he was married to a woman who had known all about his Kafkaesque predicament months before their wedding, and whose fury at what was unfolding was matched only by her husband's.

Without her – and with Victor still a distant figure in the RAF – it's possible that Tarrant might at this point have relinquished his mission, bewildered and beaten down by these first early rebuttals. But Edie was having no defeatist talk, and John took very little persuasion to carry on with the fight. His subsequent life would reveal a taste for endurance events, and the faintest stink of injustice and snobbery had always rankled with him since his childhood. Edie was right. The harder it got, the harder he'd try. Choosing his words carefully, he picked up his ballpoint and penned a second application to the Derbyshire AAA, once again throwing himself on their mercy and attaching the same dog-eared postal order for five shillings . . .

What followed for John Tarrant were the lost years, when rejection piled on rejection, when months were sacrificed to endless waiting, with diminishing hope, for the next official knockback. As a boxer, his prospects had been doomed by a tendency to walk into big punches. Now it seemed as if he was doing it again. The more the authorities spurned him, the more persistent became his claims. By his own account, Tarrant lost track of the number of times he applied to the AAA and the ABA for reinstatement, always with the same uncompromising response.

To his way of thinking it was a simple case – a moral case – which should be decided on the grounds of common sense and decency. To the officials, the man was a bloody nuisance who'd taken some grubby backhanders, broken the rules and must pay the price. They might – might – have given him more time if he'd been polite. But as the months became years, John's growing revulsion for authority figures frequently led him to deploy language which was unhelpful at best and deeply damaging at worst. 'I am quite certain that John wrote this letter when he was bitterly disappointed,' observed one bruised official following a lashing from Tarrant some years later.

And so it went. Falling through the Grove Lane letter box came a steady stream of brusquely phrased typewritten replies to John's laboured but endlessly impassioned longhand pleas. 'Your letter was placed before my Council last night,' wrote Mr R.W.A. Freer, of the Midland Counties ABA. 'I have to advise you that the application for reinstatement was refused. Correspondence is returned herewith as requested.'

'There is nothing more that my Association can do under the circumstances,' wrote Mr Stretton of the Northern Counties Athletics Association. 'The postal order to the value of 5/0d is returned herewith.'

Unable to race and paralysed by his seemingly hopeless predicament, Tarrant drove himself even harder on the high roads and lanes around Buxton. 'All the setbacks seemed to strengthen my determination,' he wrote. Up there alone, John could safely exorcise all his bottled-up furies, the rain and sleet lashing at his face in winter, the mayflies dancing on the reservoirs as the summer broke and the moors exhaled their deep, warm breath of peat. Who the hell was Mr R.W.A. Freer of the Midland ABA anyway? Why should he have governance over his fate? What did he know or care of John Edward Tarrant? All he wanted to do was run. Was that really such an outrageous thing to be seeking? What could he possibly do to bring more pressure on these people?

As his thoughts bounced from question to question, Tarrant's nightly run looped him back home, as always, to Harold Light's pebble-dashed semi on Grove Lane. For once, running – and his weekly mileage – wasn't the only thing on his mind. The plumbing job at the council hadn't worked out, and after completing his formal apprenticeship he'd quit to take up a new position in a limestone quarry a few miles out of town. Something else was different, too. Since August 1954, he and Edie had been looking after their firstborn son, Roger. Roger Victor Tarrant.

Like everything else in his life, fatherhood would have to take its place in the queue behind running. Although John would later write a moving sequence of letters to Roger – each one awash with cautionary homilies and creaky paternal advice ('Take care of yourself, lad, and lay off the booze') – he was too blinded by frustration to give Roger the time he deserved and almost certainly needed. Weekends were mostly spent working overtime or clocking up miles. Apart from one reluctant trip to Clacton, neither Edie nor Roger remembers any family summer holidays. Money was tight, but for Tarrant time was tighter.

Without his realising it, the patient months of waiting had built up into years. The start of 1956 meant that four years had vaporised since he'd first taken up cudgels against the AAA. Four years of letter writing. Four years of rebuttals. Four years of nothing. In March, he tried a new tack, seeking to circumvent the unbending AAA by signing up with the Road Runners Club, the organisers of the prestigious London-to-Brighton road race; it was a competition he would later dominate but which now hovered impossibly beyond his grasp.

'With the utmost goodwill in the world it would not be

possible . . . unless and until you became a member of an amateur club affiliated to the AAA,' wrote Road Runners general secretary Ernest Neville. It wasn't exactly what he wanted to hear, but it was something. It was the voice of a human being. 'Utmost goodwill' was surely a step forward, and, unlike every other bureaucrat he'd dealt with, Neville appeared genuinely moved by Tarrant's position. 'I have always had considerable sympathy with men like yourself who have for a few paltry pounds rendered themselves ineligible to compete as amateurs,' he wrote, signing his letter 'with every good wish – believe me'.

There was still hope. He was still only young – just 24 – and he'd been staggered by the backing his wife was giving him. Edie wouldn't fail him. Edie wouldn't walk away. Ever since their honeymoon, she had always known this was how it might be, and in the warm summer of 1956 – as Tarrant plotted furiously for a way through the impasse – she could be thankful at least that her husband was working.

The Peak District was – and still is – pockmarked by deep limestone quarries, places where a man prepared to graft could earn far better money than an aspirant plumber. As a younger man, Tarrant's Olympian mentor George Bailey had worked in them for years. Maybe it was fate that John should find himself working there too. Clocking on at 7 a.m. and back off at 8 p.m., John put in a 12-hour daily shift, broken only by a single hour's break for his snap. It was brutal, back-breaking stuff, but Tarrant seemed to enjoy its open-air physicality far more than the corporate claustrophobia of his job with the council. Humping rocks beat blocked drains any day, and at the quarry's expense the strength in his arms and upper body was now increasing rapidly.

There were other intriguing echoes of the George Bailey myth which John would have enjoyed at Ryan and Somerville's quarry. In his entire life, John would never drive a car or take a driving test. Even if he'd been able to afford a car – which he couldn't – his few experiments behind the wheel had so terrified his companions they'd urged him to stop. The local buses were unreliable, so John – like Bailey and countless working men before him – solved the problem by getting to and from work under his own steam. Three miles there, and – if he chose to finish at 5 p.m. and forgo three hours' overtime – a longer, ten-mile country route back. And just maybe, if his energy levels were high, a gentle stretch during his precious one-hour lunch break.

Along the way, there was even the occasional opportunity for him to indulge in a little mild diversionary competition. On some mornings, he'd meet with a fellow quarry-bound worker – not a runner, but a cyclist – and a ritual race would follow, with John losing the downhill sprints, before easily outgunning his two-wheeled opponent on the uphill gradients. What the cyclist never knew was that the pack on John's back was loaded with rocks to help him build up his stamina and strength, and that without them he'd probably have beaten him downhill as well.

Once at the quarry – with the stone dust sticking to his sweat like a ghostly mask – Tarrant threw himself into his labours with the same demonic energy he brought to his training, an approach which clearly rankled with his bemused workmates. 'It was piecework,' remembers Victor. 'Each worker had to fill so many trucks a day, and because John found it all so easy his workmates started to sabotage his truck to try and slow him down, or else they'd *all* be asked to fill more trucks a day. John told them that if they didn't lay off he'd work even faster and fill twice as many trucks as they were being asked to . . . I think that pretty much stopped them.'

* * *

Victor had enjoyed the military life. Although he'd completed his National Service in 1954, he had stayed on and was stationed at RAF Credenhill in Herefordshire, later to be the headquarters of the SAS. The taciturn boy who'd once gagged at a plate of cold tripe had blossomed into a darkly handsome, physically fit and highly accomplished chef. Alice Campbell would always maintain that the RAF 'brought Victor out of himself', converting bashful gaucheness into calm, quietly confident self-knowing. 'He no longer had the problem proving himself that John did. He was perfectly happy helping John prove himself and achieve what he did,' she says.

Just as they had been throughout their childhood, the two men remained extremely close. It hadn't been easy – rare home visits and the occasional postcard – but Victor had kept up to date with the news and was fully aware of his brother's predicament. Other than Edie, no one knew better just how hard John had been hit by the ban. During the early months of 1956, they had conferred regularly, frantically angling for a way to break John's case out to a bigger audience. It seemed reasonable to assume that most fair-minded people would take his side if they knew what was happening. But another thousand furious letters wouldn't get Tarrant's case into the public domain. If the snobs who were strangling his dreams couldn't be reasoned with, then perhaps they could somehow be shamed.

As spring warmed into high summer, Victor and John secretly hatched the plot which they hoped would catapult John's case into the public eye and shower ignominy on his tormentors. If it was to work, they would need to support and trust each other – just like in the old days, backs against the wall, Big Tarrant and Little Tarrant all over again. It would require cunning, courage and perfect timing. It might also get both of them into a lot of very serious trouble.

It was a simple plan, naive but deliciously audacious. If the hidebound bureaucrats of the Amateur Athletic Association wouldn't let Tarrant run in races officially, then he would run in them unofficially, gatecrashing major events to gain the public's attention, closely followed (the brothers reasoned) by widespread sympathy and support. With a fair wind, he might even win some of the races. Running alone against his stopwatch, John had proved to himself that he could match the times of the very best runners in England. All he had to do now was find a way of taking some of them on. It was a challenge which proved much harder to pull off than either John or Victor had expected.

Secretly – and highly illegally – Tarrant had already been testing himself with the Salford Harriers, a club whose mill-town origins made it sympathetic to his cause. Although his name was never mentioned in any of their results, Tarrant had performed well in their ten-mile championships and had decided this was the distance at which he would make his unofficial debut. According to *Athletics Weekly*, there were tempting ten-mile road races looming that summer in both Macclesfield and Leeds, and it was the Tarrant brothers' intention to race John in both of them. Assuming, that is, they could get him there and then get him safely out, tasks which had been assigned Victor as the duo's getaway driver.

Unlike John, Victor adored engines. In due course, he'd be 'the fourth person to own a Mini in Hereford', but in 1956 he was content with just two wheels: the BSA motorcycle which was to feature as the secret weapon in the Tarrant master plan to turn John's predicament into a subject of national debate. It was a ruse which started badly, however, and which quickly descended into farce. 'Easier said than done,' was John's subsequent deadpan verdict, and the two were fortunate that no one witnessed the comic bungling of their shambolic trial runs. Although only 12 miles separate Buxton from Macclesfield, the pair got lost in a maze of Cheshire hedgerows and failed to make the start of their first race in time. A fortnight later, on their way to the ten-mile run in Roundhay Park, Leeds, Victor's motorbike became snagged in city-centre tramlines, spilling both men onto the road. 'Fate was against us,' John recorded in his memoir, discreetly choosing not to mention the crash. 'After a series of mishaps we reached the park ten minutes after the race had started.' If it hadn't mattered so much, it would have been funny. But John would never be known for his sense of humour, and he wasn't laughing. 'It was a crushing disappointment,' he wrote. 'I was getting desperate for a race.'

It had been a disastrous start, but the Tarrant brothers had learned something. With a little more planning – and a good map – their blueprint to spark controversy had genuine potential, and Victor's motorcycle might yet prove crucial to their strategy. By travelling on the bike, they could (in theory) get right to the thick of the starting melee. With Victor up front, John could leap into action almost immediately – and then back out of it just as quickly if a speedy getaway turned out to be necessary. The finishing touch would be John's 'disguise': running shorts, vest and plimsolls concealed beneath a cap, a thick, long coat (it could be cold on a motorcycle) and trousers which could be quickly removed, hopefully without falling over.

Having blundered twice, John and Victor – desperate to preserve both nerve and momentum – cast around for a third 'party' to crash, settling on the City of Liverpool Marathon, due to be run just a few days after their tramline debacle in Leeds. It was a choice which introduced yet more risk into an already madcap equation. A marathon is a race of 26 miles and 385 yards, but John had never competed openly in a race of any distance and had never run more than 12 miles in one go in his entire life.

He knew nothing of tactics or diet, and his experience of competitive sport extended little further than the occasional morning rivalry with a Buxton bicyclist. But too much time had already been lost, and John 'could not bear the thought of having to wait until next year'. On 11 August, come what may, he would be at the start of that race. In a few days' time, Tarrant reasoned, he would no longer be fighting this fight on his own.

It was time to let Edie in on the full extent of his secret plan, and, to alleviate her anxiety, John promised he would pull out of the race the minute he started to feel the strain. Reassured, she asked no further questions, and with one day to go John put in a wearying thirteen-hour Friday shift at the quarry while Edie stitched a pocket into his running vest (for his glucose tablets) and prepared a flask of coffee and sandwiches for the adventure ahead. This time, there was to be no last-minute dash through the back streets, no 'crushing disappointment'.

Determined not to be late, the brothers temporarily shelved their motorcycle plan, and John travelled alone to Liverpool by train, arriving with a clear two hours to spare before the start, time enough to eat his butties on a sun-warmed park bench before asking a local policeman for directions to the changing-rooms. 'As I sat there munching . . . I thought a lot about the race and began to feel scared about my chances of completing the distance on such a hot day.' He must have wondered, too, whether his life would be changed by what he was attempting to do. 'He was fully aware how controversial his actions would be,' reflects Vic, 'but he was getting no help. By the time of that race in Liverpool, he really felt he had no other choice.'

As John counted down the minutes, another man had arrived at Liverpool's Lime Street Station, as determined as John to leave his mark on the 1956 Liverpool Marathon. Just like George Bailey, and like Tarrant himself, Arthur Keily was indomitably working class, a stocky, cocky 35-year-old human bulldog who would still be running marathons almost 40 years later. A blacksmith by trade, Keily had already won this race in 1954 and 1955 and was determined to travel back to Derby with a hat-trick. To John – who devoured the sports pages, memorising every runner and his times – Keily was a hero. He'd run for Britain and was everything Tarrant desperately aspired to be, and suddenly here he was, in this makeshift changing-room at a Liverpool Conservative Club, wishing strangers like John Tarrant good luck and warning everyone that it was 'the pace that kills, never the distance'.

For all Tarrant's bravado, these must have been horribly self-conscious moments. In the 1950s and '60s, marathons were not the vast mass assemblies they subsequently became. No one ran dressed as an apple pie, and the runners – who were all properly accredited – invariably knew one another well. Tarrant's unfamiliar presence would have caused a stir, but no one seemed to be asking any questions. Studiously avoiding eye contact, he slipped into his best green shorts and white vest while his sixty or so rivals worked through their pre-race stretches, each one (apart from Tarrant) sporting a number on his vest, and each one (apart from Tarrant) named on the official event card. Among them, Arthur Keily – despite not recognising this tall, unusually withdrawn stranger – had gone out of his way to wish him good luck. 'We knew there was something odd going on,' says Arthur. 'I remember him looking worried in the corner, as if he thought he was going to make a right Charlie of himself.'

But Keily could not have begun to guess at the tumult in Tarrant's head. Writing his book almost 20 years later, John could still taste the sense of absolute panic which had begun to swarm over him – pricking his skin with sweats – as the 3 p.m. start time drew near:

> I was having difficulty fastening the laces of my plimsolls. What would people think of me? Exhibitionist or crackpot? Would people understand my inborn love of running, or that for a miserable seventeen pounds earned in another sport I was being treated worse than a criminal. I could drop out and no one would be any the wiser . . . but it was too late to quit. The Mayor of Liverpool had fired his pistol.

At the starting line in Liverpool city centre – head down, trying desperately not to be noticed – John re-checked Edie's vest pocket and its cargo of glucose tablets. Not for the first time, he had cause to give thanks for his wife's unswerving commitment to what had become a shared conspiracy between three confederates. Edith had played her part, as had brother Victor, in the planning, but now, finally, it was all down to John. Four years of bile and rejection were about to be put to the test he'd been longing for.

Within a half-hour of the start, John had already glued himself to the leading group of eight, effortlessly running six-minute miles and finding it very hard not to gallop away from his fellow pacesetters. Everything he'd learned about himself running alone above Buxton was coming good. His body could cope easily and the hard gasping of the runners around him felt like the sweetest noise he'd ever heard. Why hadn't he done this years ago? Why was everyone running so slowly? After an hour, he was starting to enter the unknown, propelled there by the tsunami of adrenalin which was pumping through his body.

> I was feeling tremendously powerful . . . I began to think I could win the race . . . At around eleven miles I could not contain myself any longer and made an effort to break

away . . . No one was prepared to give chase . . . I couldn't believe my luck.

But there were others who couldn't believe what they were seeing, either. And many of them didn't like it. Screaming through loudspeakers from the sidelines as the nameless, numberless runner broke clear, race officials demanded that the unidentified interloper immediately surrender himself to the police. 'I'm Tarrant of Buxton!' he bellowed back, taking care to sidestep the apoplectic stewards deploying themselves across the road to try to catch him.

Amongst the official runners, reactions to the mysterious pacesetter were mixed. Some sided sycophantically with the stewards and pleaded with Tarrant to get off the road. Others, like the indomitable race favourite Arthur Keily, were finding the whole thing intensely amusing. 'This bloke had run past us, and we'd absolutely no idea who he was,' remembers Arthur, who at 90 years old can still recall the stir of fascination which John's first run caused. 'We were running in his wake and people alongside the road were saying, "You ain't going to win this one, Arthur. There's a bloke well in front of you."'

As the miles ticked by, and as confusion grew, the Liverpool spectators – sensing an underdog with a story to tell – had become fascinated by the stranger's crabby running style and by that nervy novice's way he had of constantly glancing back over his shoulder. There was something endearing about the air of desperation this ferociously concentrated young man seemed to be floating in. There was something comical about the way he'd periodically overtake the vanguard outriders and pilots on their pushbikes before realising his mistake and falling back behind them. So what if the snotty stewards and the rozzers were after him? All the better, in fact. Whatever he'd done, he was still a bloody good runner, and he was showing that old-timer Arthur Keily a thing or two about marathons.

Despite the crowd's support, Tarrant's isolation and inexperience were costing him the race. Since the start, the roadside feeding stations had refused to offer him liquid refreshments, and on an already hot day he was beginning to suffer badly from dehydration. Worse was to come. Reaching for his glucose tablets, he found they'd fallen out of Edie's pocket, and, with the stewards still denying him drinks, John's race was almost but not quite run. In the controversial months to come, he would have Victor as his second to steer him through his darkest moments out on the road or track. Here, in Liverpool, he had a stranger to thank.

At the 15-mile mark, he'd been unexpectedly adopted by 'a big Irishman' on a bicycle. The man rode alongside him and reported that his two-minute lead was dwindling fast, and that he'd run the first 15 miles in 1 hour and 26 minutes. It was a thrilling pace, but it was far too quick, far too soon. Tarrant was cramped and exhausted and fading fast. At 19 miles – completed with no refreshments whatsoever – his pace had slowed to a stumbling walk, and the pursuers who'd trailed in the stranger's wake for so long were finally able to sweep past. 'Well done, lad!' shouted Keily, as he brushed Tarrant aside and pressed on towards his third victory in as many years.

As runner after runner surged by, Tarrant slumped, humiliated, at the side of the road, the electric thrill of his debut suddenly reduced to the nagging practicality of how to collect his clothes from the finish line at Anfield in time for his train back to Buxton. He'd started the day a nobody and he'd finished the day a nobody. It was over. He'd failed. Stuff running. Sod boxing. Sod and damn it all. It was all over. Or it would have been but for Tarrant's anonymous Irish Samaritan. After vigorously massaging John's legs, the stranger popped into a nearby shop, reappearing with a bottle of Lucozade, which helped John stagger another five anguished miles towards the finish. 'More walking than running. Sitting down for long periods in between. By then every runner in the field seemed to be passing me,' he remembered. 'They all seemed so fit, so full of running . . . I was feeling really fed up and a long way from home.'

At 24 miles – twice as far as he'd ever run before – he could go no further. Almost every runner was ahead of him, and the only thing left moving on the road was the ambulance which slowed down to offer him a lift. Slumped in the back of the van – dehydrated and catatonic with exhaustion – John drank so much orange juice he was violently sick, a foreshadowing of the wretched mid-race vomiting that would plague his running career.

In the immediate muscle-bruised despair of the race's aftermath, Tarrant wanted nothing more than to slip back into anonymity and start all over again. But it was far too late for that. Long before Arthur Keily had crossed the line to claim his hat-trick, it was the 'mystery man' who had captured the headlines. That same Saturday afternoon, the early sports edition of the *Liverpool Echo* had run a story (under the headline 'Refuses to Quit') about 'Torrance of Buxton' (*sic*), branding him the 'marathon interloper' who was still leading the field at 15 miles when the paper went to print.

Several hours later, there wasn't a sports reporter in the city who didn't want to know more, and as he headed wearily for his train 'Torrance of Buxton' was ambushed by a posse of journalists determined to unlock the secrets of the man with no name – and no number. It was the moment John had been thirsting for, and at an impromptu alfresco press conference he unburdened himself of his story with the relief of a man who believed absolute right to be on his side. 'I got a big kick out of this, and felt very important,' he later confessed. Courtesy of the *Daily Express*, 'the ghost runner' was born.

Within 48 hours, almost every national paper was carrying John Tarrant's story. 'Odd Man Out Led the Field', trumpeted the *Sunday Graphic*. 'Gate-Crasher Led', revealed the *Sunday Pictorial*. 'Mystery Solved', claimed the *Daily Mirror*. 'Mystery Runner Owns Up', reported the *Daily Herald*. Even the sturdy *Buxton Advertiser* eventually cottoned on to the celebrity in its midst – albeit a week later – running a story about the 'local man who startled organisers' in the 'marathon with a difference' alongside a picture of John, a very anxious-looking Edie and wide-eyed son Roger. But it was the *Daily Express* which most acutely assessed the real power of John's story, and it was they who came up with the tag by which he would forever be known.

In the story carried on 13 August, their 'Express staff reporter' was able to boast how he'd spoken to, and identified, 'the ghost runner' in the Liverpool marathon. 'Here is the story of a man who knew where he wanted to go and thought he knew how to get there,' declared their strapline, sitting above copy which described John as a 'runner with a heart as tough as the rocks he carves in the quarry'. Everything was there. Everything he'd so badly wanted people to hear. John's desperation to be cleared to run officially. John's meagre earnings as a scratch boxer. John's poverty. John's deep belief in his own ability as a class runner. It wasn't subtle – John didn't do subtle – but even allowing for the filter of a Fleet Street staff reporter's notebook, the words sounded real and rang with the fresh-minted anger of a man unlocking a lifetime's dam of resentments.

'I ran to convince the AAA that I am a purely amateur runner and race for the love of it . . . I needed to show that I had the ability . . . but the AAA refuse to recognise me.'

From now on this would be the mantra which John would repeat, almost word for word, publicly and loudly, to anyone who was prepared to listen. Overnight, he'd gone from a hopeless ex-boxer to a national cause with a voice, a family . . . and a face. Alongside their article, the *Express* had given readers their first glimpse of a sockless Tarrant in a picture captioned 'Oh, my poor feet'. He didn't look like a man to be messed with. He didn't sound like he was going to go away quietly.

It had half-killed him, and he'd failed to finish, but the Liverpool Marathon had been a transforming experience for John. For more than half the race, he'd led an international field. Strangers had cheered him and clapped him on the back. Words couldn't express what it felt like to be out there, surging forwards from the front – at least not any words he knew – and every sports page had carried his story. Like some outlaw legend, he'd even acquired an alias – 'the ghost runner' – which he would actively cultivate, and which would become synonymous with the name of John Edward Tarrant.

Any doubts in his mind about running – or the fight ahead – were gone forever. He was 24 years old and time was pressing. The Rome Olympics were barely four years away, and he'd set a place in the British team as his target. Now that his story was out there, he felt confident the authorities would concede and that the whole sorry saga would be swiftly resolved and forgotten. If it wasn't, then he'd ruthlessly exploit his new-found status, and the ghost runner would run illegally again and again until his case was won. After Liverpool, running would be the priority around which he constructed his life. Until further notice, his work and family would take second place.

Deep within their headquarters at Torrington Place in London, the very officials whose ears he was seeking were getting their first real inkling of a distant provincial problem.

Within a few weeks' time, they felt absolutely certain, it would burn itself out. Rules were rules were rules, and they couldn't be allowing a professional into their ranks. But how unreasonable of the *Daily Express* to give him so much space. Weren't they supposed to be on our side?

Chapter Four

The Ghost Runner

1956

He didn't know it, but John Tarrant was not alone. All over Britain – and in northern England especially – there were other young men bridling against the ancient, ingrained hypocrisies of the country in which they were growing up. Too young to have fought in the war, they would be too old to enjoy the fruits of the next decade now fizzing with promise on the horizon. Instead, they had found themselves trapped between the post-war Labour dream and the predictable return to power of the Tory toffs and landowners. By the late 1950s, Attlee and Nye Bevan were gone, replaced by Old Etonian smoothies like Anthony Eden and well-meaning duds like Harold Macmillan. The old order seemed to have efficiently reasserted itself, and young working-class upstarts were being taught a lesson in durability.

It all made for an awkward time to be a rebel. By the mid-'60s, the floodgates would have opened. The day was coming when merely to be young guaranteed you a ticket to the cultural revolution. But in John Tarrant's time, the malcontents were few in number, and their sense of post-war dissatisfaction lacked cohesion or common purpose. Although the newspapers would label them the 'angry young men', there was never a manifesto or a formal movement, never any momentum for change. Nor was it terribly clear who they were or what they were angry about. Mostly their rancour seemed to stem from a stew of vague resentments: a feeling of neglected grammar-school-boy provincialism; a fondness for the unsung heroism of working-class life; or simply bitter frustration at being excluded from the resurgent Tory establishment's secret inner circle.

In Alan Sillitoe's 'The Loneliness of the Long Distance Runner' (1959), the teenage borstal-boy hero deliberately loses a cross-country race with a rival prison merely to irritate his jailors, the message being that it isn't the runner who has lost but the establishment which has been beaten. Not that John Tarrant ever read Alan Sillitoe, John Braine, John Osborne, Kingsley Amis or any of the other literati whose scorn for the status quo qualified them as angry young men. Much closer to home was a fictional anti-hero whose bloody-minded anti-authoritarianism could have been modelled on Tarrant himself.

Since his first appearance in *The Rover* in 1949, the character of Alf Tupper – 'Tough of the Track' – had become a British comic-book legend. Like John, the fictional Tupper was a self-made Northern runner who travelled to his races by train and whose running career was defined by his constant battles with the men in blazers at the Amateur Athletic Association. Like John, Tupper had worked as a plumber and like John (as revealed in later prequels) he had spent most of his childhood in a home. But what they shared most, Tupper and Tarrant, was a complete distaste for the petty hierarchies and self-deluding authority figures which infested their sport.

It was a coincidence that Tarrant and his comic-book doppelgänger were so alike, but it was certainly no accident that Tupper chimed precisely with his times. Like Sillitoe and others, his creators had perfectly captured the beginnings of the collapse of the age of deference. Not a movement, but a fundamental mood change, one which would profoundly affect how John waged his war and how his adversaries would seek to retaliate.

Since he'd returned to Buxton from Liverpool, and despite his initial burst of notoriety, Tarrant's morale had slumped. Absolutely nothing had changed. Every few weeks, he would still complete an application to either the AAA or the ABA, enclosing his five-shilling fee, and every few weeks he'd get his money returned, together with the same doleful reasons for his rejection. True to his word, he'd intensified his training, even switching employers to find more time for his precious road work. His new job wasn't as well paid as the quarries, but Tarrant didn't care. Working as a labourer on the railways meant that he could finish at 5 p.m. with time to squeeze in a ten-mile run before his tea. On Saturdays, he'd run 20 miles, and on Sundays – when the passenger trains were forced to crawl past the maintenance gangs – he'd reluctantly work.

Knowing how prudent Edie was, they probably wouldn't notice the drop in his weekly pay packet. And if they did, he'd be perfectly happy to trim back. It wasn't as if they had a car or ever went out. It was perhaps as well. Within a few months, John had given up on the railways to work as an attendant at Buxton's public baths, which, on £7 10s a week, enabled him to run not ten but twenty miles a day. Shortly after that, he switched yet again, to a company making asbestos brake linings and a job which guaranteed every weekend off. 'It's very difficult for a dedicated athlete to find ideal employment. One that will give him enough time to train properly,' he argued later. Those were words with which Edie was to become very familiar.

But it was John's failure to reactivate the ghost runner – not Edie's diminishing weekly shopping allowance – that was giving him the most cause for despair. By Christmas 1956, five months had slipped wastefully by, and still the ghost had not been seen since Liverpool. Thankfully, the press remained periodically intrigued by his story ('Told the Truth – So Now He's an Outlaw' was the December headline in a *Daily Mirror* feature), but unless Tarrant started needling the authorities again, his campaign would have stalled before it had ever really started. The following year, he resolved, would truly be the year of his freshly minted alter ego.

In the build-up to Christmas, while Edie wrapped Roger's presents, John studied the race calendar for 1957, picking out the six high-profile races he would target. During the holiday, he'd dutifully sit and eat his turkey – he might even treat his old man to a bottle of pale ale – but, while Buxton was listening to the Queen, Tarrant would be up on the high roads, checking his times and clocking up the miles. 'His dedication was unbelievable. It was his whole life,' remembers Victor, who was once again being drawn into his brother's ever-thickening conspiracy.

On New Year's Eve, with 'The Kilt Is My Delight' entertaining the throng around Ted Hockenhull's crackling television, John and Victor got their heads down early for a dawn start and a very long drive. Determined to kick off the year with a flourish, Tarrant had decided to gatecrash a 13-mile road race being run between Morpeth and Newcastle. If all went to plan – if he didn't get lost on the way – it would put the ghost back on the nation's sports pages.

By almost every measure, however, the mission was a failure. The pair had made the start in time, but Tarrant had finished 46 embarrassing places behind Arthur Keily, the same man who'd annihilated him in Liverpool. 'I was his idol,' says Arthur, modestly, 'but he never, ever beat me.' It didn't seem to make any sense. John's training had been harder and more scientific, and at ten, fifteen or twenty miles he knew he was capable of better. His one consolation was the apparent absence of newsmen. Finishing 47th would hardly have enhanced his mystique, and Tarrant knew that the line between cult figure and laughing stock was a fine one. Luckily, there'd been no real fuss from the officials, either, and as the deflated Tarrant returned to Buxton to lick his wounds and Victor sped back to his RAF kitchens in Hereford, their hope was pinned on the spring for a change in their fortunes.

In early April, he was back. At a fifteen-mile road race in Nottingham, he leapt numberless from the crowd, holding a commanding lead over Arthur Keily and a gaggle of panting stewards for eleven miles before slumping to a sixth-place finish. As he crossed the line, a storm broke out. Following a complaint from 'an international athlete', Keily was disqualified for using an unrecognised professional – John Tarrant – as his pacemaker. 'I treated it as a huge joke, which indeed it was,' recalls Keily. 'I said, "If Tarrant was in the race to pace me, where was he in the last five miles when I was all on my own?" It was sour grapes from an established international runner.'

The judge's decision was reversed. Arthur Keily's name was restored as the rightful winner. John Tarrant's name, however, was nowhere to be seen on the official results. According to the records, a Mr Wood from the Rotherham Athletics Club had finished in sixth place, not John Tarrant. It was a sobering moment. As far as officialdom was concerned, John was a non-person – a ghost – whose performances didn't count and whose presence in races should be strenuously resisted.

Attitudes on both sides were hardening rapidly. Tarrant's antics were clearly infuriating the top brass at the AAA, and he simply had to be stopped. Tarrant, on the other hand, was having the time of his life. However much they airbrushed the histories, Tarrant knew he'd finished a creditable sixth behind five top-class athletes. The whole experience had utterly transformed him. Imminent despair had been squeezed out by hope and excitement. He had also found himself embraced by a new community of supporters.

John was never a gregarious, clubby person but at Morpeth and Nottingham, amidst the buzz and tension and pre-race chatter, he'd felt welcomed by his fellow athletes. From what he could see, the road-runners were all just like him anyway. Not remote scholars using big words like the glamour boys of the track. Not Oxbridge like Bannister and the rest of his four-minute-mile cronies. Just ordinary lads, working every hour God sent to put food in their families' mouths and raise the train fare to the next race. Brickies and factory workers. Colliers and railwaymen. Brummies and Geordies and Scousers. Unpretentious, unglamorous lads running for love, not money, and who spoke and thought just like him.

There was barely one now who didn't know his story, and, from what he could tell, they almost all wanted him reinstated. They could see how he'd got himself into this mess. No one begrudged him his few quid as a boxer, and, apart from the odd stuck-up grumbler, they all wanted him to run. Even Arthur Keily – his nemesis out on the road – had gone on the record as a supporter of John's cause. 'He was upset and he was right,' he remembers. 'What was happening to him was diabolical.'

It was crucial to Tarrant that he had this collective blessing. Dodging the stewards was tricky enough, but if John's rivals had taken against him, the challenge of running as a ghost would have been insurmountable. At any time, they could have nudged him out or tripped him up. Even if he did always turn down their offer of a beer, preferring to head off alone or with

Victor, Tarrant felt wanted. The previous summer, when he'd started, there'd been so many terrifying unknowns. One by one, they had slipped away, but getting this far had exhausted his well of courage. Out on the road, with the validation of his comrades, he felt confident enough to continue. And after the low-key skirmish of Nottingham, the days couldn't go quickly enough before the next battle in his one-man war.

Easter Monday, a mere three weeks away, was already looming as the ghost's next big day. Huge crowds, a quality field and a small army of the Northern Counties AAA's most officious officials were expected for the prestigious Doncaster-to-Sheffield Marathon. Perhaps it was as well that Tarrant felt so secure with his co-runners. For his latest outing, he'd chosen one of the most high-profile long-distance events on the sporting calendar. Everyone knew that he would be sure to try to gatecrash it. And every single man sent to officiate would be out to stop him succeeding.

Over the months to come, the brothers would gain more and more experience of the stratagems needed to get John into races. Although they sometimes travelled in Victor's Mini, they still went for two wheels rather than four whenever possible. It was head-numbingly cold, but it was also a lot cheaper on petrol, and a motorcycle could slalom through parked cars and spectators, getting John within a whisper of the start. If they arrived early, and if stewards were thin on the ground, Tarrant would risk the official changing-rooms. 'These would usually be in a school hall or a community centre, something like that,' says Victor. 'By this time, the other runners were really pleased to see him. They would never have shopped him. He was a celebrity.'

If the way into the changing-rooms was barred, the brothers doubled back to find a quiet spot where John could switch into his running kit unseen, and warm up, before sneaking back to the start on Victor's bike, John wearing his long thick coat and cap, invisible amongst the growing crowd. If they'd travelled in Victor's Mini, John would stay in the car and change in that. It was never very dignified – and it was an abysmal way to spend the precious minutes before a big race – but the two men had no choice. 'We somehow had to get as close to the start as we possibly could, because John couldn't show himself until after the starter's pistol, which meant the other runners had all got a head start already,' says Victor.

In a few years' time, Tarrant's knotted nerves and wretched liquid bowels would literally bring him, repeatedly, to his knees. At this time – when John was still just a novice – the running was the easy part. In the early summer of 1957 – heady with optimism and anticipation – the anxiety which always pecked at John's confidence evaporated quickly out on the road. It felt good to be the man with no number. He felt safe running at speed in the pack, where the stewards couldn't reach him.

His incurable need to always run from the front was risky, but ahead of him, or riding close by, would be Victor on his motorcycle, and Victor could always take care of business. Years afterwards, they both still chuckled about the day someone had tried to pull John out of a race by his arm. 'I was following behind on my motorbike and I drove it straight at this bloke, and we both ended up sprawled on the road. I was shouting, "Let him go, let him go," and John was shouting, "It's all right. Go on, go on." But I drove at him anyway,' confesses Victor. 'He had a trilby on.'

It was an important detail. In the world-view which prevailed among road-runners, it seems, a man's social standing could be determined by his headwear: lowly working men and their kind wore caps of the flat variety; the stewards who marshalled the runners invariably wore black suits and ties, white shirts and trilbies. If it was true, there would be trilbies aplenty at the Doncaster-to-Sheffield Marathon. John Tarrant's notoriety – and apparent popularity – had made him the AAA's public enemy No. 1. Any further embarrassments needed to be avoided. As the days ticked away and the race approached, the pressure on both John and Victor Tarrant began to build.

With four days to go, John had never felt better. Helped by Ron Ford, a friend from Buxton, Tarrant had measured out a debilitating 24-mile course above Buxton, linking a series of exposed hilltop roads. In filthy weather, on the Wednesday before the race, with Ron leading the way on a borrowed motorcycle, John had completed the distance in 2 hours and 24 minutes – never deviating from the six-minute miles he hoped would provide the platform for eventual success. 'I was delighted with my form,' he wrote.

Meanwhile, John's brother had been busy, too – refining their subterfuge with yet new levels of cunning. Since leaving Derbyshire, Victor had himself quietly discovered the joy of running and had joined up with a local club, the Cheltenham and County Harriers. Knowing that his brother would be greatly helped by a detailed map of the route – one that showed the locations of manned checkpoints – he'd entered the race under his own name, intending to pass the official information pack on to John. The organisers' reply revealed just how keen they were to keep his older brother away:

> At our committee meeting held last evening it was reported that a man of similar name to yours living in Buxton had been entering races when he was not officially attached to an athletic club . . . To avoid any upset on the day, could you please confirm that you are a member of the Cheltenham Harriers, and that you are eligible to take part in this

Marathon? The Committee emphasised that the Mr Tarrant of Buxton would not be permitted to run on Easter Monday.

But 'Mr Tarrant of Buxton' was not to be stopped. On a dirty, damp April morning – the roads glossed by dark, greasy puddles – Victor navigated his Mini through the terraced red-brick back streets of Doncaster. Squeezed inside were a silent and apprehensive trio of outlaws. In the rear sat Ron Ford, roped in as an extra pair of eyes. Cramped in the front passenger seat was John, shivering fretfully, with his black running plimsolls clenched between his knees. Only Victor seemed to have full mastery over his nerves, calmly locating the changing-rooms at a local school before ordering his brother to stay put while he and Ron checked out the security.

With the rain pinging eerily on the car roof, John sat in dread awaiting the return of his co-conspirators. They'd been too long. There was a problem. Maybe the car had been followed. Where the hell were they? When Ron and Vic eventually scuttled back to the car, he could tell from their faces that something was badly wrong. On door duty they'd found a race steward with the express instruction not to allow 'the ghost runner' anywhere near the changing facilities. In his hand had been a recent photograph of John.

It was a serious escalation of hostilities. If photographs had been issued to stewards, the task of getting John into the race would be even tougher. Finding a quiet street on which to park nearby, the three men sat in misted-up silence as John wrestled himself into his running kit, trying desperately to focus on the race ahead. At least they'd got this far. If John kept his head down, if he walked to the start between Victor and Ron, they should still be all right. Under the cover of a growing crowd, the trilbies couldn't possibly pick out every face.

They were in luck. Huddled in a cold Yorkshire drizzle, an anonymous grey scrum of spectators had stepped out in their winter coats and were congregating, collars up and caps on, beneath a black tide of umbrellas. It couldn't be better. In the monochrome morning light, everyone looked exactly the same. Oddly, a man with a placard – 'Christ Died For Our Sins' – was making his way to the start line, and as the 11 a.m. pistol inched closer John headed that way too, sandwiched between his confederates, a regulation raincoat and flat cap concealing the blue singlet and white shorts beneath. *All he wanted was a number.*

If he raised his head just an inch, he could see the other runners; feel the invisible snap of their tension; smell the liniment warming on their calves and thighs, rising strongly above the acrid bite of burning tobacco. *A lousy number on a lousy vest.* Out of the corner of his eye, he saw another runner arriving late, face set stern, hair greased back, the number 22 pinned to the belly of his vest. Arthur Keily. Bloody Arthur Keily. John's voice hissed out towards him. 'Arthur. *Arthur.*' Keily turned sharply to try to locate who was whispering his name. 'There he was,' he remembers, 'standing near the start in a big topcoat all ready to dive in. John Tarrant. My ghostly shadow.'

With seconds remaining, there was no time for pleasantries. A moment's silent eye contact between the two men was enough. In a race which Keily would later call 'a battle of the giants', he was not remotely troubled by John's presence. 'I felt as calm as a child to slumber soothed,' Arthur remembered in his autobiography. Tarrant, on the other hand, could scarcely contain himself. After the stewards had scanned the crowd for ghosts and satisfied themselves that all the runners had numbers, the Mayor of Doncaster fired his gun.

To the mayor's horror, pandemonium broke out all around

him. From the crush somewhere behind, a cadaverous, dark-haired man had emerged, throwing his coat and cap to the pavement before leaping off in the wake of the official field. *It's him! It's him!* Laughter spread through the crowd, and a handful of stewards, clutching clipboards and holding tightly on to their hats and spectacles, clattered frantically down the road in pursuit. Within minutes – with their shouted remonstrations fading quickly behind him – John had buried himself in the pack, and before even one mile was completed he was once again running shoulder to shoulder with Arthur Keily.

'It was a nice cool day, and I felt in good form,' remembered John, who tucked in and introduced himself to the runners around him.

> They made me very welcome and were most concerned to know if I had a second to care for my feeding requirements and if not they were prepared to help me out. I felt relieved to learn that they did not hold anything against me . . . that they were right behind me in my fight for justice.

Once again, in this early part of the race, most of the runners were right behind Tarrant on the road as well. Entirely self-taught and lacking race experience, John only felt comfortable when he ran hard from the front. He knew how strong he was and reasoned that so long as he could keep going there was no better place to be. But it was a tactical affliction which was to hamper John throughout his entire career. At critical times, in crucial races, he would find himself drained and helpless when his rivals attacked. Not just once but time after time he would flop out, unable or unwilling to take another step.

To his fellow runners, it was naive and incomprehensible; only Victor and Edie really knew why he did it. What he was doing wasn't about simply taking part. Tarrant was only there to win. If he was a winner, he felt certain the authorities would have to climb down. If he was a loser, he was terrified they could afford to keep on ignoring his letters. As a winner, the press would write about him and rally to his flag. As a loser, he would command pity but never respect. When John lost his head and charged to the front like a bull, it was desperation which drove him there, not tactics: a terrible all-consuming fear that time was slipping away, and with it his chance for redemption.

Even out here, pounding the dismal streets through Rotherham, he couldn't escape the indignities of his predicament. At every checkpoint, a man sitting inside a loudspeaker van pointed out that the runner with no number was an unofficial competitor who had no right to be in the race. Much as the crowd cheered – much as Victor and Ron urged him on – this wasn't how it should be. Slinking along like a criminal. Not for seventeen measly quid, it shouldn't. At 18 miles, trailing the leader by 100 yards, John could no longer hold himself back. The mists descended, and he was off. 'It was a shocking expenditure of energy for which I was to pay dearly ... at the speed I was travelling it was only a matter of seconds before I drew level.'

Two miles later, John was spent, and the inevitable, compact figure of Arthur Keily loomed over his shoulder. Tarrant was done. With one mile to go, he was still holding on to sixth place. By the end – reduced to a stagger – he'd crumbled back to eleventh, almost ten minutes behind Keily, whose winning time had set a new course record. In John's broken state, it required Victor to point out the milestone which had just been passed. Putting pain and failure aside, Tarrant had completed a marathon for the first time, albeit at a price. 'Poor, gallant John. He was in a really bad state after that race,' says Arthur. 'Always was in fact. Used to really knock himself about a bit.'

If it were possible, the day got worse. Washed and changed – some wearing smart blue Great Britain blazers – the official runners were making their way to Sheffield's Channing Hall, clutching invitations to the post-race banquet, in Arthur Keily's words 'a proper spread . . . tip-top meal . . . waiters and everything'. The great and the good were all there, councillors with handlebar moustaches and aldermen in their chains. Even Mr J.C. Kennedy, president of the Northern Counties AAA, was on hand to help present Keily with his cup.

In the fading light outside, hearing the thunderous applause from within, a crestfallen John Tarrant wondered what to do. Through those thick doors were both his friends and his enemies. The people whose love he craved and the people whom he believed to be persecuting him. If he'd been dressed for it – if he'd had one of those flashy blazers – maybe he'd have gone in. But Victor and Ron were waiting; Edie would probably have the tea on; and it had already been a long, strange day. Sometime – as a winner – perhaps he'd be back. As he turned to leave, Arthur Keily was once again there at his shoulder. 'I told him, "You'll be all right in here with me, lad. You can be my guest," but he wouldn't come in.'

Tarrant had lost and was shattered. Although he'd crossed the line in 11th place , his name was missing from the published results. Officially, a Mr Frank Lucop of Hull had finished where John had. As if his aching body wasn't bad enough, now this. He'd always known they'd deny him, but it still hurt more than a sockful of blisters. As the three men drove thoughtfully back across the Derbyshire hills, they each must have wondered whether the 'ghost runner' trick had run its course. The following day would provide their answer.

Under a large picture of the leading runners, singling out 'Mystery Man Tarrant', the *Sheffield Telegraph* had praised him for his 'brilliant' run. Given that the *Telegraph* had organised the event – and had earlier written to Victor saying that 'Mr Tarrant of Buxton' could not compete – their sudden turnaround was mystifying. Not that John was quibbling. The *Telegraph*'s reporter had quoted him kindly, apologising to the organisers for any embarrassment, whilst insisting that his 'ghost running' was his only way of 'bringing my claims before the sporting public'. Even more helpful were the words the *Telegraph* had coaxed out of Arthur Keily shortly before he'd disappeared into the Channing Hall for his free plateful of post-marathon potted beef. 'I feel every sympathy with Tarrant and I should like to see him running with official blessing,' he'd said.

It was only a few words, but it was a pivotal contribution to John's case. Arthur Keily was nearing the end of an illustrious domestic and international career. Like John, he was an uncompromising, blunt-spoken working man. Unlike John, he had met and was able to communicate with some of the key figures pulling the strings behind John's ban. What Arthur said held weight, and in the months to come – backed overwhelmingly by his fellow runners – he wrote repeatedly to the AAA pleading Tarrant's case. 'The way this man was treated was disgusting,' he says. 'I wrote several times but never got any replies.' The silence was symptomatic of the authorities' refusal to budge, but it didn't really matter. Tarrant was no longer alone, and someone, somewhere was getting the message.

He was now into his third job in a year. Less than 12 months before, he'd been humping rocks into trucks at a limestone quarry. By the summer of 1957, he was spending the days in his swimming trunks, blowing the whistle on underwater petting and dangerous dive-bombing at Buxton's public baths. For a man who wanted only to run, the hours indoors must have seemed endless, every minute ticked off, every thought fighting against a hateful chlorine cacophony. Three days a week, he'd finish at 5 p.m. (on the others at 7.30 p.m.), and then he'd be away. On the dot. Clear the pool of kids and into his kit. Ten miles before tea. Fifteen miles if he was feeling good.

If Edie was surprised that John was prepared to earn less in order to run more, she didn't say so. It wasn't ideal living with her father, and she'd have liked a council house of their own, but at least John had a job, and she'd learned not to fight where running was concerned. Victor had always said John wasn't materialistic. Good job he wasn't. Now she knew that when it came to work he wasn't very conscientious either. Bloody lazy, some said, but Edie didn't think that was fair. Until this ghost-running thing was resolved, he'd never settle. She still believed in him, and he'd still have her support. One way or another, though, it would need to happen soon. It wasn't easy bringing up a boy on your own.

In July, John and Victor were off on their motorcycle again, riding 40 miles in a deluge to gatecrash a race in Northwich. Once again, Arthur Keily was in the line-up and – for the fourth successive time – Tarrant was unable to best him. Keily's public support, however, had begun to show results. John now had new, even more influential supporters. The *News Chronicle* would shortly be swallowed up by the *Daily Mail*, but it was a newspaper proud of its liberal voice, and in Tarrant it had found an underdog – an angry young man – worthy of its radical spirit.

In a series of tough articles, *Chronicle* writer Roy Moor was taking every opportunity to lash the authorities for their refusal to reinstate the ghost runner. 'Come on AAA,' he pleaded. 'Give the boy a ticket. He's earned it.' It was good knockabout, tabloid stuff, but at Northwich the brothers themselves also detected evidence of a thaw in higher places. Although, as always, Tarrant's name was obliterated from the results – he finished eighth – the animosity from the stewards felt muted.

Hereford, 1960. John, Edie, son Roger and Victor's Mini.

Private John Tarrant marches to a new record with fellow TAs Ken Flowers (left) and Derek Davies. (courtesy of Ken Flowers)

The all-conquering Hereford TA runners *c*.1961.
Victor is in the front row, second from left; John is in the back row, on the far right.

'He'd always want to hammer you.'
Reinstated and virtually unbeatable
– Tarrant in his pomp.

November 1966, Cardiff. A new world record at 40 miles.

Ned Waring, Tarrant's indefatigable benefactor. (courtesy of the family of Ned Waring)

A ghost in New York, 1967.
(courtesy of Tom Osler)

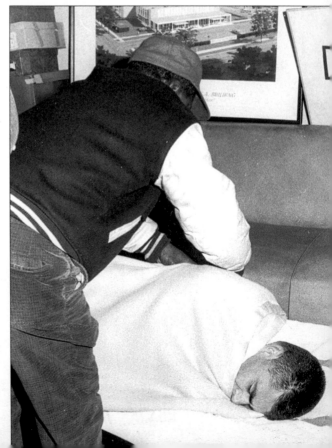

Jet-lagged and weary: Tarrant
on a camp bed hours before
ghosting in the USA.
(courtesy of Tom Osler)

Durban, South Africa, 1968. Tarrant basks in his notoriety.
(courtesy of Independent Newspapers)

Dave Box and Dave Bagshaw,
Tarrant's great long-distance rivals.
(copyright unknown)

Dave Box: the ego of a potentate, the body
of a Greek god. (copyright unknown)

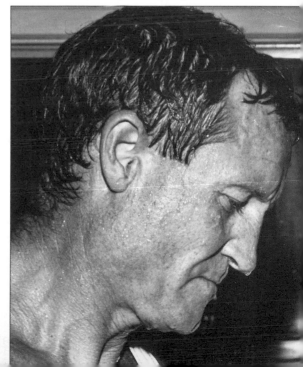

October 1969. John embraces Edie seconds after setting a new world record at 100 miles. (courtesy of *Daily Express*)

Rajendra Chetty. 'You are made in the mettle of great men,' he told John. (courtesy of Rajendra Chetty)

Finishing the Comrades in South Africa in 1968 – the fourth place that never was.

South Africa, 1969.
Running out of steam in the Comrades.
(courtesy of Independent Newspapers)

Posing with the Goldtop Trophy in 1971, only hours after his first massive haemorrhage.

Hereford Football Club, 1974. A gaunt-looking Tarrant runs for the last time. Victor (in the white jumper) keeps time.

Tarrant even told Roy Moor that 'one official actually wished me luck in my bid to be accepted'. It wasn't much, but it was a start, and four weeks later, at Holbeach in Lincolnshire, it got even better.

Privately, what some enlightened local AAA officials were realising was that Tarrant's presence in a race guaranteed them dollops of free advance publicity and much bigger crowds on the day. Nor was it very difficult for race organisers to get the attention of the press. In the '50s and '60s, people didn't read newspapers, they wrestled with them. A typical Fleet Street daily was more like a sail than a collection of articles – a vast flapping broadsheet with acres of space for sports news from almost any level. Jostling alongside First Division football news might be the school rugby scores from Bridlington or the Rutland women's hockey league tables. It was invariably tedious, but it was what people expected, and it sold. There was no appetite for celebrity tittle-tattle, only information and statistics, and every Sunday afternoon an army of freelance stringers would ring in with their weekend copy, hoping for a bite from a sports editor with five blank pages to fill by midnight.

More than 50 years later, that world has almost entirely disappeared. The races have mostly gone; the stringers have hobbled away; and the niche sports and their scorelines have retreated to specialist magazines and the Internet. It's almost impossible to imagine anyone getting to hear about a John Tarrant in today's football-dominated tabloids, let alone his performance in an unremarkable seven-mile road race on the edge of the Wash. But back then real-life Alf Tuppers didn't come along every day, and certainly not one with a chip on his shoulder the size of Stockport.

Tarrant was good copy. Tarrant sold. There was never a

shortage of hacks to help steadily embellish the myth, employing emotive headlines and carefully staged photographs. Here was John getting changed alone behind a tree. Here was numberless John standing tellingly apart from his fellow runners at a starting line. By 1957, fascination with Tarrant's story was so widespread that his presence on a stringer's beat ensured a guaranteed payday – assuming, that is, you knew Tarrant was heading your way in the first place. And that – up till now – had been the hard bit.

In August 1957, Tarrant received an extraordinary letter from a Mr R.E.S. Clay, the secretary of the Holbeach Athletic Club, inviting him to a modest seven-mile road race at the town's annual sports day in Lincolnshire. By John's recent standards, it was a backwater event, but the implications of the approach were huge. For the first time, a recognised official had asked him to participate in an accredited race. Although it was clear that Tarrant would be competing unofficially, the welcome seemed genuine and sincere. It was also a very shrewd recognition by Mr Clay that an avalanche of peer opinion was fast swinging behind the ghost runner and that Tarrant's presence, if leaked, would do nothing but boost the profile of his meeting.

With just a few days to go, the stringers got busy feeding suspiciously well-informed stories wondering whether John Tarrant might be heading to Holbeach. 'Will "Ghost" Runner Gate-Crash Big Race?' asked the headline above an article which reported a record surge of last-minute entries from 'Newcastle, Doncaster, Stockport, Leeds, Norwich, Sheffield and St Albans'. From all over England, the running fraternity were flocking to get a peep at the controversial ghost. Tarrant himself, meanwhile, was making a typically shambolic hash of his own 120-mile journey to Holbeach. With Victor unavailable, he'd caught the train to Nottingham, missed his connection and then hitch-hiked the final fifty miles, arriving ten minutes before the race was due to start. 'My cash wouldn't run to a taxi,' he told reporters. Waiting to greet him was the enterprising Mr Clay, whose confidence had now grown sufficiently for him to hand Tarrant a card marked 'GHOST' to pin onto his red vest.

Never before had John experienced such curiosity and affection. The trademark hat and long coat were not required. There would be no hot-faced stewards in pursuit. Even the start had been delayed to allow him time to recover from his travels. It felt odd to be lining up with all his fellow runners, odder still that his perennial rival Arthur Keily was nowhere to be seen. But even without him, there was no fairy-tale result. Egged on by the bemused Lincolnshire crowd, John managed third place. But after such a favourable build-up, it felt like yet another failure.

Maybe if he'd got there under a little less stress. Maybe if Victor had driven. Maybe he should decide which bloody distance he was best at. He was glad that Mr Clay was happy, and flattered that the papers were calling it 'the best meeting in the event's ten-year history'. But 12 months after diving into that Liverpool marathon, he still hadn't got a single victory under his belt. On the grapevine, there was unsubstantiated talk about his reinstatement, but nothing concrete. Nothing he truly believed. It was time to do what John always did when progress had stalled. It was time to change his job.

It has long struck most travellers as an odd boast, but for years the Peak District settlement of Chapel-en-le-Frith has welcomed drivers with a sign proclaiming itself 'The Home of Ferodo Brake Linings'. From its leafy workshops on the edge of the town, the company – now part of US conglomerate Federal-Mogul – has always been one of the region's biggest employers.

Since 1897, it has been supplying the world with 'friction products'. Most of Buxton's male workforce seems, at some point, to have gravitated there for a job. George Bailey worked there. Even John's father, Jack, was briefly on their payroll.

In the 1950s, every car, bus and even train was fitted with curved metal plates shod with heat-resistant asbestos which when forced into contact with a rotating wheel drum brought the vehicle slowly to a standstill. By today's standards, the technology was clumsy, but it was effective, and in 1957, having sampled almost every other job in Buxton, Tarrant found his way to the company's gates. As always, it was the time he wouldn't be working which seduced him: straight eight-hour shifts with the promise of every Saturday and Sunday free unless he fancied some overtime. Never would he work harder for his days off.

By his own account, he was taken on as a 'machine operative'. According to his colleagues, he had the worst job in the plant. Working in a factory yard – invariably alone – John's task was to hack off the stubborn asbestos residue from train brake plates worn down on New Zealand's railways before being shipped back to Ferodo for relining. Even by John's standards, it was a foul and filthy way to make a living. To loosen the old asbestos, each plate needed to be heated up in a furnace. John would then scrape the remnants away before sweeping up the dust and tossing it into the fire. 'I used to cringe when I saw what he was doing for a living,' remembers fellow worker John Sherratt. 'It was a truly horrible job.'

But Tarrant wasn't thinking about the job. He was thinking about running. Work served merely as a necessary but deeply inconvenient backdrop. His job at Ferodo might have been lousy, but it suited him perfectly. The stretch of the A6 between Buxton and Chapel-en-le-Frith couldn't have been better for his training. Rising steeply up out of the town, past a couple of pubs and the golf course, the road ran due north for three miles to Dove Holes, where John swung left, dropping sharply through narrow country lanes to the factory just in time for clocking on.

As he'd done when he worked at the quarry, he took to stuffing a haversack with house bricks or large books and running to work with it on his back. On the uphill stretch – despite the handicap – it wasn't unusual for him to overtake the local bus, looking up with a pained smile to see his fellow workers jeering at him through the windows. In his lunch breaks, he'd be out again, changing into his kit in a shower room behind the Ferodo canteen and then out by Chinley, up over the edge of Eccles Pike and back through Chapel marketplace to work. Most days he'd run alone, but if their shifts matched, John Sherratt would join him, struggling to keep up but fascinated to know more about the loner with the diabolical job.

'In those days,' he says, 'I was an apprentice in the electrician's job. I was also in the Salford Harriers, which I know John was interested in, but he was a much, much better runner than me. After those lunchtime runs, it was showers, butties and straight back to work. That was it. At the end of play, he'd be off again and running home to Buxton. We'd get the bus, which left within minutes of knocking-off time, and by the time it had climbed up to Dove Holes we'd just about be catching up with John.'

By mid-October, he was ready to ghost again. Despite the constantly swirling rumours about reinstatement, there had been no communication from the AAA, and his campaign had slipped off the back pages. This time, he would run right under the noses of the sporting establishment. This time, he would take the fight right into their snooty Southern back yard. Since leaving the children's home, Tarrant had steered clear of the

Home Counties, but the prospect of a ten-mile race in Walton-on-Thames was proving too tempting to resist. Dragging another local runner, Pat Grundy, along for the ride, John caught the early Saturday train south to St Pancras, where he was met by a sportswriter from a national newspaper. 'He picked us up and we went out to the track in his car. I'm also pretty sure it was the same journalist who drove us back to the station,' recalls Pat.

In all probability, the journalist was the dependable Roy Moor, whose coverage of the race spread across four columns of the next day's *News Chronicle*. Behind the scenes, Tarrant had been colluding with senior Fleet Street figures, sensing correctly that the AAA were looking for a way out of their increasingly embarrassing dilemma. It didn't matter that he managed only 17th in a field of 135 runners. What counted for John was the universally sympathetic myth-building coverage which followed his every appearance. At Walton, according to the newspapers, he'd changed behind a bush, shaken hands warmly with his fellow athletes and then dashed numberless into the race to avoid grumpy officials. 'The effort cost him £5 for train and hotel expenses but there's certainly no doubt about John's amateur spirit.' So said the *Daily Express*.

According to Moor's article in the *Chronicle*, it was now only the ABA who were holding out against Tarrant's complete exoneration. 'Red Tape and ABA Keep Tarrant Waiting . . . But Officials Give Him Hope', claimed the headline. It was progress – of sorts – but to Tarrant's incandescent way of thinking it was the same desperate, sordid nonsense. Only when the Amateur Boxing Association had forgiven him for his teenage sins in Buxton would the AAA tag along and junk their ban. Hadn't that been the exact situation 15 months ago? Apart from a reputation, what, precisely, had he gained?

Two weeks later, on a late-autumn Saturday at Woodbank

Park in Stockport, he slipped quietly into his ninth race as a ghost. It was the annual Salford Harriers ten-mile track championship. No journalists had been alerted, and the few officials in attendance turned a Nelsonian blind eye to John's presence. Tarrant was a friend, and a cause true to the Harriers tradition. There'd be no cap and coat required here. They even lent him a pair of running shoes after he discovered his own were still back at home in Buxton. Forty laps and fifty-six minutes later, despite the hell of a rain-sodden grass track, John Tarrant had won his first race for ten years. As always, he'd run from the front, but for once he hadn't flagged. Pebble-dashed with mud and chilled to the marrow, he'd kept on going, lapped the entire field and beaten the second man in – the record book's *official* winner – by two clear minutes.

It was a thrilling private moment, the necessary vindication of all the superhuman effort and stress which had preceded it. But it was far too little, far too late. Less than two weeks after his victory, John Tarrant contacted his friends in Fleet Street and told them he was giving up his fight for reinstatement. 'I must accept defeat,' he was reported as saying in the *News Chronicle*. 'It is an impossible task. I have decided to give up running. I am 26 and time is not on my side.' He'd made his point. Finally, he was a winner. From now on, the ghost would haunt only the hills around Buxton – running for company with lads like Pat Grundy and fading slowly out of sight, like all those distant Olympic dreams.

'The laws on amateurism are comical to behold,' proclaimed the *Chronicle*, aghast that Tarrant had 'given up the ghost'. They were right. The rules which had governed amateur sport since the 1880s were so riddled with hypocrisy, so infected by unfairness and inconsistencies, that it was almost impossible to understand let alone defend them. To belong to the Amateur

Rowing Association, an aspiring member had once needed to be able to demonstrate 'gentlemanly status' alongside proof that he had never done 'menial duty'. A professional cricketer could compete as an amateur, but it was absolutely forbidden for a rugby player who had taken money ever to compete again under the laws of rugby union. In the late nineteenth century, the fledgling AAA – forward thinking as ever – had even pursued legal action against athletes falsely claiming to be amateurs; the unlucky ones were prosecuted for fraud and condemned to six months' hard labour.

It was a problem with its roots in class and snobbery, but it was an issue of such bewildering complexity that John Tarrant had done well to come this far. Others had given up much sooner. Scottish athlete Tom McNab had been only a student waiter when he'd won £5 in the jumps at a 1956 village Highland Games. 'A schoolboy folly,' he calls it, but the result was a lifetime ban from international athletics. Derek Ibbotson, on the other hand, was a no-nonsense Yorkshire superstar who, in 1957, set a new world record at the mile. Such was his fame and consistency that he would personally choose the prizes before competing in a race, knowing full well that he would win. 'If we needed something for the house, then that's what I'd get,' he says. 'I remember a set of crockery very well. Ninety to a hundred pieces . . . That year was my big time. Forty-five races and forty-two wins. I could ask for an appearance fee, because there were very few like me who could get a crowd in. The organisers knew what they were going to get, and I wasn't going to turn out for nowt.'

Money. It was always about money. John Tarrant knew of McNab and had run against Ibbotson. In his weary retirement statement, he'd pulled no punches but named no names. 'There are many top-class amateurs competing today who are not bona fide amateurs,' he'd said. Everyone knew what went on.

Everyone knew it stank. As Tarrant saw it, the whole amateur 'thing' had been orchestrated in the nineteenth century by rich boys from Oxbridge who felt distaste for the money and gambling which underpinned crowd-pulling sports like pedestrianism – joyous and earthy working-men's events which drew thousands to watch characters such as George Hill, who in 1815 walked fifty miles a day for three weeks on the fields of London's Blackheath.

Hidden away in Britain's public schools, a counter-ethos had emerged: the cult of the gentleman amateur, which hinged on the belief that the working man could not be relied upon to compete fairly by virtue of his suspect appetite for pound notes. To exclude these unappetising men of 'menial duty', and to protect this selectively British notion of 'fair play', sport had slowly been codified under the guidance of the so-called gentleman-players.

In 1880, the Amateur Athletic Association had been formed with its chilling (for John Tarrant and others) definition of an amateur as one who since the age of 16 'has never competed for a prize or monetary consideration in any sport or game . . . or staked a wager or bet in which he was an entrant . . . or taught athletic exercise for pecuniary consideration, or in any way exploited his ability for profit; and who has never taken part in any competition with anyone who is not an amateur'.

Nor was it just athletics. The bogus pursuit of lofty and regressive aristocratic sporting virtues was everywhere. Amateurism's central creed was that participation was its own reward and that no performance motivated by financial gain could ever command merit or respect. In rugby union, it meant working men were banned from claiming back their wages if the sport required them to miss work. In football, it saw the formation of the Corinthian Casuals, a squad of former public schoolboys pledged never to train or compete for honours. So wedded were they to the so-called ancient Greek ideal that, in the 1890s – when the penalty kick was introduced – they opted to withdraw their goalkeeper whenever one was conceded. For a Corinthian to gain benefit from an act of foul play was simply not cricket, old boy. Better to lose than play the game to win.

It was a line which had held fast throughout the first half of the twentieth century, perpetuated by men whose wealth shielded them from temptation. Tarrant well remembered George Bailey's tales of being shoehorned into steerage en route to the Los Angeles Olympics. He'd been confronted by too many cut-glass accents, and chased by too many men in black suits, to be under any illusions about what kind of people governed his sport. Privately, he poured scorn on the lot of them. Publicly, he struggled, against his instincts, to maintain his dignity. As Tom McNab saw it – now merely a spectator at the 1958 Commonwealth Games he'd hoped to compete in – the whole shooting match was, he says, 'laced with hypocrisy and malice'.

'The officials felt morally superior to people who earned money. To them, professionals were on a par with criminals. And yet the upper classes – who didn't need money – were the ones who'd created and now sustained the rules. Locally, you sometimes had clubs who took these attitudes on and were even more intense in their devotion to the amateur codes. These were people of no human quality. We talk about sport dignifying the human condition, but these people did the opposite of this. Every now and then, there'd be someone they didn't particularly like and they'd be thrown to the wolves.'

What made it unbearable for Tarrant, was that by the 1950s the edifice of amateurism – so meticulously constructed on the playing fields of Harrow and Eton – had become riddled with cracks and inconsistencies. For the organisers of glamorous weekend track meetings, big names meant big crowds. In 1948, the official AAA championships had sucked in almost 50,000 people. The *News of the World* and the *Daily Telegraph* were pouring sponsorship into the sport. Events at Stamford Bridge, Belle Vue and White City were hugely popular, but only when they lured top athletes onto the billing. And that would happen only if someone was prepared to slip them a brown envelope, let them pre-select their prizes and handsomely cover their costs. 'The authorities didn't get to know what you got,' says Derek Ibbotson. 'It would have taken too much time and money to find out.'

Amateurism as the Corinthian Casuals had practised it was dying. No one was withdrawing their goalkeeper any more. Shamateurism had taken its place, a murky halfway house in which the strong got stronger – and richer – and the weak got a good hiding. 'The people who were paying this money out were the people who'd later be banning you,' fumed Tom McNab. 'The whole thing was totally corrupt.'

Road-runners had always been sport's poor relations. Mostly, like Alf Tupper, they were working blokes, grafters whose factory jobs left little spare time – or cash – to train, travel and race, particularly if they were also keeping a family. Their events were unfashionable and generated no income, either for them or the AAA. No one had to buy a ticket to stand on a sticky, wet pavement and watch 50 unknown men run past in vests. The open roads and public highways suited them best, because it cost them nothing and their fellow runners were honest and bullshit-free.

On the night before a race on the Isle of Man, with one runner unable to find lodgings, Tarrant had happily surrendered his mattress and slept fully clothed on the bedsprings. On another occasion, down to his last ten shillings (fifty pence) and ravenous after a race, Tarrant had put the money in a charity box and forgone the meat pie he was craving. Men like this were much closer to an authentic amateur ethos than those gentleman-players whose participation in sport was underwritten by a trust fund or a professional qualification.

As Mel Watman, a former editor of *Athletics Weekly*, puts it, 'Their motivation was "I want to run for my country" and that was all.' It was ironic that in Tarrant's case such altruistic simplicity had – in Tom McNab's words – been lobbed to the wolves. It was fortunate, however, that, as John stewed miserably through the winter of 1957 and 1958, the poor relations of athletics were about to find their voice. And the first of those voices to be heard was his wife's.

On 16 November, shortly after Tarrant's 'retirement', a missive from Edie headed the letters column in the influential *Athletics Weekly*. 'I am proud to be married to a man with so much courage and determination,' it said. 'Running has become a part of John's life and I know he would be unhappy without it. You have not seen the last of the Ghost Runner yet.' It was a brave, and characteristically self-sacrificing, endorsement. Marriage had never been kind to Edie Light. Spare cash was elusive, domestic privacy was non-existent and – as Pat Grundy saw it – she'd married 'a very, very selfish lad'. But Edie wasn't listening. People could say what they liked. Until her husband got what he was entitled to, she'd put up with his mood swings and swallow her pride during the long, lonely days and companion-free nights.

Seven days later, it became clear just how much her short letter had helped. A deluge of correspondence had fallen on the magazine, prompting it to respond with a strongly worded editorial which said that:

> From the letters received from all parts of the country it
> seems that public opinion is very much on the side of John

Tarrant . . . space will not permit the printing of even a fraction of the letters received, many of them lengthy.

The following month, a rival magazine – *The Athletic Review* – offered its own, even more daring support for his case:

An honest, clean-living man with the courage and tenacity of John Tarrant would be an acquisition to the ranks of amateur athletics. If [the AAA] really want to give Tarrant an opportunity . . . then it is to be hoped they are doing everything to persuade the ABA that no good purpose will be served by adopting an uncompromising attitude on the matter.

Pressure was building. What had started almost six years ago as a festering private correspondence between Tarrant and his local AAA officials was now an increasingly public war of words. 'Let Justice Be Done', bellowed one headline. 'Alter the Rules – and Quick', said another. But it wasn't as simple as that. Both the AAA and the ABA were squirming in the ruinous mire of their own outdated rulebooks, publicly unable – and secretly unwilling – to make the changes which would let Tarrant in. According to Mr Jack Piggs of the Northern Counties AAA, in a letter to *Athletics Weekly*, the very idea that the rules could be amended, let alone broken, was 'a sentiment with which I thoroughly disagree'. 'To break our agreement [with the ABA] would be a very serious matter,' he added.

It was the same dog-tired old sticking point, the same grotesque abhorrence of change. Until the boxing authorities accepted Tarrant as an amateur, the athletics authorities were powerless to act. The only hope now for Mr Piggs and his like was that the row would somehow dribble to a standstill and that John Tarrant (and his troublesome wife) would shut up.

But by February 1958, there was absolutely no chance of that. At an emergency session of the Amateur Boxing Association's London council, Tarrant's application for reinstatement was again 'turned down flat'. John's immediate, furious response was to reactivate the ghost.

Fired up by the huge outpouring of support, he'd already cut short his retirement, popping up briefly to ghost a race in Hull before returning home to find a letter from the BBC inviting him to appear on *Sportsview* with David Coleman. Despite the warm support of the national press, it would ultimately be the new fad of television, not print, which broke the farcical deadlock. Through gritted teeth, Tarrant had clung on just long enough to arrive in a new age, an age in which the governed seemed to be adapting much faster than the governors.

The huge television audience which watched David Coleman interview John Tarrant in February 1958 saw an unpretentious, dedicated sportsman make a simple, moral case for his reinstatement. It probably helped that he was quizzed while running around a country park in the West Midlands. It certainly helped that in Coleman he'd found an empathetic supporter, happy to use his increasingly popular programme to express his personal backing for Tarrant's case. 'You deserve to win your fight,' he said. 'You are the most genuine amateur it has ever been my privilege to interview.'

Back home in Buxton, it was an appearance which caused momentary discomfort for Tarrant's son, Roger, unable to comprehend how his father could be on television whilst simultaneously sitting next to him on the family's cramped sofa. There was laughable confusion, too, at the Amateur Athletic Association. Uncertain, with his case so delicately poised, whether to accept the BBC's fee, John had written to the AAA for advice. By return, he was told that 'an athlete cannot accept refund of loss of wages in connection with any athletic activity . . . it will therefore be necessary for you to return to the BBC the sum of £1 18s [£1.90].' Legitimate expenses, with receipts, were acceptable. Precious lost earnings were not. And since he'd paid a cabbie a tip, and forgotten to claim for a meal on the train, Tarrant was once again out of pocket. 'In spite of my feelings I had to refund the money to the BBC,' lamented Tarrant in his memoir. 'Strange how the powers that be would not allow me to refund my [boxing] earnings to retrieve that "mistake".'

But John's out-of-pocket expenses were a side issue. Appearing on television had galvanised his campaign and put an unstoppable spring in his step. Over the next few weeks, he gatecrashed two more races, finishing comfortably within the leading group each time. In April, he was back in Yorkshire, rerunning the Doncaster-to-Sheffield Marathon but losing yet again to the effervescent Arthur Keily.

In Buxton, a petition had been raised, attracting thousands of signatures, and bundled off to the AAA's headquarters in London. In magazines and newspapers, more articles were retelling the heroic story of the ghost runner – the blighted young man from the North whose shirt carried no number and whose name never featured in any official results. Finally, in the glossy photo magazine *World Sport*, came the single piece of journalism which would shatter the line held for so long by the British athletics establishment. The irony was that, when it arrived, it came from the pen of one of its own most trenchant and traditional conservatives.

Subsequent generations would know his story through the film *Chariots of Fire*, but in the 1950s Harold Abrahams was the darling of British athletics and a passionate advocate for unpolluted amateurism in his sport. Educated at Bedford, Repton and Cambridge, he'd overcome anti-Semitic hostility, emerging as a national hero after winning the 100 metres gold medal at the 1924 Paris Olympics. In almost every detail, he was the diametric opposite of John Tarrant. The ghost runner's wife was a part-time cleaner; Abrahams' was a D'Oyly Carte mezzo-soprano. John's brother was an RAF cook; Harold's two brothers had both been knighted. Abrahams himself had served in the army and been captain of the British Olympic team. But although Abrahams would be a lifelong opponent of professionalism, his training in law had given him an acute sense of what was right – and what was clearly not.

Looking forensically at Tarrant's case, he swiftly identified the important anomaly which had lain buried there since the very beginning. If John had never belonged to the Amateur Boxing Association – as he had always insisted – then he'd broken no rules, and therefore the ABA's reciprocal agreement with the AAA was completely irrelevant. As Abrahams succinctly put it, 'You cannot suspend or disqualify someone unless he comes under your jurisdiction.'

It was a brilliant piece of repositioning. Whilst roundly condemning Tarrant for receiving his £17 as a boxer, Abrahams was still able to say that – according to the letter of the AAA's own rulebook – his application could be reconsidered without any reference to the ABA. 'Whether it *will* reinstate Tarrant remains to be seen,' he added carefully, 'but there are cases far worse than this where the AAA has readmitted to the ranks runners who had, for instance, competed in professional meetings.'

It was a calculated and decisive intervention. Abrahams already sat on every key committee in British athletics. Everywhere he looked, he saw people rattled and confused by Tarrant's persistent ghost running. If it went on much longer, who knew where it would all end? Since 1926, Abrahams had served on the AAA's general committee, and he was the chairman of the British Amateur Athletic Board, which governed participation in overseas events. For more than 30 years he'd been an athletics correspondent for the *Sunday Times*. His books on training and competition had inspired countless athletes. He'd even been a timekeeper on the day Roger Bannister ran his sub-four-minute mile. No voice carried the same weight or would initiate such an immediate response.

Less than a month after his article, a letter arrived for Tarrant – 'without warning' – at Grove Lane in Buxton. It was a short, unsigned note from the Northern Counties AAA – just 41 words – offering no trace of regret and not one line of explanation:

> I beg to inform you that you have been reinstated as an amateur by the Handicapping Board of Control and are therefore eligible to compete at athletics meetings held under the laws of the Amateur Athletic Association from this date forward.

For a moment, Tarrant literally could not believe what he was reading. Through rare tears, the words blurred, and he passed the letter to Edie, asking her to read it aloud – slowly – so he could be absolutely sure he wasn't dreaming. Still unconvinced, he rang Roy Moor at the *News Chronicle* asking him to check that it wasn't a hoax. After so long, it wasn't easy to trust this single bleak sentence constructed with such lack of charm. To John, it had always felt personal, and the letter simply confirmed it. They hadn't liked what he'd done, or where he'd come from, and they loathed him for what he'd said. Now, at the death, what else could he expect?

But he'd won. That was all that mattered. Forty-one priceless words, however sterile, would suffice, and – for fear they'd vanished – he got Edie to read them one more time. And then, for good measure, he read them again in silence.

The next morning, the works bus over to Chapel-en-le-Frith would have no chance keeping up with him. Wings on his pumps, he'd have. The day's filthy graft would fly by in a confusion of hopes and plans. He was finally free to join a club and get some proper coaching. In just two years' time, they'd be picking the British team for the 1960 Rome Olympics and he'd be on that plane. He knew it. He could taste it. Instead of sneaking around like a fugitive in his long coat and cap, he'd stride into the arena, head held high, hair creamed back, wearing a jacket emblazoned with the Union Jack.

As he folded the precious letter into his wallet, his only private sadness was that he didn't think he'd ever need the ghost runner again. He was wrong.

Chapter Five

'Dear Tarrant'

1958

The two years which followed John's reinstatement would be the happiest in his tragically short life. As a child tearing around Tooting Bec Common, there'd been moments when the thrilling simplicity of his existence had made him breathless with joy. But Lamorbey had killed all that. Since the children's home, he'd often felt marooned in a life over which he had little control. Everything had felt so fractious and complicated: his mother dead so young; his father remarried; the move to Northern England; Victor upped and gone; and John marooned in a house of babies and smoke. Boxing had given him a few pleasant jolts, but look what good it had done him. Marriage and fatherhood – they'd been all right too, but nothing – nothing – had ever felt as sweet or as simple as this.

At this time, his horizons – like his energy – appeared to be boundless. There was no distance he wouldn't travel and no discomfort he wouldn't endure simply to run and race with his fellow athletes, no longer as a murky ghost, but as a recognised equal and – as the months passed – a rival to be feared. Wherever he went, he was feted and welcomed, a celebrity of sorts: the ordinary bloke who'd stood up for what was right and planted his metaphorical fist on the noses of the sport's stuck-up London squares. If he wasn't careful, people would even pinch his running shoes while he was in the showers. The ghost runner's plimsolls. Fancy that.

Almost overnight, John's heavy-browed frown changed places with a broad, toothy smile on a face topped by cropped spiky hair. Every press photograph taken before Tarrant's victory had dwelled on crusader John: dour, humourless and simmering. Every picture taken now showed a man at ease with the world, a man with a number finally flapping on the front and back of his vest. Behind the satisfied grin, however, Tarrant's manic fire burned as furiously as ever. For years, he had likened his situation to that of a criminal condemned to hang without trial. Now, in the delirium of his reprieve, he found it impossible to restrain either his impatience or his appetite.

The year before, in 1957, his training runs had added up to a respectable 2,151 miles. By the end of 1958, he'd outstripped that total by 600 miles, and from here on the figure would climb almost every year, peaking 12 years later at 5,033 miles. 'From the day of my reinstatement I never thought of finding an excuse for missing a session,' he wrote. What with John away most weekends – racing anywhere from the Isle of Wight to Barnard Castle – it was Edie and Roger who'd become the prisoners, not John. 'In our courting days [she'd] never complained,' he argued in his memoir. 'She was well prepared for it when we married.'

It was no more, or less, than Edie had expected. John hadn't needed to ask her to take up his campaign. She'd been as disgusted as he was by the rotten treatment he'd endured. There wasn't any future in hoping that he'd change, and – truth be told – she wanted John in Rome almost as badly as he did. A little more romance would be nice, but she wasn't holding her breath. John would do precisely what John wanted to do. And in most respects, he was a fine husband. He might sulk occasionally, but he would never raise a hand or verbally abuse her. He would do his best to put food on their table. He would always thank her for the unflinching support she gave. She, in return, would be the haven where John could always find safe refuge. Sometimes it meant she felt more like a mother than a wife, but that was the deal. Marriage was compromise. *Woman's Own* said as much every week.

According to them, a wife's place was in the kitchen, where 'day after day you made with your hands the gift of love'. Looking around her Buxton council estate, no one else's marriage seemed that much different. Most seemed a great deal worse. Drudgery was the only offer on the table. It was what men wanted. One recent survey had shown that a man's top criterion for a perfect wife was 'good housekeeper'. Another had found that women stuck at home worked 15-hour days, doing everything from sweeping out the ashes in the morning to tucking the kids up at night. It wasn't much, but it was a job of sorts, and Edie felt John would surely slow down eventually.

Not this year, though; not in 1958. At 26, Tarrant was terrified that his best days were already behind him. Every race, every training session, had a new point and purpose. For years, the 'team' had been just John, Edie and Victor, but that was no longer enough. John's illegal status was gone, and with it the crippling restriction on his joining a recognised athletic club. After a hiatus of two years, he reactivated the application to the Salford Harriers which had started all the trouble.

It was a perfect fit. Tarrant's chosen club had a bloody-minded nonconformist streak which had always tickled him. When he'd trained with them, everyone had had a face or a voice like his. Ordinary fellas. Salt of the earth. Older members told him how they'd sold their pet rabbits to raise the bus fares to races, how they'd won their wedding rings as prizes or pawned their racing medals for food. He'd heard how the Harriers had been set up by a Pickwickian entrepreneur called Harry Hardwick to make money at the turnstiles and how, in the 1920s, he'd lured one top runner to his club by making him the landlord of a Manchester pub. This would be rebel air he'd be breathing. Within hours of his reinstatement, his application was in the post. If the Salford Harriers had been good enough for George Bailey, then they'd do very nicely for him.

Five days later, John was on the train to Liverpool with the Harriers team, his excitement uncontainable and a welcome telegram from the organisers of a 20-mile road race in Huyton folded neatly in the pocket of his trousers. Just a week before, he'd been planning to gatecrash this same race in his coat and cap. Now, on a loose slip added late to the official programme, he could see his own name in print. 'Mr J.E. Tarrant (Salford H)'. He was real. He existed. He could mingle nonchalantly with the stewards and the athletes, share their facilities and peck at their cheese sandwiches without fear of rebuke.

In the changing-rooms, he looked coyly at the other runners, just as they looked at him. Some he knew. Some he didn't. A tall lean lad about Tarrant's age was talking loudly in a broad West Riding accent. John asked around, and was told the man was a new runner called Bernard Gomersall. Someone to keep your eye on. One for the future, maybe. Others were crowding in late from the train. Friends, foes and familiar faces. Everyone wanted to shake his hand and clap his back. Two years ago, he'd slunk in and out of this same city as a ghost. Today, even the suits wanted to know him. It was hard not to laugh, impossible not to smile. And to complete the sense of déjà vu, here was little Arthur Keily, grinning from ear to ear – Tarrant's jinx, Tarrant's bogeyman, Tarrant's five-time conqueror. 'Hello, John,' he said.

Out on the road, in blustery spring conditions, John felt like a different man. Shorn of worry, his running came easier, and by the halfway mark he was clear of the field. The day just kept on getting better. For the first time in his life, he was the official leader of an official race, wearing a number rather than the furrowed forehead of a fugitive. Unable to restrain his excitement, John had run too hard, too early. Why did he always do that? Without even looking, he knew who he would see next. For the sixth time in two years, the brilliantined figure of Arthur Keily appeared cheerily at his side, followed shortly by Arthur's younger brother Joe. Ten miles later and John's race was over; he surged home in third place, four infuriating minutes behind the brothers from Derby.

This time, John wouldn't need to miss out on the post-race meal. He was proud of his podium place – it boded well for the future – and he'd every intention of enjoying his moment. The Keilys were there. So was that lanky newcomer Bernard Gomersall. Suddenly, everyone was standing and cheering and filling the room with applause. It took a second, but then John realised the ovation was for him.

'I can remember it quite distinctly,' says Bernard Gomersall. 'We'd all been sympathetic but felt there was nowt we could do about it. Rules were rules. I think everyone was glad it was over for him and wanted to show it.'

The day's only sadness was that the Salford Harriers hadn't won the team prize. According to the AAA race officials, Tarrant's application to join the Harriers couldn't possibly have been processed in time, and therefore his third place didn't count towards their team score. It was spiteful and petty and it was untrue. John even had the acceptance letter from his new club to prove it. For once, though, he let it pass.

He'd been freed to run, but he wasn't daft. He knew there'd be no favours. The trophy would go to the Derby team instead: yet more silverware heading to the Midlands and the groaning sideboard of Arthur Keily. Over the coming year, Tarrant would trail in behind Arthur two more times, and when Keily finally hung up his road shoes on New Year's Eve 1960, his record against John Tarrant was intact. In eight races he'd taken on the ghost, and in eight races he'd vanquished him.

There would be many similar rivalries over the years, and many cracks at revenge or redemption. The entire country was stitched together by a series of carefully coordinated road races, most of which have now disappeared. Hereford-to-Ross-on-Wye, Exeter-to-Plymouth, Liverpool-to-Blackpool, Windsor-to-Chiswick, Doncaster-to-Sheffield, the prestigious London-to-Brighton and countless others linking smaller towns in fiercely contested annual events. Each had its own character and reputation – some infernally hilly, some tediously flat. Each had its own specialists and race favourites, and each was measured off at its own, often absurd, distance: the Tipton 12½, for example, or the Macclesfield 10.

It was no surprise that John had kept feeling Arthur Keily's hot breath down his neck. By ensuring that the major race dates didn't clash, the organisers could be confident that the very best runners could usually attend. Providing they could put in some overtime and work up the rail fare, the same itinerant circus of road-runners would be lining up every weekend, anywhere from Tyneside to Cornwall. For the truly dedicated, this wasn't a hobby, it was an all-devouring lifestyle, requiring military-style planning and a wife who liked her own company.

Most of the runners – especially on the Northern circuit – were blue-collar grafters with inflexible jobs. Very few could afford a car, and, on top of the religiously observed training regimes, there were endless, convoluted cross-country train journeys in airless, smoky carriages. By late Sunday evening, weary runners would be falling onto dark platforms all over the country, discharged from the milk trains and slow trains and stopping trains which had carried them home. For the town's insomniacs, Tarrant was a familiar spectacle, staggering back into Buxton – last train of the weekend – too shattered to speak, his dawn shift at the brake factory just a few hours away.

For some, like Bernard Gomersall, it was all too much. 'I would love to have run more. I'd love to have run races like the Exeter-to-Plymouth, but I just couldn't afford to go there. My wife wasn't working at that time. We had a daughter. We just couldn't afford it. There might have been backhanders on the track, but for the pure road-runner there was nothing. No money in it. None. It was ferociously amateur.'

Even later on, the year after he'd won the feted London-to-Brighton race, Bernard would need to work a Saturday's overtime to fund the trip south to defend his trophy. Such were the harsh practicalities of amateurism. Much as he'd have loved to join the nomadic fraternity, Gomersall simply didn't have the cash. John Tarrant, meanwhile, was trying very hard not to let his own impecunious circumstances – or the presence of a wife and four-year-old son – stand in the way of anything.

In June, he was on the Isle of Wight, finishing fourth, with a personal best time for the marathon. In August, he was running in a Leeds ten-miler, the same event he'd been heading for when Victor's bike had got comically snagged in the tram tracks. In September, he was up at Morecambe bagging a gold-plated travelling clock and silver tankard for his second-place finish in a 20-mile road race. In November, he again won the Salford Harriers ten-mile track championship, not as a secret entrant as he had been the year before but as an official competitor whose name could be engraved alongside those of the trophy's previous winners, one of whom, John noticed, was the man whose advice he'd sought right back at the start: George Bailey, the Buxton Bulldog.

Bailey had done his best by Tarrant. It was just unfortunate the way things had turned out. To everyone watching Tarrant now, he once again looked like a man badly in need of some sage advice. As Christmas loomed – little more than six months after his reinstatement – he had become incapable of taking a rest. The quality of the opposition no longer seemed to matter, and the distances he was running showed no pattern. Six miles or twenty-six – just so long as he was running. In his own mind, he was sure the wins and the results would come, but to everyone else it was clear that Tarrant needed help, and that without it John might very soon slip out of sight altogether.

Everyone around the Salford Harriers knew Joe Lancaster, and Joe Lancaster might be the answer. Joe was Northern, no-nonsense, old-school, a railway goods clerk who would run 13 miles to work and 13 back and think nothing of a few extra miles after his lunchtime sarnies. Joe had survived TB, and a childhood calliper on his right leg – 'Joe Limpy Lanc' they called him – but he'd still gone on to set world records, running more than twenty-two miles in two hours in 1955.

Illness and ill fortune had scuppered his chances of running for his country, but he didn't seem unduly bothered. Proudly, he'd tell you that since 1942 a day hadn't passed without a cigarette. 'I had a wonderful father,' he'd say. 'On the day of my first wage, he said, "Now, get to the shops and buy your own packet of Woodbines."' It was a story he was still telling well into his 80s, and although it was hardly in keeping with Tarrant's monastic inclinations, the two men became close.

The previous year, Joe had written a powerful and poetic article pleading John's case to the authorities. In it, he'd spoken of the mysterious joy of running, with its 'freedom of action, mind and soul . . . that expression of power, of well-being, the competitive spirit, disappointments, triumphs, aches, loves, that is LIFE. Why should this, our way of life, be denied to anyone who wishes to share it?' That was *it*. That was what it felt like. Tarrant knew all those words. He just couldn't put them in the right order like Joe had done. It was as if someone had crept inside his head and plucked out his feelings.

Tarrant had clipped Joe's article and stored it carefully in his fast-thickening file of cuttings. Sixteen years later, in his own deathbed paean to Joe Lancaster, Tarrant would repay the favour. Joe, he wrote, was 'the bravest athlete I have ever known . . . another case of a world class distance runner not getting his due recognition'. The 'other' runner Tarrant was referring to was himself. But in 1959 he was still a long way from world class, and Joe 'Limpy' Lancaster was the man who might start the transformation from angry also-ran to someone who – like himself – could set standards unmatched by anyone else in the world. That was if John would listen, and there was no guarantee of that.

The classroom would be the high roads of the South Pennines, beneath watery skies twittering with nesting skylarks. Whenever they could, the two men would run together, side by side, searching for the rhythm and the stride which would bring consistency to Tarrant's fitful performances. From the beginning, it wasn't an easy task, and whilst Tarrant was happy to take advice, he was eager to stress that the relationship was a casual one and that Joe had not become his coach. Not in any formal sense, at least. Sometimes he'd let Victor tell him what to do, but he wasn't keen on instruction.

It was probably as well. Privately, the older man found John's approach perplexing. Joe's philosophy – 'Nothing too startling, because that's how horses are trained' – couldn't have been more ill matched to his pupil. From what Joe could see, Tarrant only had one gear, and that was gallop. 'He was strong and incredibly willing,' he recalls, 'but he never paced himself properly. In a long race, you work up through the field. Maybe get in the first ten, hit a steady rhythm and watch the others fall out. But John always went all the way.' Even in training, John could never bear to be second. 'It was like he was only ever really in a race against himself. He was always so desperate to prove himself, and once he got to the front it just sparked him off. Some runners were crafty – brainy – but John wasn't one of them.'

He'd been told often enough, but John wouldn't listen and was deficient in self-control. The way Joe saw it, Tarrant's best hope was to stick to the longer distances. Over 26 miles, his immense natural strength might cancel out his self-destructive tendency to stampede himself into exhaustion. Knowing that it was the marathon which John had set his heart on for the Rome Olympics, the two men focused on mileage and endurance, and in the spring of 1959 – as the last snows melted on the High Peak – the tentative green shoots of a strategy began to peep through.

A fractionally improved time in the Doncaster-to-Sheffield marathon was followed by a blistering run in the Bury and Radcliffe 21. John had also won the Harriers 10,000-metre track championship, and in April he'd beaten Joe Lancaster's own club record to take the five-mile title in a record time. It was promising, but it still wasn't enough, and Tarrant knew it. Headlines like 'Buxton Runner Wins Again' would only count for anything if the wins were in blue-riband distance events watched by Great Britain's team selectors.

Out on the hills he began to wonder whether his job was standing in the way of his plans. If he didn't have to work these wretched shifts at Ferodo, he'd have more time for training and he wouldn't be so knackered setting off on the train on a Friday night. Buxton wasn't exactly ideally placed, either. Much as he loved the fells and had been galvanised by them, he was ready for a switch of scene. He hadn't chosen Derbyshire himself in the first place; it had just happened. If he could find something better, it was time to go. Time for a fresh start. If needs be, he could stay in touch with Joe by letter.

Seven years had passed since Victor had joined the RAF, and just as Alice Campbell, his teenage crush, had predicted, the service life suited him. After completing his National Service, he'd stayed on as a chef and was filling military stomachs at Credenhill. Although superficially the brothers remained alike, manhood had amplified their differences. Neither was naturally sociable, and to strangers they could both appear taciturn, shy and reserved. But where John was anti-authoritarian and brusque, Victor was calm, placatory and self-knowing. His RAF years had raised his already high levels of diplomacy and charm – qualities which had weakened Alice Campbell's resistance almost a decade before, and which, in Hereford, were still working their magic on the opposite sex.

Cruising the local NAAFI, Victor would pull out the tag at the back of his woolly jumper if he spotted a particularly attractive new female recruit. He hadn't yet met the girl who didn't offer to tuck it back in for him. Unlike his older brother, however, Victor had been careful to avoid anything long term and was comfortable in his roving bachelor shoes. Tantalisingly, there had been one special girl – a sleek-figured runner with lustrous dark hair – but she'd gone off to America with someone else. For the rest of his days, he'd keep her picture over the gas fire, but he'd keep his life largely to himself.

Although his gentle manner and chiselled film-star looks ensured he was never lonely, Victor never married, ultimately preferring his own company, or that of his dogs, to anyone else's. Even in his mid-70s, en route for a life-saving heart bypass operation, Victor declined an ambulance and opted for the bus to the hospital from the end of his street, telling neighbours he was going on holiday, back in a few days. Victor hadn't needed an Edie. 'I don't think that marriage is a natural state,' he says, living the life of a self-sufficient recluse in a hidden-away bungalow called 'Marathon', surrounded by stopwatches, bottles of pills and curling photographs of the brother he adored. 'We'd have died for each other,' he says, and he means it.

Despite their differences and the years apart, the two had remained exceptionally close. At the children's home, it had been John's job to look out for Victor. In adulthood, the roles had been reversed. 'They were always talking to each other. Always,' remembers Edie. Without Victor's backing, the ghost runner would simply not have happened, and whenever his duties permitted he'd drive up in his latest motor car to see his extended Buxton family and check on the fluctuating fortunes of his brother.

Something, he felt sure, wasn't quite right. From the triumphant cuttings John fastidiously clipped and posted, he already appreciated that the performances – whilst erratic – were steadily improving. He also thought that under Joe Lancaster's guidance John's impetuous brilliance might finally get him somewhere. But Victor knew his brother and could sense the perennial twitch of his impatience, even from Herefordshire. Motoring over to collect him from Ferodo at Chapel-en-le-Frith one Friday evening, he brooded over what he might do to help.

Victor would never forget what he found that day. So much noise and grime and dust. It was shocking for him to imagine John at this place, arriving breathless from his morning race with the works bus, his lungs hungry for breath and sucking at the factory air. He'd had no idea this was how John was working. When he'd left Buxton ten years before, his brother had seemed destined for a life spent repairing immersion heaters. Not this. 'When I picked him up that day, you could smell the asbestos on him. I said, "You can't do this." He said he couldn't get a job anywhere else. I promised him I'd try and get him a job down in Hereford somewhere. Somewhere nearer me. I wanted to rescue him, and I'm convinced that if I'd left him, he'd have gone down long before he eventually did.'

A half-century later, the memory could still stir him to anger, and, although no direct medical evidence exists to support his view, Victor remained convinced that the cancer which eventually killed his brother had its roots in John's 18 months at 'The Home of Ferodo Brake Linings'. Other Ferodo workers would later use the courts to blame the company for their asbestos-ravaged lungs, but John Tarrant would be dead by then, and Victor's opinion would stay rooted in his gut rather than in science.

It wasn't just the lousy job. Victor and John had missed each other. Seeing John that Friday at Ferodo had provided Victor with the pretext he needed to bring them back together. Returning to Hereford, he wasted no time putting his rescue plan into action. Alongside his RAF duties, he was also a part-time soldier in the Territorial Army and a pillar of the Hereford TA's hugely successful and desperately ambitious athletics team. In the summer of 1959, the city's sprawling TA Centre was in need of a caretaker, a handyman, someone to cut the grass and buff the parquet in the drill hall, and preferably someone who didn't feel out of place in a pair of running shoes. One word from Vic and his brother was on his way down for a chat.

If they'd known more about Tarrant's plumbing abilities, they might have thought twice. But it wasn't his manual dexterity the TA's top brass were interested in; it was his feet. For once, John Tarrant was the perfect candidate for a job. The work would be easy, and most of it would be conducted outside in the fresh air of the Welsh borders. As soon as he'd shown the senior officer a few glowing newspaper reports, the job was his. It would be good for morale to have the legendary ghost runner around the place. Now all John had to do was get back to Buxton and convince Edie it was the right thing. She'd know it was for the best. He wasn't expecting her to put up much of a fuss.

John was right. Much as it hurt her, Edie could see the logic of leaving Buxton, and – apart from her family – she had few ties to sever. Roger hadn't started school yet. She'd never worked in the town, and the absence of privacy in her father's house was becoming unsustainable. Nor would she be sorry to escape the delicate atmosphere which had built up between her and John's family living around the corner. As she saw it, there had always been a 'strange feeling' about her in-laws' place on Sherwood Road. Decades later, even Roger could remember that it had been 'worse than untidy . . . a tip'. In his own childhood home on Grove Lane, you could never quite escape the ammoniac whiff of Brasso. In the home of his grandparents, Jack and Maysie, the air was still as thick with tobacco smoke as ever. 'Mum just didn't get on with Maysie,' he says. 'There's just no way she'd have stood for that.'

The Tarrants, on the other hand, were secretly amused by Edie's obsession with cleanliness, and behind her back Jack enjoyed a joke at his daughter-in-law's expense. On one occasion, after picking up their grandson for a Sunday walk, Jack and Maysie scathingly reported to John's half-brother David that Edie had given them a cloth to wipe Roger's shoes should they get muddy on their stroll. It was harmless stuff, and John was always careful not to get too involved. Atmosphere and arguments were never his cup of tea. But Edie could feel the tension, and it made her decision that much easier.

By September 1959, John, Edie and Roger were ready to leave. In his memoir, Tarrant described how they'd 'decided to sell up in Buxton', although it's hard to see exactly what they were selling. Tarrant had always travelled light; they owned no luxuries and possessed precious little else likely to test the capacity of a removal van. For almost a year, they'd have to live in a caravan at Breinton, on the edge of Hereford. After that, they'd be moving into the caretaker's tied house – their first real home – at the TA Centre on Harold Street, behind the town centre.

As they left Buxton, John and Edie would have had very different thoughts. Edie had known nothing else; she was a Buxton girl, and it wouldn't be easy to get back. She knew no one in Hereford – not a soul – apart from Victor, and what would happen if John started drifting from job to job again? Where would they be then? How would they live? Would she see even less of him than she did already? One subsequent friend remembers that just a few months later Edie was spotted waiting at a bus stop in Hereford; she was alone and she was crying. It seems the answers to some of her questions had already come in.

John didn't share his wife's doubts. He'd found himself in Buxton by accident, and – in many ways – he'd be glad to see the back of it. Finally, he had a job which suited his running, and, better still, he had Victor to keep him on track. Edie and Victor and him. The old triumvirate. Perfect. In nine months' time, the selectors would be picking the marathon team for the Rome Olympics, and the way things stood Tarrant knew he didn't have a prayer. Sweeping Buxton out of his system – with all its bad memories of boxing and bans – would give him the impetus he needed.

He'd miss Joe and the Salford lads but would always go back for their annual championships, and whenever he could he'd run proudly in a Salford Harriers vest. He'd miss the fells, too, but Buxton not at all. The young lad who'd once been battered there by Johnny Hough seemed like another person. The place had changed and appeared to be sliding downhill. The old certainties and splendours were decaying. Even the thermal baths were falling apart. No one seemed very interested any more. Only a few timeless institutions were standing up well against modernity. Down across the green from the Town Hall – where John had first put up his fists – Y-fronts were still on display in the crowded window of Potters, and inside – where every available inch was crammed with sensible clothing – Edie's dad Harold was still on hand to parcel up your items in crisp brown paper and string.

His son-in-law's new job wasn't that much more taxing, but John was content. Hereford bustled pleasantly, and the county's green, rolling hills provided a satisfactory substitute for the Peak District. So long as his workplace was kept clean – to military standards – no one was on his back, and even John could change the occasional light bulb or push a broom around the parade square. Anything too technical and he'd call Victor in to help. After they'd moved into the red-brick Victorian caretaker's house, he was round there every Friday anyway, to watch *Bonanza* and eat a fish-and-chip supper with Edie and young Roger.

The gardens were a different matter. John had no patience for flower beds and roses and eventually persuaded another TA officer to take them over, just as he'd persuaded Edie to give him a hand with the regimental brasses. It was two less things to do on an already undemanding list of responsibilities. So long as he was running well, no one was going to complain. Not when their regimental sergeant major, Jack Owen Jones, was so happy.

From the outset, the Territorials had made it clear that they wanted John for his running, not for his aptitude with a screwdriver. As well as training part-time soldiers, RSM Jones was an ex-runner who fantasised about turning his Herefordshire Light Infantry athletics team into the most feared and successful outfit in the land. More than anything, he wanted to win the British TA Championships, and, like a football manager, he was shameless in recruiting 'soldiers' who could form part of his pampered gladiatorial elite. Victor was already on board. So were two other classy local runners, and part-time squaddies, Derek Davies and Ken Flowers. Now that John Tarrant had arrived, RSM Jones had secured his dream team. Over the coming years, these four men would win him his precious national trophy six times in succession. Soon, his cabinet would be overflowing with trophies, and Edie would have a job on keeping them clean.

For the first time in three years, Tarrant had ceased to have any news value. As far as the public were concerned, he had vanished into obscurity. Since his reinstatement, only the sports pages had been following his steady emergence as a distance runner. With the ghost persona surplus to requirements, Tarrant's news value had quickly faded. Shortly after his arrival in Hereford, however, he was embroiled in an astonishing event which once again splashed his name all over the national news pages, and which provided him, for just a few brief minutes, with his first-ever world record – one which he secured carrying a sub-machine gun and walking 110 miles in full army kit.

In order to run for its teams, John – like his brother – had signed up with the Territorial Army. Occasionally pulling on a uniform was a bearable penance, but very little else about army discipline appealed to 23737365 Private Tarrant. Nature had not designed him to have orders barked in his face. He loathed going away on camp; the rifles confused him; the kit cleaning irked him; and the loudmouthed bullies in charge stirred up far too many unpleasant memories. That autumn, however, a craze had erupted within the services which chimed with his masochistic instincts and turned him overnight into a local hero.

In September, a Royal Marine had set a new world marching record, covering 110 miles in 36 hours and 27 minutes. A fortnight later, two regular Army sappers had knocked a further two hours off the time, and one week after that more than thirty servicemen – in different parts of the country – set out to claim a world record which was clearly there to be obliterated. Among them were Private John Tarrant and Lance Corporals Ken Flowers and Derek Davies – three of the four crack runners in the TA's all-conquering team.

Wearing borrowed boots a size too big, John tore into the mission with his customary lack of finesse. Starting at Hereford, the trio had covered twenty miles in five hours when Davies pulled out, his feet lost somewhere inside an immense bubble of blisters. A few miles further down the road saw the two survivors apprehended as deserters near Cardiff but released after questioning. After 18 hours, Ken Flowers withdrew with a strained Achilles tendon, leaving only John to keep going, carrying a Sten gun on his back and sustained by sausages, eggs, tea and mountains of oranges.

As night fell on the return leg from Cardiff to Hereford, Tarrant's progress was impeded by thick fog. 'Even if I have to crawl I'm going to make it,' he told reporters. After more than 24 hours' marching, he was almost done in. Foot powder and fresh socks were applied – along with hot soup and vigorous massages – and John was up and off again. Three hours later, he'd covered a hundred miles, and with just ten miles to go he began to complain, with masterly understatement, that his 'body senses were beginning to dull'. It was the cue for his team of army helpers to play one last desperate card, 'singing and whistling popular marching songs' to urge him to the finish.

Even this cheery caterwauling wasn't enough. In the toilets at Abergavenny bus station, Tarrant was spotted coughing up blood, and with three miles left, the local paper reported, his 'face became hollow and contorted . . . his eyes oblivious to what was happening'. For a moment, his team of helpers seemed certain he would pass out. Reports of a new record had just filtered through. Another army team had completed its 110-mile march in 30 hours and 45 minutes. If John could cover this last awful stretch in 55 minutes, he'd beat that time and recapture the world record, but to do that he'd have to be moving, and he was at a standstill.

Not for the first time, it was Edie who saved the day. Fetched to the scene by a local reporter, it was his wife's presence which stirred Tarrant to his ruined feet. 'Like a man inspired', he stumbled forward again, followed now by a ragbag convoy of cars, pedestrians and bicycles. At 2.20 p.m., after more than thirty hours' almost continuous marching, he'd left himself twenty-five minutes to walk one infuriating, agonising mile. 'Bent and crying, he staggered on,' wrote the clearly emotional *Hereford Times* reporter, 'but with 50 yards to go [Tarrant] heard cheering . . . and marched to the finishing line like a soldier going to battle.'

For several hours, John Tarrant was a world record holder. His time of 30 hours and 36 minutes had beaten the day's earlier record by 9 minutes. It was also a staggering four hours quicker than the record established only one week before. In the sergeants' mess at the TA's Harold Street barracks – with his swollen feet propped up on an armchair – Tarrant sipped from a pint glass of shandy. Alcohol had never suited him, and he'd probably leave it for someone else to finish later. He'd never forgotten the night someone had spiked his drink with spirits. Horrible. You couldn't be too careful with alcohol, and there really wasn't anything to celebrate.

Shortly after Tarrant's new best time, a 20-year-old RAF airman had knocked off the 110 miles between Norwich and London's Marble Arch in 30 hours dead. It was cruel, but that was the problem with records. There was always someone younger going to come along and take them away. Gold medals were different. Gold medals were for keeps.

'All I want to do now is go to bed,' said John, who was slung across a colleague's back and carried to his slumbers. It was RSM Jones doing the lifting. He didn't want any more damage inflicted on his prize asset. There was an important army race coming up the next weekend, and, judging by the state of Tarrant's feet, his caretaker was going to need Monday off to recuperate.

In fact, laid low by double pneumonia and exhaustion, John didn't run again for almost two months. Like so many of Tarrant's highs, it had been a bittersweet encounter with success, no sooner tasted than snatched away. The escapade had also been characteristically haphazard in its execution. John had never walked or marched long distances before – let alone in full army kit – and he'd only decided to enter two days before the three men set off. If he'd learned anything, however, it was that Hereford was suiting him. At the age of 27, he felt stronger than ever, and he'd secretly enjoyed the epic quality of the distance. Intense physical pain and mental anguish had never bothered him. They were simply the necessary side effects of his chosen sport.

As his friend and rival Dave Box says, 'As a distance runner, you've got to be able to take a bloody good hiding. You've always got to remember that if you're suffering, then the runner alongside you is suffering as well.' Those pains Tarrant could manage. It was the pains with their origins away from the road which troubled him the most, and as the 1960s got under way they returned with a jolt.

Invigorated, he'd started the new decade like a man reborn, winning races all over England and Wales, in Hereford, Manchester, Brighton, Bury, Newport and Cardiff. He was winning at ten miles and he was winning, in record times, at twenty miles. He was even coming home first in cross-country races and had been crowned the British national TA champion over a seven-mile course. Things couldn't have been better. His form was building nicely, and by May he was looking unbeatable in almost everything he entered. Just so long as he was fit in July, that was all that mattered. On the 9th, he'd be running in the annual AAA Marathon at Welwyn Garden City, and traditionally there had always been a guaranteed seat on the plane to the Olympics for the winner. One good race there and he'd soon be eating spaghetti in a nice smart blazer just like Arthur Keily's.

That spring, however, John had begun to hear rumours which filled him with dread. People were saying that his reinstatement allowed him to run *in* Britain but not *for* Britain, and that as far as international athletics was concerned he was still *persona non grata*, a tainted amateur who'd taken money for boxing. Desperate for reassurance, he wrote to the British Amateur Athletic Board, the arm of the AAA which looked after overseas competition. By return post, on 18 May, he got the reply he had most feared. After two happy, halcyon years, Tarrant's honeymoon was over. The letter had been written and signed by the BAAB's secretary, Mr Jack Crump.

> Dear Tarrant . . . I recognise to the full your obvious
> keenness to obtain your international vest but I am afraid
> that the international rules on this matter are very clear
> indeed. No one who is a reinstated professional may take
> part in international athletic competition. This is not a rule
> of [our] making but it is an international rule which applies
> throughout the world . . . in these circumstances it would
> appear to me that you can never achieve your objective of
> running for Great Britain . . . I realise what a disappointment
> this will be to you.

Shaking with fury, Tarrant folded and reopened the letter
rereading it time after time, desperate to find a crack in its
armour. But there was none. Over the coming weeks, he would
study it so often that holes formed along its creases and the
edges frayed slowly away. In his own words, his 'whole world
collapsed' in that single moment. 'Dear Tarrant'. Whoever
started a letter like that? Didn't a working man qualify for good
manners?

Demanding more detail, John was told that the problem lay
with the IAAF – the International Amateur Athletic Federation.
It was their rules which governed athletics overseas, and no
mechanism existed for an appeal. It was even worse than he'd
thought. It was a nightmare beyond imagining. 'Due to my
honesty,' he wrote, 'I had lost the best athletic years of my life,
and now faced the prospect of not realising my true potential.
Society often gave murderers a second chance but for seventeen
miserable pound notes I was condemned for life.'

Since early 1958, Tarrant's life had been near perfect. The
wounds of his 'lost years' had healed, and he had learned how
to convert endeavour into victory. In an instant, the scars were

torn open. This time, the enemy wasn't even on his doorstep; instead, it was some convoluted multinational committee. These weren't people; they were vapours. Every time he reread the letter, its message seemed worse and its language more patronising. 'Dear Tarrant'. A fellow human being had written these sentences, and at the bottom of the now-ragged missive was his name. Crump. Jack Crump. This would be the man upon whom Tarrant would focus all his rising bile and bitterness.

If he expected to find a stereotypical Oxbridge gentleman – of the type Alf Tupper so mercilessly hounded – Tarrant would have been disappointed. Like John, Jack Crump had spent a part of his childhood in Tooting, the son of a machine printer who'd alternated between unhappy jobs spent agitating for strike action and long spells of enforced unemployment. 'My father,' confessed Crump sheepishly in his autobiography, '[was an] artisan in that he worked with his hands.' Jack Crump, on the other hand, was a grammar-school boy who'd longed to play football but was undone by an irreparable knee injury at 21. Not for him a job with his hands. Instead, he sought empowerment through the worlds of business and sport; a social climber and natural committee man, he rose effortlessly in both spheres.

Whether it was a flower show, a dance at the village hall or a walking competition, Jack Crump would be there pushing paper and pulling strings, as fastidious in his application of the rules as he would shortly become in British athletics. In his autobiography, he would proudly recall how one of his early track events in Mitcham had been organised with such rigour, that 'Mr Ted Vowles had refused to accept a penny for the ammunition he had used in his starter'. Few things in life riled Jack Crump more than the pollution of the Corinthian ideal by money. Unfortunately for John Tarrant, he was the most powerful man in British athletics.

Throughout the 1950s and early '60s, nothing happened in track and field sports which Crump didn't know about or control. There was scarcely a pie which did not contain one of his prodigiously powerful digits. As the secretary of both the AAA and the British Amateur Athletic Board, he not only ran the Great Britain team at overseas and domestic events but was also in charge of its selection. Whenever British athletes boarded a plane, it was Jack Crump who had put them there, and Jack Crump would be travelling with them first class. If there was a smoked salmon and caviar reception at the other end, or a trip to a Japanese teahouse, Crump would almost certainly be there, too.

Journalists dubbed him and his kind 'the blazerati' and wrote scathingly about Britain's posse of 'freeloading' travelling officials. Autocratic, moody and paranoid, Crump was also loathed by large numbers of the athletes in his control. After the Tokyo Olympics in 1964, when the British sprinter Robbie Brightwell had said, 'We must rid athletics of these little men,' everyone knew who he meant. The pair had clashed bitterly over team selection, and Brightwell had led an athletes' boycott of the BBC after Crump had denied athletes a share of the broadcaster's fee, warning that to do so 'might involve breaches of the amateur rules'.

To Brightwell, Jack Crump was 'a conundrum', a fossil from another age. To Crump, behaviour like Brightwell's was incontrovertible proof that money was a contaminant, a bad thing. In 1956, the IAAF had relaxed the rules to allow athletes a daily allowance of 14s 6d (72p) when running overseas for their country. Despite widespread astonishment, Crump had even opposed this. 'At the risk of being considered not "with it", I regret the introduction of this payment,' he stated in his autobiography. Crump, on the other hand, was entirely free to make money out of the amateur code he was now so diligently enforcing.

Since the late 1940s, writing under a pen name, he'd been regularly supplying the *Daily Telegraph* with paid articles about athletes and athletics, whilst taking fees from the BBC for his radio commentaries at major track meetings. To embittered outsiders like John Tarrant, it seemed rank hypocrisy to be deriving significant financial gain from the highly policed activities of amateur athletes. To Jack Crump, the payments were merely the legitimate spoils of a life entirely dedicated to his beloved sport. 'I have no intention of justifying my actions in regard to my journalistic activities,' he wrote, 'for I do not need to do so.'

There was something else about Crump's earth-shattering letter which rankled with Tarrant, apart from its tone. On the letterhead, the name of the BAAB treasurer was given as Harold Abrahams CBE, the same revered Olympian whose carefully argued article in 1958 had helped blow away the cloud of Tarrant's ban. It seemed utterly mystifying. How could these people return something with one hand only to rip it back with the other?

The answer was that Tarrant the ghost had unknowingly rocked these establishment figureheads far more than he'd realised. Reinstating him had been merely a pragmatic tactical concession in a rearguard war against change being fought by people like Crump and Abrahams on an increasingly hopeless front. Professionalism was coming – athletes were finding their voice – but not on their watch. Not if they could help it.

To have allowed Tarrant's domestic martyrdom any more publicity would have been foolish, and by freeing him to run in Britain they'd capped a potential rebellion. Most likely, they reasoned, he'd stick up there in the North and they'd never hear from him again. But here he was, winning races, talking openly about the Rome Olympics and looking like an issue waiting to explode in their faces all over again. This time, they'd hide behind the international rules. Tarrant simply would not be permitted to run overseas or represent his country. That wouldn't happen on their watch, either. Lest there be any doubt, Jack Crump sent his letter.

Had John looked closer, he'd have discovered how tightly the web had been spun around him and how utterly hopeless his position had become. As well as his seat on the BAAB, Harold Abrahams was an influential member of the IAAF, the international organisation whose rules forbade Tarrant from competing overseas. The IAAF's long-serving president was Lord Burghley, an Old Etonian and former Governor of Bermuda who had competed in the 1924 Paris Olympics with friend and fellow Cambridge scholar Harold Abrahams.

It was Burghley who'd sprinted around the Trinity quad before the college clock struck 12 times. It was Burghley who was said to have circled the deck of the *Queen Mary* liner in just 57 seconds wearing normal everyday flannels. There were no council plumbers here. No two men more perfectly embodied the fast-decaying Edwardian notion of the properly educated gentleman-player, and no two men wielded such immense influence over one sport. Between them and Jack Crump, there was not a single chink of light where amateurism was concerned. John Tarrant, whoever he was, was going nowhere.

In Tarrant's Hereford home, Crump's letter had worked its terrible spell. For the second time in three years, John's spirit was crushed. In the long winter months before his reinstatement, he'd briefly slung away his running shoes, only to be revived by the urgings of his wife. This time, the situation seemed more hopeless, with no obvious mechanism for protest, legitimate or otherwise. The man who had broken the news would be the man picking the British team for Rome. So to whom did he appeal?

Tarrant's dream felt run. Denied even the chance of representing his country, there seemed little point in continuing, and for several dark weeks, he trained with the slouch of a beaten man. In his head, out on the road, he composed vicious, acid retorts. Back home, he'd commit them to paper, sending some but wisely seeking advice before posting others. Derek Davies, his fellow territorial, saw one of them and told John it couldn't possibly be sent. 'It was written to "Dear Crump" and it was blasphemous,' he says. 'I told him that Crump would sue, but at this point John was developing tunnel vision. It was getting to be John, John, John.'

It was not in John's nature to be down for long. Instinctively, he probably knew that a bloody correspondence with Crump would be futile. John's longhand and biro versus the electric typewriter of Jack Crump's secretary. Lined Woolworths notepaper versus the embossed letterhead of the British Amateur Athletic Board. It wouldn't be a contest, and he'd no time right now for a war of attrition. Alone on the rolling Herefordshire hills, he persuaded himself that the authorities might once again be shamed into reversing their position. The public was on his side. And by not running, he'd be handing victory to Crump on a plate. Since he was also in the form of his life, he had every chance of rubbing a few noses in some dirt.

He pulled out his training diary. Less than two months remained before the race he now simply had to win: the AAA Marathon Championship, the event which guaranteed automatic Olympic selection to its winner. If he could squeeze in two high-quality races before that, Tarrant was convinced he'd have regained the necessary physical sharpness to win. With his mind cleared of obstacles, his mood surged. On a warm spring bank holiday Saturday, he travelled to Ryde on the Isle of Wight for the first of the two big competitions he felt sure would bring him right back into contention: the 28th Isle of Wight Marathon. Two hours and thirty minutes later, he'd run himself into the headlines.

On a beautiful June day he'd been unbeatable, winning the race his way – from the front – easily holding off the rest of a high-quality field. From stunning 8-mm colour film shot that afternoon, it's clear he was in the prime of health, running with a smile along idyllic lanes, past ladies from the Women's Institute wearing cardboard placards around their necks, 'Plain water' offered by one, 'Black Currant' by the other. As always, his arms flap from side to side like divining rods, but – in his white vest and shorts – the rhythm looks easy, and when he slumps into a blue and white deckchair at the finishing line, with a cup of tea, he looks capable of doing it all again.

A few days later, *Athletics Weekly* was ecstatic. Tarrant, they said, had knocked six minutes off his personal best and 'put himself into the top flight of marathon runners'. It was not at all what Jack Crump would have wanted to hear, and barely a week later his mood might have worsened. Running for Derbyshire at the British Inter-Counties Games in London, Tarrant had struck again, winning the 20-mile road race in Victoria Park with a career best time of 1 hour 48 minutes, despite hot and draining conditions.

Electrified by his successes, and increasingly confident of victory at the all-important AAA Marathon, John wrote to his old Salford Harriers mentor Joe Lancaster for last-minute advice. Control yourself, stick with the leaders for 17 miles and then go for it, he was told. It was what Joe had usually said. It was also what John usually chose to ignore. This time, though, he'd shackle his temperament. He'd simply have to. There hadn't been a race in his life which had mattered so much.

* * *

At Welwyn Garden City, 9 July 1960 arrived fresh and blowy, with the sniff of a sensation in the air. Around the Gosling Stadium – which the marathon runners would enter for their final few hundred yards – reporters were on the lookout for the ghost, just as he was on the lookout for them. 'I got the impression they all wanted me to win,' he recalled. 'One reporter promised to make it the athletic story of the year if I did.' For Jack Crump, looking on from the stands, that was an outcome too uncomfortable to contemplate.

Someone would surely beat Tarrant, and failing that Crump would simply reiterate the facts: that this was the IAAF's ruling, not his, and that Tarrant deserved a great deal of sympathy. The source of his discomfort, however, was busy telling journalists that he'd 'never felt fitter or more confident in his life'. Looking down the names of his 60 top-class rivals, John saw nothing to dent his self-belief. He'd beaten some of these men before, and he'd beat them all today. 'No other position meant anything to me; to finish even second would mean that I had failed.'

From the gun, the pace was fast, and John was happy. Tucking closely into a group of seven front-runners, he'd gone effortlessly through the five-, ten- and fifteen-mile markers, gradually shedding most of his rivals along the way. As always, he felt overcome by the gnawing compulsion to break clear, but Joe's advice was holding good, and he reached 17 miles before making his move. 'Never before had I felt so full of running,' he remembered. Everything was going like clockwork.

According to the pre-agreed plan, John surged strongly into the lead, quickly gaining more than 200 yards on the pack behind him. 'Tarrant was in one of his killer moods and looked all over a winner,' reported one magazine two days later. '[He was] running with extreme verve and not in the least distressed,' observed the *Daily Telegraph*. But at 19 miles, the landscape of the race was utterly transformed by a monsoon-like deluge. As the sky blackened and the air temperature plummeted, Tarrant began to feel twinges of cramp, and around 22 miles a 'ginger-haired fellow in a white singlet' flew past him and on to victory. Nothing John tried could get him back into contention. Although his time of 2 hours and 25 minutes was his best to date, he'd trailed in a bedraggled and broken second, more than two minutes behind the winner – a 22-year-old draughtsman from Coventry called Brian Kilby.

Despite the widespread plaudits for his performance, Tarrant ranked it 'the biggest disappointment of my athletic career'. The virtually unknown Brian Kilby would be going to the Rome Olympics – not John Tarrant – where he'd be running alongside Arthur Keily in the official British marathon team. Unbowed by his failure, John fled Welwyn greedy for new challenges, every sinew twitching with the confidence of nine victories in twelve outings. In mid-August, he caught the train north to Liverpool, heading back alone to the event where it had all started four years ago. From Lime Street Station, he found his way to the changing-rooms on foot, through early-morning streets left empty under persistent drizzle, on every doorstep a pair of milk bottles running with rain.

The 1956 marathon already seemed like several lifetimes ago. The pale-faced ghost who'd outrun the mystified stewards was now lean and tanned, his hair shaved up the sides but still thick on top; he carried not a morsel of fat, the contour of his muscles hard and perfectly defined beneath his broad boxer's chest. As they had always done, the other runners welcomed him – but with respect added to the curiosity of before. There was something intimidating about this new John Tarrant. His eyes seemed even deeper set, their mood even harder to read in the sunless shadow of his brow. It wasn't any perceived lack of courtesy which unsettled people – John was always unfailingly polite – it was just that he seemed so reluctant to engage, to open up or even relax. 'He was so very introspective,' remembers one contemporary. 'For all the outward show of aggression, there was this real vulnerability. To be honest, I don't think he'd ever learned how to communicate.'

Alongside the smoke-blackened columns of St George's Hall, under flat Mersey skies – the conditions perfect for running – Sir Ernest Stacey, chairman of the Liverpool Conservative Association, fired the gun to start the city's 13th consecutive marathon. This time, there was no need for the coat or the cap. Wearing the number eight on a bright red vest, Tarrant ran freely past the bubbling crowds, untroubled by officials or loudspeaker vans.

Four years before, with just two miles to go, John's race had ended in the back of an ambulance. This time, there was no stopping him. Looking fresh and strong, he entered Anfield football ground for the final few hundred yards; a huge crowd stood to applaud him as their winner. Over the crackling tannoy, they were told that Tarrant had run 2 hours, 22 minutes and 35 seconds, shattering the previous record by almost 5 minutes. Another rumble of applause broke out, and Tarrant told them, 'Liverpool crowds are great . . . the public has been with me all along.'

It was a bravura run – easily the best of his life so far – but it had come too late to have any bearing on Rome. The deadline had long since passed. Two weeks earlier, the Olympic team had been officially announced by Jack Crump, and no one had expected any miraculous reprieve. In John's view, it was the country's loss as much as his. For Keily and Kilby, it would in any event be an Olympics they would quickly want to forget. Running in temperatures of 100°F in the shade, Keily hobbled across the finish in 25th place. He was passing blood and weighed a stone less than when he'd started. His time of 2 hours and 27 minutes was worse than Tarrant's second-place performance at the AAA Championships. Kilby himself fared no better. He crossed the line 29th in just under 2 hours and 29 minutes.

On paper, it looked as if the better man had been left behind. Back at home, watching events in Rome unfold on television, Victor Tarrant grieved quietly, feeling that his brother had earned his right to be there, that his strength would have seen him through the heat, and that he was both younger than Keily and more streetwise than Kilby. But no one who'd endured the sapping conditions in Italy truly believed this, and even if Tarrant had beaten Kilby at Welwyn Garden City, the authorities would never have allowed him to go. It was folly or fantasy for Vic to think otherwise.

John Tarrant had taken money for boxing. He'd been banned from competing overseas, and would never be picked for a national team. Even if Crump had wanted a change in the rules – which he almost certainly did not – there were others ahead of Tarrant in the queue. Sentiment favoured Victor's brother, but the facts told another story. He'd run the marathon brilliantly throughout 1960, and was now authentically world class, but seven British long-distance runners had run better. Even if John had pipped Brian Kilby to the tape in that July downpour, Crump, in all probability, would have taken somebody else.

As he travelled back to Hereford from his triumph in Liverpool, John thought about the one face which had been missing in Liverpool, and the one person he now knew he would never beat. Soon after his exertions in Rome, little Arthur from Derby would call it a day. In his 40th year, worn down after pounding 27,000 miles, he'd come to the end of the road.

But Tarrant himself was far from finished. At 28, he was

reaching the physical peak of his life. It was time to look forward and think afresh. But where and towards what? Every hard-won step seemed to end at another locked door. What could he do to leave his mark more indelibly on the world? Something epic, something unique? As yet, as his train back to the borders rolled south through Ludlow and the blooming Welsh hills, he didn't have the answer, but it would not be long in coming.

Chapter Six

'The Ageing Maestro'

1961

John Edward Tarrant had changed. Where there had once been doubt, there was swagger, and his adolescent reticence had late-flowered into smouldering, self-righteous truculence. Physically, he had altered too. The man who'd sprung into Anfield Stadium the previous August, slicing lumps off the old Liverpool Marathon record, bore little resemblance to the slack-shouldered boy of those Buxton wedding photographs.

Thousands of miles of lonely running had refashioned his once lanky body into a formidably muscled force of nature. The shoulders were broader, the chest deeper and more powerful. It was ironic given his back story, but his physique closely resembled that of a lightweight boxer, the boxer he'd once wanted to be but never was. Even his famously hollow cheeks had deepened, appearing darker and more concave than ever, the skin leathered and baked by his countless hours under the sun.

In his caretaker's dungarees, grumpily pushing an orbital polisher across the TA's gymnasium floor, he looked older than his 29 years, the eyes flatter and harder, their twinkle diminished by the joyless years of frustration. In his running kit – wearing the period's thin-soled road shoes, through which one felt every blemish on the highway – he exuded brute sporting menace. Incomparably polite before the gun. Irrepressibly competitive after it. 'Beyond fanatical' is how one of his contemporaries described Tarrant during this period.

Being John Tarrant had never been particularly easy. Trying to be one of John Tarrant's friends was almost as taxing. Although he'd kept his links with the Salford Harriers – and still caught the train north from Hereford once a year for their mud-caked annual championships – John remained an outsider, usually preferring his own company where there was the least risk of exposing his social clumsiness. Since he scarcely drank, and still shunned cigarettes, the common ground he shared with fellow runners was severely restricted and generally stopped at the changing-room door.

Living in Buxton, that hadn't mattered. He'd been the ghost runner then, running for himself and training, mostly alone, in his mental cocoon up on the moors. In Hereford, it was different. Although it wasn't in his contract, he'd got this job solely on the understanding that he turned out for the Light Infantry athletics team. For once, he would have to share his running – and his training routines – with relative strangers. Given the sclerotic hardening of his character, no one expected it to be easy. It would help that RSM Jones had assembled such a formidable array of talent, but it wasn't what John wanted and it was still a very great distance from where he'd planned to be.

There was one consolation, however. For the first time in his life, Tarrant would be running regularly with his brother. In the years they'd spent apart, Victor had developed into an accomplished and elegant athlete, a county champion at various distances, with the keen grasp of coaching and tactics

182

which John signally lacked. Alongside these two, making up the core of the TA's winning squad were Ken Flowers and Derek Davies, the two men who'd tried but failed to stay with John on his self-destructive 110-mile march 18 months before.

The walk had been an ominous warning of things to come. Thrown together, they would achieve extraordinary results on the road – and across country – but it would almost always be Tarrant who finished at the front, and the dreadful physical toll it imposed on him would become as depressingly familiar to John's teammates as his first-place finishes. Outside his immediate family, no one would ever get to know John quite so well as Flowers and Davies – and no one would gain such repeated insights into his method, his moods and the puzzling first signs of his troubled health.

Throughout the previous year, the four of them had been almost invincible. As the 1961 season began, they continued to dominate, with Tarrant winning the individual honours, and strong combined performances from Victor, Flowers and Davies ensuring that 'the Terriers' invariably walked off with the team medals as well. 'Most races we entered we'd win,' remembers Flowers, 'but John wasn't really a team runner. John was always for John. He'd either be in the first three or way down the field, having run himself into the ground. Unlike the rest of us, he wouldn't battle for third or fourth place. If John couldn't win, as often as not he'd be out. Only one thing mattered to John Tarrant, and that was John Tarrant.'

Tarrant's new teammates might have been surprised, but Victor wasn't. 'My brother was selfish because he'd had to be' is the younger Tarrant's assessment. Only Victor – and Edie – were ever permitted a glimpse of a softer side. After an argument, the brothers challenged each other to a race of two laps around the heavy turf of Hereford racecourse. At the finish, they were neck and neck in a time of 15 minutes (which remains unbeaten), but Victor always knew who'd won. 'I was down on my knees spewing up, and John was jogging happily nearby. He could have beaten me if he'd wanted to. He just chose not to.' It wasn't often John was so magnanimous. Even when he was boxing in Buxton Town Hall, Tarrant had loathed the pointless humiliation of defeat. Only winners got noticed. Nothing else mattered. But, in Hereford, it wasn't simply John's egocentric running which generated tension within the group.

Although it was rarely discussed, Flowers and Davies – as Welshmen – had each earned an international vest. It was the single honour which Tarrant craved more than any other – and it still seemed as far away as ever. Had he needed the motivation to drive either man into the ground, this would do nicely. These days – if he was being honest – he thought about little else. Even in training, it rendered him impossible to live with. As Ken Flowers puts it, 'If you'd cut John in half, he'd still be running.'

'He said to me one day, "Whereabouts in Abergavenny do you live?" I told him. He said, "I must have passed there the other day." He'd run from Hereford to Ross-on-Wye: 14 miles. Ross to Abergavenny: another 24. Abergavenny to Hereford: that's over 60 miles. I said, "What do you do for refreshments?" He said he knocked on strangers' doors for a drink and got an apple or two from an orchard.'

At first, it had been brilliant. With John on board, they were all winners, and the army's top brass indulged their every triumph. On weeknights, while the rest of the TA's poor saps learned how to drill and to dismantle their Lee–Enfield rifles, the golden boys were excused duties and sent out to train in their black army pumps. Around Hereford, there wasn't a country lane they didn't know, and every gradient, curve and straight had its value in seconds, an intimate compendium of routes and times to be re-engaged every time they trotted from the dismal parade ground and fled towards the hills.

Out towards Fownhope, perhaps, then left following the signs to Dormington, their heads bobbing above dense hedgerows, the fields hemmed in by rowan and ash, and for company an occasional deer, startled as they navigated back towards Hereford just as darkness fell. Tarrant's overpowering presence, however, had seriously unsettled the happy equilibrium which had existed before. They all wanted to win, but John's desire was something else completely, something alien, almost feral in its intensity.

Even Victor had changed since John had arrived from Derbyshire. When the brothers were together in a crowd, they'd occasionally communicate in a secret back-slang – the ancient code of their Sidcup children's home – from which all outsiders were excluded. As Ken Flowers saw it, some of the joy was being sucked out of what they loved. 'It was hard for me to like John. Really hard. It was very rare you'd see him laugh. I felt he resented that I was an international and that he wasn't. Vic tells me John admired me. But I just can't believe it. Not that I ever had an argument with him. He wasn't someone you'd argue with really. He was a bruiser. He looked like a boxer, not a runner.'

It wasn't easy to intimidate Ken Flowers. He was a robust, gutsy little Welshman – one of five brothers – who loved soldiering and had spent a year in Korea witnessing things which fifty years later could still reduce him to tears. It took a lot to wind him up, but, time after time, John Tarrant succeeded. 'Training on the hills, he'd literally sprint up them. Any kind of training and he'd kill you. He'd give no quarter. He'd always want to hammer you. I don't think he knew what gentle was.'

On one occasion – during a wintry cross-country race near Cheltenham – Flowers was crossing a fence when a yank on his vest dragged him down into a ditch. When he clambered up, there was the muddy mark of a running shoe planted squarely on his chest. In the autumnal gloaming, just beyond the fence, he could make out the back of a rival runner striding fiercely into the distance. It was John Tarrant.

Another time, Flowers was leading the county six-mile championship and had lapped every other man bar one: John Tarrant. 'As the last lap started, John looked over his shoulder, saw me and took off like a greyhound, sprinting to ensure I didn't lap him too. It took so much out of him that he ended up in a state of collapse and got overtaken for second place. I got the feeling it was because I had my Welsh vest. Because he could never run for his country, he was making this point . . . He was a strange mixture, was John. He was beyond fanatical. Something else was driving him, but what it was we'll never know.'

There was no great secret. Time was driving John, festering in John, distorting his perspectives. Validation had become a constant, insatiable need, an addiction. Every lost second was a failure. Self-worth was entirely bound up with victory, however small that victory, be it on an evening training run or against an international field. It helped that things were going so well with Ken, Derek and Victor, but everyone knew Tarrant's heart wasn't in it. What really counted for him were the solo honours – the big prizes. It couldn't have been worse that, as the racing season unfolded in 1961, Tarrant found himself at the wrong end of two highly publicised beatings by much younger athletes.

In every other respect, the year had started well. Writing in the *Sunday Telegraph* in January, no less a luminary than Christopher Chataway – Roger Bannister's pacemaker in the first sub-four-minute mile – had slammed Tarrant's continuing exclusion from international competition. 'In his capacity as a policeman of sport he [Jack Crump] should emulate his local constabulary who no doubt turn many a blind eye on . . . the weirder pieces of legislation left on the Statute Book.' The support was welcome, but out on the road Tarrant was struggling to justify his tag as the lost hope of British athletics.

In the annual AAA Marathon, he'd lost for the second year running to Brian Kilby, trailing in more than 30 minutes behind his rival. Shortly afterwards, he'd headed for Liverpool – the memories swirling as always – hoping victory in the marathon there would lift his battered spirits. At Lime Street Station, he'd met up with Joe Lancaster, his old Woodbine-smoking mentor, and from a following car Joe had coaxed and cajoled his former pupil as the race unfolded through Liverpool's sun-baked streets.

Once again, though, a younger man was ruining his day, a runner he'd never seen or heard of before. At 20 miles, Tarrant and the unfamiliar, beak-nosed youth were running shoulder to shoulder, the pace frenetic and the rest of the 50-strong field nowhere in sight. From the sidelines, fearing self-destruct, Joe frantically urged the rampant Tarrant to ease up: 'Let Ron take the lead! Let Ron take the lead!'

It was an invitation the pixie-like stranger didn't need to hear twice. At 24 miles, with a shrug, he was gone, leaving Tarrant to cross the line in second place. 'Ron', meanwhile, had cadged a lift back to Manchester, where he was so knackered he was propped up against a bus stop until he was ready to walk the last few yards home. Tea that night would most likely be chips cooked on a paraffin camping stove in his flat.

He was 22 years old and he'd never run further than 15 miles before that day. His name was Ron Hill; he'd go on to compete in three Olympic Games, set a marathon world record in 1970 and still be running every single day of his life into his 70s. He would become everything Tarrant had always wanted to be. But then Ron Hill had never earned £17 as a boxer, and Ron Hill didn't live under a persistent black shadow which refused to go away.

In late summer, the old issues flared up again. Not content with domestic glory, the army had quietly entered a three-man TA team – John Tarrant, Flowers and Davies – to compete against a top field of international runners in a marathon at Enschede in Holland. When word of their plans reached 54 Torrington Place – London fortress of the British Amateur Athletic Board – Jack Crump summoned his secretary, Miss Tupholme, and dictated a letter to the Hereford top brass.

It was regrettable, they were told, but Tarrant simply could not travel. The situation was perfectly clear. Unless the international rules changed, he was forbidden from competing anywhere in the world except England, even if it was for a team selected by the British Army. Crump's message was unequivocal. Tarrant should be happy with what he'd got. If he turned up with his kit in Holland, there'd be a stink so strong it would cross the Channel.

At the gloomy caretaker's house in Harold Street, Hereford, the news came as no surprise. Tarrant had been thrilled to get his first passport, with its hard blue cover and its shiny promise of overseas adventure, but he'd never really believed it would happen, not even when the plane tickets arrived. Much as his commanding officer might huff and puff about civilian pen-pushers, it was Crump who prevailed in the tiff which ensued. Tarrant's freedom to run – or lack of it – was a matter for the athletics authorities, not glory-seeking military types. If the army wanted a team at Enschede, there really wasn't a problem – just so long as John Tarrant wasn't a member of it. A few days later, RSM Jones broke the news to Ken Flowers and Derek Davies. The trip was off. No Tarrant, no team.

It was yet another humiliating disappointment. Furiously, Tarrant dashed off a letter to Jack Crump full of such libellous venom that it was forwarded swiftly to the BAAB's lawyers as Crump sought protection 'from charges which are constantly levelled against me without any foundation'. Although John's letter was never kept, it seems clear he'd lambasted Crump's newspaper earnings, employing language that 'was of such a nature' that the BAAB supremo felt obliged to take advice. It was folly of the highest order, but no one who'd seen the recent changes in John was remotely surprised.

The transition from anger to untrammelled bitterness was complete, and Tarrant no longer felt compelled to restrain his views, in person or in print. It made him feel better and it made them – whoever they were – feel worse. To that extent, it restored some balance in his world. What made this letter particularly imprudent was that, foolishly, he'd begun to hope he might secure a place in the British team for the 1962 Commonwealth Games in Perth, Australia. If he was right – and he wasn't – it didn't seem wise to be insulting the man who'd be picking the team. But in his 30th year this was what Tarrant had become: a man forever swerving blindly between wild despair and misinformed optimism.

For the next few months, an ominous silence prevailed. No reply came back from Jack Crump, and John stubbornly refused to investigate why. Once again, it would be Edie who broke the deadlock. After two lonely years in Hereford, it would at least give her something concrete to do. With eight-year-old Roger installed at school – occasionally quizzing his money-strapped parents about his lack of a brother or sister – the days dragged around the desolate Harold Street barracks.

To help John out, she'd always lend a hand with his cleaning, and their home – with its precise rows of brass ornaments and running trophies – was as immaculate as Grove Lane in Buxton had ever been. But Hereford wasn't Buxton, and Edie's homesickness was chronic. A few friendships had developed – one with Derek Davies' wife, Heather, would prove lasting – but Edie had always been in John's shadow, was a poor mixer and now lived on an army base surrounded by men in brown uniforms. Knowing that John needed her mettle was a lifebelt in a sea of sadness, and she grabbed it – as always – with both hands.

Throughout that October, there was a snowstorm of correspondence between Torrington Place and Harold Street. As yet unaware that John had potentially libelled him, Edie wrote secretly to Jack Crump, pleading for her husband to be considered for the Commonwealth Games. In his reply, Crump drew Edie's attention to John's allegations, explaining that until those remarks were formally withdrawn, then the matter would stay in the hands of 'the appropriate committee'. As far as the Commonwealth Games were concerned, the position was unchanged. According to the International Amateur Athletic Federation, John's boxing in Buxton meant he had 'automatically disqualified himself' and therefore could not compete in Perth.

Tarrant took the hint. Swallowing his pride – and with Edie breathing down his neck – he penned two grovelling letters to Crump, the first one retracting his remarks and the second seeking Crump's support for any rule change which might help Tarrant break free of his trap. It was the cue for two pages of patronising pomposity from the vindicated honorary secretary of the BAAB, Mr J.C.G. Crump OBE JP:

> I think your true character is shown in your letters and I
> am quite certain you did the right thing in telling the AAA

of your former status as a boxer. After all, you know there
are some things in life more important than an international
vest and I think a completely clean conscience is one of
them . . . if we can help you in any direction you have only
to let us know.

Tarrant held his tongue and got back on with his polishing.

The following February, John Tarrant turned 30. If there were
celebrations in Harold Street, they were quiet ones. Since
Christmas, John had been troubled by a knee injury and had
already travelled to Wolverhampton – at the regiment's
expense – to receive injections. For the first time, he'd been
forced to curtail his incessant training, and the ensuing sense
of helplessness exacerbated his natural seasonal despair at the
steady evaporation of opportunities.

By the spring, with the knee restored, he was like a caged
cheetah. Everything he'd ever heard from officialdom seemed
momentarily forgotten. With his uncanny gift for self-deception
– and his unflinching faith in natural justice – Tarrant persuaded
himself that one more year of high achievement would force a
change of heart somewhere. Apologising to Crump didn't
mean he'd given up on his dream, and Crump was a bloody
idiot if he thought it did. Without a thought for the consequences
of failure, Tarrant plunged himself into the 1962 race season
like a man possessed.

It would be another year of frustratingly mixed fortunes –
every bit as unsatisfactory as the one which preceded it. Despite
stunning wins in three marathons, he slumped badly in others,
and to almost everyone who knew him it looked like Tarrant
was running too much. There was also an entirely new problem
to contend with. After 20 miles of the perennially important
AAA Marathon at Welwyn Garden City, he'd been forced to

leave the field temporarily with stomach trouble. By the finish, there were six better – and much stronger – men ahead of him, among them the event's habitual winner, Brian Kilby.

In the immediate aftermath of defeat, no one seemed too concerned by John's physical distress. Whilst it was unusual for someone to suffer mid-race diarrhoea, it wasn't entirely unheard of. Prior to this race – incredibly – John had never once taken liquid refreshment during a marathon. Even those runners who did take drinks were strictly forbidden from having their first until ten miles had been completed; little wonder Jim Peters had collapsed so famously in the 1954 Commonwealth Games, surrendering a three-mile lead through dehydration, or that Arthur Keily had lost a stone in weight during the Olympic marathon in Rome.

At Welwyn Garden City, under Victor's guidance, John had agreed, as an experiment, to drink liquids during a race for the first time. John's 'corpse reviver' they called it, a precisely engineered cocktail of clear Corona lemonade, one teaspoon of salt and three tablespoons of glucose powder. As they travelled home, the brothers speculated on whether this new concoction might have destabilised his digestive system. Or had he simply run himself out of form? Whatever the cause, it was soon forgotten. In an irksome year of contradictions, it seemed the least of his worries.

Despite his optimism in the spring, 1962 was petering away miserably in a series of marginal late-season triumphs. In August, he'd won a 30-mile road race in London, and a week later he'd set a new record in the Tipton 12½. It didn't matter that in his own mind he was running brilliantly, because no one was watching. Crump and his kind had seen to that. They'd won, and he'd lost. 'Tarrant – The Forgotten Man – Wins' ran one newspaper headline, but it was the *Hereford Times*, not the *News Chronicle* of old.

It seemed horribly unfair. To be forgotten was incalculably worse than being a ghost. To be a local hero was no substitute for being a national one. And yet no one else in the world bar Tarrant had won three races at marathon distances that year. 'It was frustrating to be so fit and yet have nothing left to conquer,' he said.

Like the mythical Sisyphus, Tarrant had been consigned to a remote place and forever condemned to roll the same rock up the same hill, unnoticed by the world. Running for the Hereford Light Infantry was all very well, but it was hardly a Great Britain blazer. The goals he aspired to still remained impossibly out of reach. The races he was winning were the same races, year in, year out. It didn't matter that he was getting faster and more ruthless any more than it mattered how quickly Sisyphus rolled his rock. Not enough people cared, and the audience had drifted away. The weekend stringers who'd once trailed the phantom runner with their notebooks had moved on to fresher stories. Denied the bigger stage he craved, Tarrant was shrinking out of sight, loathing invisibility almost as much as he hated losing.

Apart from anything else, it was humiliating. In May – after winning the Isle of Wight Marathon – he'd contacted the BBC, inviting them to re-interview him on the subject of his international ban. Writing during a break at a dreary TA camp at Tavistock in Devon, he'd practically begged them to put him on *Sportsview*. In their reply to '23737365 Pte. Tarrant, Plasterdown Camp' he was told that 'having covered your position on one occasion, and it having been covered by newspapers on many occasions, we cannot see an occasion when we would be able to tackle the subject again'.

It was lousy English, but it was no more than he'd expected. He was used to condescending put-downs from figures of authority, and everyone knew the BBC paid the AAA handsomely for exclusive television rights to its athletics events. Call it hypocrisy, call it what you like, but a conspiracy theorist like Tarrant hadn't really expected the BBC to rock any boats to help him out. The David Coleman thing had been a one-off. From what he could see, all the toffs were in it together. BBC. BAAB. IAAF. String any letters together you liked. It didn't really matter. None of them had ever done him any favours, and none of them ever would.

As the autumn approached, Tarrant's mood darkened. He had always disliked the cross-country season, and without the adrenalin of the road – or the flattery of press interest – he appeared incapable of maintaining the hope which had sustained him through the thrilling summer cycle of competition. The endless dark tunnel of winter training gave him too much time to think, and, lost in those thoughts, Tarrant kept reaching the same conclusion. Enough was enough. In late October, he let it be known that he was calling it a day.

'There is no point in going on,' he told reporters. 'If you want to get on in athletics you must move south, where one good race is as good as twelve up in the north.' Breaking the news of his 'retirement' in a letter to his father in Buxton, Tarrant heaped scorn on Jack Crump, asking 'how many officials will be jumping on the bandwagon for Perth without having raised a sweat . . . in a country that boasts that its justice is the fairest in the world, I think I have had a raw deal.' From now on he would 'run to keep the weight down', but that was all.

As she had done so often, it was Edie who unilaterally took John's crisis to the next level. Writing furiously to Jack Crump, she tore into the nonsense of amateurism, ridiculed the international regulations, near canonised her husband and practically ordered the BAAB chief to contact John direct, expressing whatever qualified regret he could muster.

Two days later, he meekly obliged. 'You have striven against great disappointments with tremendous courage,' wrote Crump, before adding that 'however bitterly you may have expressed yourself . . . you will appreciate that in carrying out the rules of the IAAF, the British Board had nothing against your personal integrity or character.'

Every sentence oozed relief. Crump must have believed the Tarrant story was finally over – one less thorn in a world of them. All summer long, the amateurism row had plagued him in the national press. None of what had been written had been kind; most of it had been vitriolic. Arthur Rowe, the champion shot-putter, had been banned from amateur athletics for life after switching to the professional code of rugby league. He was a blacksmith, and, perfectly reasonably, he needed to make a living.

Even the *Daily Mail* was scandalised, saying, 'sport in Britain [is] a tyranny with a prodigious amount of anomaly.' Every high-profile blow made it harder for Crump to do his job, but Tarrant's retirement was a help. He could afford to be expansive in his sentiments. Offering John and his wife all good wishes, he signed the letter with a flourish and dispatched Miss Tupholme to the mailroom. It was a letter which would soon be read by millions.

Driven by vanity or mischief – most probably both – he leaked Jack Crump's missive to Peter Wilson, a blunt-speaking, crusading columnist on the *Daily Mirror* sports desk. Four days later, every one of Crump's private words to Tarrant were printed verbatim in a full page *Mirror* spread. 'This is the wickedness of rigid amateurism,' Wilson's report began. 'The Tarrants of this world get little enough encouragement in their country. LET THEM AT LEAST HAVE JUSTICE.' It wasn't the first time the *Mirror* had taken up Tarrant's case, nor would it be the last. But it would be, by some distance, the most caustic of the many articles Peter Wilson penned on the runner's behalf.

For Tarrant himself, it necessitated one more apologetic missive to Jack Crump – to which Crump replied wearily (marking his letter 'personal and confidential') expressing 'great concern and resentment' at John's release of private correspondence to 'a bitter opponent'. As far as both men were concerned, the matter was now closed. It was Christmas – the time for ritual forgiveness. It was also the moment that John Tarrant, after six weeks of 'retirement', decided he couldn't give up running after all. Seeing his case splashed all over the *Daily Mirror* had once again charged him with hope. And for that – with impossibly majestic irony – he had no one to thank but Jack Crump himself.

There would be many big headlines in 1963 – the Great Train Robbery, Kennedy's assassination, the Beatles – but Tarrant would feature in none of them. He was unable to rediscover the fitness or the hunger of previous years, and the months slipped away in a mood of uncharacteristic torpor. By December, his training log would show 3,100 miles – his highest annual tally to date – but he'd entered few races and won almost none of them. On the Isle of Wight, going for a fourth successive marathon win, he'd been hit by a car mid-race and fared no better than thirty-third, ending the day on a stretcher surrounded by St John Ambulance medics. Even the Hereford Light Infantry's all-conquering square-bashers – Davies, Flowers and the Tarrant brothers – found it impossible to sustain the magic of previous years. RSM Jones's once invincible team was drifting slowly apart.

No one was quite sure where it had gone, but John's mind was elsewhere. Puzzled indifference seemed to have swapped places with Tarrant's trademark anger. Even his incessant correspondence with Jack Crump had become apologetic and familiar. It was always 'Dear John' now and never 'Dear Tarrant', and Crump's signature had reduced itself to the simple endearment 'Jack'. Like weary boxers unable to land the killer punch, it seemed they had beaten each other into mutual respect.

Hindsight would make it all so much clearer. In 1963, each man was at his own personal crossroads. For Crump, the old certainties were collapsing fast. Behind the scenes, Britain's amateur athletes were gathering strength and organising, rising up to challenge the Victorian codes which governed their sport and which required them to live and compete in penury. One group of them – the short-lived British Athletics Union – would take up Tarrant's case, meticulously questioning the small print of the IAAF regulations which were holding him back, but failing – like Tarrant – to make any progress whatsoever. 'Our meeting with Jack Crump and Harold Abrahams was like the Mad Hatter's tea party,' they told him. 'They did not budge one inch.'

But bigger things were shifting now. Within 18 months, Crump would have retired as BAAB secretary, humiliated by a full-scale athletes' mutiny before, during and after the Tokyo Olympics. The following year, broken and exhausted by his public humbling, he died suddenly at the age of 61. Despite it all, he and Tarrant had never once met.

It was touching that, towards the end, the older man had tried to reach out to John, knowing instinctively that his own days at the BAAB were probably numbered. Tarrant had been an honourable foe. A bloody nuisance but still a decent, plain-talking, and courageous sort. Not like these new johnny-come-lately long-haired upstarts with their big ideas and demands. Privately, Crump had always felt rather sorry for the fellow, and lately he'd said as much out loud. But the world would fall apart without rules, and athletics was a better sport without money. It seemed harsh for seventeen quid, but there you had it.

Meanwhile, John Tarrant was reaching some life-shifting conclusions of his own. He'd talked to Victor and they both felt the same. The fading of Crump marked the end of a phase for Tarrant, too. At last, he could let the Olympics and the Commonwealth Games go. They'd passed him by. But the marathon wasn't the only race he could run. Pounding the Peak District had made him powerful and strong. Winning races nationwide against brilliant men had made him stronger. But where John Tarrant was concerned, 26 miles simply wasn't enough.

It was time to make the switch from the loneliness of long-distance to the splendid and total isolation of ultra-distance. Not twenty-six miles but twice or four times that distance, races which took twelve hours or twenty-four, not three.

It's hard to find ultra-distance events today, and those which remain attract very few spectators. Watching 40 athletes trudge endlessly around a track can be hypnotic but is rarely compelling. At a typical race in Keswick, Cumbria – staged in 2009 – only a few mums with prams and curious retirees looked on as 40 supremely fit runners set off to run 24 hours non-stop around a public park under the rusty autumnal brow of Skiddaw.

They've travelled from four continents to be here, men and women together, aged anything from twenty-five to fifty, a community of like-minded and fiercely competitive athletes, each one utterly dedicated to the tyranny and madness of endurance. Not a lot has changed since John Tarrant inhabited this strange world.

No running style is the same. One woman shuffles; another

slides her feet like a skater. One man raises his knees boyishly high; another appears bent like a crab with a blockage. Some are sustained by jelly babies and Hula Hoops; others wolf down jars of custard and rice cakes. As the race starts with collective whooping at 1 p.m., it's almost impossible to believe that for 24 hours only toilet stops will break their rhythm, or that they'll trudge silently through the long, cold night, lost in the soothing soundtrack of their iPods, until the frosty dawn greets them and a mere seven hours' running remain.

At the finish, very few people have dropped out, and the winner – still capable of standing and joined-up speech – has run more than 140 miles. One by one, they cross the line and the computer chips in their vests finally stop clicking up the miles on the race computer. As they slow to a merciful halt – each checking readouts on their stopwatches – they mostly seem fresh and bouncy, unconcerned that Keswick has ignored them or that the outcome will feature only on niche Internet sites.

Amongst the tight-knit group of runners here today – from India, Canada, New Zealand and elsewhere – the name John Tarrant provokes little response. Few people have heard of him or his achievements in the sport which now consumes them as it once devoured him. Only an elderly timekeeper can step forward with a memory, a man called Eddie Gutteridge, whose name will feature again much later in this story. Towards the end of his life, John had once stayed at Eddie's parents' house, and a younger Eddie had watched him run for 100 miles, open-mouthed and awed by the force which Tarrant had become.

As he gazed around the now-still sunlit park, golden leaves tumbling from the trees, it was as if Eddie had felt a ghost. 'I can see him now,' he remembered, 'running along like an automaton, wearing sticky tape around his shoes to hold them together. Utterly unaware of anything. Unstoppable. Brilliant. Not one of this lot could have touched him. He'd have taken every single one of these runners to the cleaners.'

Tarrant would certainly have felt at home among this intensely driven fraternity. No one craved approval more than he did, but his preference was for honours, not audiences. A naturally introverted man, he thrived in the strange solitude of long-distance – amongst the same breed of athletes who travelled to Keswick in 2009 to run trapped with their thoughts for 24 invisible hours. Running like this – often in terrible pain – had never been a problem for John Edward Tarrant. It was what he'd been doing practically his whole life – just not at these extraordinary, almost unfeasible distances.

Tarrant's proposed switch had other attractions. Unlike today, the 1960s and '70s were still a heyday for ultra-long-distance, and there were regular, well-publicised events which attracted huge interest from a public fascinated by such prodigious feats of masochism. Although the numbers of runners – by modern standards – were usually low, the press interest was disproportionately high. Everyone liked to read about world records, and in ultra-distance – where the human variables were so unpredictable – the records were in constant turmoil, with times improving not just by seconds but by minutes. Gold medals had eluded Tarrant, but records might not, and since these epics invariably attracted international fields he'd be racing in the sort of company he'd been deprived of. Rejuvenated, refocused and determined to make his mark, he couldn't wait to get started.

To begin with, it wasn't easy. Troubled by his knee, Tarrant struggled throughout 1964 to find any consistent form. Running the extra miles wasn't hard – Tarrant could knock off 40 miles on any weekend morning just for fun; the problem was knowing how to pace the miles along roads which were very rarely flat. It helped that Victor had decided to try his hand at ultra-distance, too. John's brother had always been more curious about tactics, and travelling the country together in Vic's motor was like the good old ghost-running times. The bad old times – the years at Lamorbey – were never mentioned.

In September, the brothers turned up at the Woodford-to-Southend 37, finding time for a pre-race natter with an ex-Olympian who sagely whispered, 'Remember, it's the pace that kills, never the distance.' It wasn't the first time – or the last – that Tarrant had been given this advice. Arthur Keily had trotted out the same line in Liverpool eight years earlier. But, for once, it seemed to stick. On a baking hot day, he looked around after 30 miles to find himself clear of the field, despite cramp in both thighs and 'fluid squelching around' in his stomach. Reduced to a plod, and fully expecting to be overtaken, he crossed the line first, in a time of 3 hours, 56 minutes and 54 seconds, 10 minutes inside the previous record. To John's absolute delight, Victor finished just four places behind him.

Once again Tarrant's enthusiasm could not be contained. Two weeks later – against Victor's advice – he took the train to London alone, spending a sleepless night in the Union Jack Club, a hostel for demobbed servicemen in a back street near Waterloo station. Throughout the night, drunken ex-squaddies lurched into his room stinking of cigarettes and someone else's sour perfume. When the milk train rolled in – or the Royal Mail train rolled out – Tarrant turned nervously on his grubby pillow as the entire building seemed to tremble under the orange wash of the street lights.

Well before dawn, he'd checked out, changed at the second-class swimming baths on Great Smith Street and was standing on Westminster Bridge – fretfully shaking and frozen half to death – waiting for Big Ben to ring seven times and for the world-famous 54-mile London-to-Brighton road race to begin. On all sides of him in the September murk were 50 top-flight athletes, 12 of them from overseas. From his athletics magazines, he recognised the extraordinary Ted Corbitt – the black New York runner, now 44, who'd run for the USA in the 1952 Olympics. In the half-light there were others, mostly illustrious strangers but among them a tall man with a Yorkshire accent whose face he knew: Bernard Gomersall.

Bernard had been there in Liverpool that first glorious day of Tarrant's reinstatement. He'd clapped and cheered after the race with Arthur Keily and the rest of them. But Bernard was a star now, bright-eyed and brilliant and back to defend his title. Still shaking off the memory of his sleepless night rocked by trains, Tarrant could have been excused a moment of self-pity. 'The forgotten man' was alone, had no second to help him, no idea whether he'd finish the distance, and still felt sore from his victory in Southend barely a fortnight before. Victor had been right. He wasn't ready for this. By contrast, the stringy Gomersall – wearing his trademark maroon vest marked simply 'Leeds' – seemed wired with serene confidence.

'That race – the London-to-Brighton – was always the most important race of my year,' remembers Bernard. 'Nothing else mattered. Everything I did was geared to it. Starting in November, I'd begin preparations for the next one the following September. Altogether I ran it nine times and never dropped out once. Once I'd set off at my six-minute miles, I could keep that up for five hours. In that respect, me and John were chalk and cheese.'

Shivering on the starting line – without anyone to advise him or supply him with refreshments – Tarrant could hardly have felt less prepared in his life. Impulse had taken him to Liverpool as a ghost in 1956. Now the same urges had brought him here almost ten years later, better known but no better prepared and as dependent as ever on the indomitable will that had got him this far. This time it would not be enough.

From the gun, he found it easy – 'like a training run' – with the leaders sharing stories and Gomersall nobly sharing his drinks. At 20 miles, he even made one of his familiar breaks. But at 40 miles, he was hauled back and overtaken and was running alone, exhausted and uncertain of his position. By the finish, he'd clung on to fourth place, albeit seventeen long minutes behind the jubilant winner, Bernard Gomersall.

'From that race forward,' recalls Gomersall, 'Tarrant was the last person I considered a rival. In my eyes, he was reckless. When the gun went, he was usually away, and because I couldn't match that my approach was, "He's gone. Just let him go." The odds were that at the three-quarter mark you'd find him blown up at the side of the road.'

Gomersall wouldn't always get it right – John Tarrant would shortly secure sweet revenge – but a periodically bitter rivalry had been born in Brighton which would dominate the next few running years of both men. For the time being, it was benign. John had been thankful for Gomersall's kindness during the race and was a wiser man for his beating. With what energy remained, he limped along Brighton front for an ice cream before returning to receive his Newcomer's Cup for fourth place from the Mayor of Brighton. It would look well alongside the others back in Harold Street. Victor and Edie would be proud of him.

It had never been in John's nature to dabble. In all things – apart from work and family – Tarrant was an obsessive for whom half-measures had no meaning. As an aspirant boxer, he'd returned night after winter's night to Ted Douglas's dismal Stockport gym. As a 'ghost', he'd travelled tirelessly to get his case heard. After reinstatement, he'd fought alone for his chance to run for Great Britain. If he'd not been denied so often, it might have been different. The way Gomersall sees it, Tarrant was incapable of compromise because running was his only means of revenge: 'All the time, the race – the win – was his way of getting back at people. He couldn't relax like the rest of us. He was always trying to get somewhere. The rest of us didn't have to.'

Now – almost overnight – ultra-distance had become the new master to which everything and everyone in his life must yield. At the TA Centre – yet another job he'd come to loathe – he'd manipulated his work schedule to free up more daylight hours and was running thirty-two miles three times a week. To build up his strength, he'd added a gruelling regime of hill sprints: timed high-speed bursts of 220 or 440 yards uphill followed by slower jogs back to the bottom.

Not until he was satisfied would he stop. Not until his muscles knotted, his lungs burned and the spittle ran down his neck into a vest drenched with sweat. Only then, when he felt content with what his body could do, would he stop and go home to the family he'd not taken on holiday since 1959, the year he'd won best knobbly knees at Clacton Butlins on the only proper family holiday they'd ever really had – or would have. These years won't come back, he told Edie. I'll be old a long time.

There'd been no formal break with his TA teammates, but Tarrant's racing days with the Hereford Light Infantry were over, too. 'He'd wanted me to move up the distances with him, but I wasn't that interested,' says Derek Davies. 'It was only because I had a car and he didn't. I wasn't stupid.'

In the spring of 1965, John's freshly inspired dedication

began to pay off. In May sunshine, he lined up outside the Odeon cinema in Exeter, where a solitary policeman guided runners to the start of the 44-mile road race to Plymouth. Less than five hours later – despite the route's sapping 3,000 ft of ascent – he struggled in exhausted, having ripped twenty minutes off the course record. Four weeks later, he won the Isle of Man 40, noting with private satisfaction that the record he'd shattered this time had been set the previous year by Bernard Gomersall. Finally, in mid July, the two men found themselves together again – side by side outside Liverpool's St George's Hall for the 48½-mile road race to Blackpool.

Nine months before, on Westminster Bridge, Bernard had been the favourite. No one, it had seemed, could touch him then. Not since July 1963 had the chirpy Leeds clerk been beaten. But this day, under settled skies, and with Victor running alongside him, Tarrant felt confident. The previous September – for the London-to-Brighton – he'd been in a strange place, overawed and sleep-deprived. Liverpool was different; it felt familiar. It was the city which had launched him, and it would surely be good to him today. He was right. The following morning the national newspapers went into battle with each other for superlatives.

Gomersall had been 'crushed by iron man Tarrant', concluded one. Gomersall had been 'annihilated', said another. According to one observer, Tarrant had manifested 'the constitution of a horse', delivering a win which was a personal 'disaster for Gomersall'. It was tub-thumpingly over-the-top prose, but it revealed a wellspring of Fleet Street curiosity about John which hadn't been tapped since his ghost-running days. He'd not been forgotten; he was still their favourite crusty underdog, their Alf Tupper with attitude. As he crossed that line on Blackpool prom ten minutes ahead of his Yorkshire rival, he'd felt the old self-righteous strut surge back. Three stunning victories in three months had silenced his devils. For years, he'd been marooned and rudderless. At last, he had some purpose again. He also had a world record squarely in his sights.

For ultra-distance runners, it was their Everest, their four-minute mile. Ever since the 1950s, the very best of them had been trying to dismantle the 40-mile track record of 4 hours, 4 minutes and 34 seconds – a time requiring 160 laps of such sustained concentration that no one had come close since South African Gerald Walsh had set the benchmark in 1957. Forty six-minute miles would bring the record inside four hours, and although he was hardly renowned for his controlled running, Tarrant was certain that his outstanding 1965 form could take him to glory. Assuming, that is, his boxing past didn't once again stand in his way.

As always, the situation was muddy. To give himself a chance, he'd decided to challenge the record at Santry Stadium in Dublin – a track known for its fast times – a trip which required Tarrant to cross into territory administered by the International Amateur Athletic Federation. Before travelling, John had put in a formal request for permission, which had caused consternation amongst London's governing elite. With Jack Crump now off the scene, the red-hot Tarrant file had been passed to his replacement at the BAAB – Arthur Gold – and Gold didn't seem to have a clue whether Tarrant's ban from competing internationally extended to any solo activities he might pursue under his own name or whether it prevented him only from representing Great Britain. Promising to get back to him, Gold scurried off in pursuit of clarification. Tarrant, meanwhile, hopped on the Liverpool ferry – alone and without a permit – and went eagerly in pursuit of a new world record.

It was his first time out of the country and he was a wretched bundle of nerves. Fully expecting Gold to drag him from the boat, he arrived in Dublin after dark on Friday, 19 August and travelled by cab to a bed and breakfast directly opposite the stadium, the home of his hosts, the renowned Clonliffe Harriers. The club's charismatic secretary Billy Morton had reassured a fretting Tarrant that there would be no trouble from the authorities, and Tarrant had warned the *Daily Mirror* to expect a new world record.

From the beginning, John had made no secret of his 'baggage', and no aspect of it worried Morton in the slightest. The way Billy saw it, Tarrant's illegal status was a disgrace, and since Morton positively thrived on irritating British sporting grandees, the Harriers were thrilled to have the famous rebel in Ireland. Tarrant seemed like an honourable man – he was paying his own way – and wanted nothing more than his chance on an iconic track which had already staged the 'greatest mile race ever': the night in 1958 when five runners crossed the line in under four minutes.

After a night's sleep, John stepped into the Irish sunshine seeking his place alongside those record-holders. None of his family was there. Apart from a handful of timekeepers, no one was watching. Perhaps it was as well. Less than 30 laps into his attempt, Tarrant's bid was in tatters. With just seven miles completed, he was forced to leave the track with the same mysterious 'stomach trouble' which had plagued him three summers before. After fifteen miles – and now woefully off world-record pace – he'd been violently sick and lay one mile behind Noel Henry, the gifted Clonliffe runner who'd volunteered to be John's pacemaker.

Three desperate miles later – after a second attack of diarrhoea – Tarrant was finished. Gasping with exhaustion, white-faced from the exertion of his sickness, John clamped hold of Billy Morton and pleaded with him for a second attempt. Morton urged him to reconsider, but Tarrant maintained he couldn't stay in Dublin for the week he'd need to recover fully. Edie would put up with many things, but John getting sacked wasn't one of them. Reluctantly, the Irishman agreed to supply two fresh pacemakers the following Monday evening. Whatever was wrong with Tarrant would need to be cleared up within 48 hours.

Two days later, word of John Tarrant's exploits had circulated and the number of spectators had swelled to six. After less than two hours, they saw him pass the twenty-mile mark looking strong, fortified by sweetened tea and Irish humour from the astonished trackside Billy Morton. In a lifetime of athletics, he'd seen nothing quite like this and never would again. Barely two days before, Tarrant had been virtually carried from this track, bilious and beaten. Now here he was reaching thirty miles in two seconds less than three hours and still tantalisingly on pace to take the world record.

Slowly, however, Tarrant's monumental effort started to crumble. Every lap was taking longer and the diarrhoea was back. All hope of the record was gone unless he could run the last five miles in thirty minutes, and there was no chance of that. The best he could hang on for now was a finish, and for 20 excruciating laps he dragged himself on, yard by lonely yard to the end, the only man on the track, racked by cramp and stomach-ache, unable either to stand or control his vomiting as he crossed the line in 4 hours, 11 minutes and 11 seconds.

It had been vintage Tarrant. Running through unimaginable walls of distress, the lifelong fury of his will had prevailed. His time had been the third-fastest ever run at forty miles, and he'd established a new Irish record. But what had seemed miraculous to Morton, and the handful of onlookers, was a matter of profound disappointment to John. The notion of heroic failure had no place in his lexicon. He'd achieved nothing and the adventure had left him 20 quid out of pocket. It was consoling that Gold hadn't arranged to have him yanked from the track, but Tarrant was crossing the Irish Sea with fresh worries that simply wouldn't go away.

Almost everyone who'd ever run with Tarrant knew about his stomach problems. Up till now, no one – not even John – had taken them too seriously, and his repeated mid-training attacks of the runs gave them all a rare chance to leave him behind. 'It was a standing joke to be honest,' recalls Ken Flowers. 'On training runs, when he had to drop his shorts, me, Victor and Derek would take off down the road like hell – really pushing on – but sure enough he'd still catch us up pretty soon after.'

It was a problem which could strike anywhere, at any time. 'We used to do a 13-mile run around Hereford,' remembers Derek Davies. 'One time, about a mile from the finish, John said, "I've got to have one," and he nipped into a driveway which turned out to be the road up to the local police headquarters.'

For Victor, the problem had even become a part of their normal race routine. When nature called – and when Victor was acting as his brother's second – he'd be ordered ahead in his car to find a well-hidden spot where Tarrant could defecate unseen. When there was no cover to be found, Victor would retrieve a large overcoat from the boot and hold it protectively around his brother while he squatted weakly to do his business.

Publicly, John made light of it and went along with the jokes. Privately, the anxiety was starting to eat into his self-confidence. Ever since his ghost-running campaign, Tarrant had suffered from nerves before big races, but until these last few years it had never affected his ability to run. It wasn't the embarrassment which worried him. Not in the least. If someone saw him taking a crap, that was their problem. He had no qualms about crawling behind a hedge. This was a man's game, and things had to be done. But this felt like more than the unsavoury by-product of nervous tension. Maybe it was just a phase he was going through, a side effect of the intense strain these greater distances were exerting on his body. Tarrant would give it another couple of races and then seek some advice.

Over the following months, the situation got worse. At race after race – throughout 1965 and 1966 – Tarrant was forced to withdraw, often bent double with pain, unable to recover the vital minutes lost during his numerous humiliating toilet stops. Paradoxically, the crisis had come when he was in the best competitive shape of his life. In September 1965, at his second London-to-Brighton, John had left Gomersall floundering in his slipstream for 40 brilliant miles, until his guts had brought him to an agonising standstill. That night at the post-race banquet, Tarrant's health was the sole topic of conversation. Noel Henry, the Irish talent who'd paced John in Dublin, listened in eagerly to the gossip. 'We all seemed in agreement,' he remembers. 'The iron man John Tarrant was finished. How wrong we were.'

Three weeks later, there was more despair. After 23 miles, John crashed out of his third attempt at the elusive 40-mile world track record, unable to do any more than clutch his knotted stomach as Lynn Hughes, the vibrant son of a Welsh miner, swept in with a new British best of 4 hours, 5 minutes and 52 seconds. Through gritted teeth, Tarrant paid his respects to the latest young pretender, but these were desperate times. In May the following year – after a winter of methodical training – John slipped back into Dublin but proved unable to run more than 17 miles of his fourth dismal shot at the 40-mile record, incapacitated once again by bowels which ran like water. Never again, he told reporters: 'It is too much of a financial and mental strain.'

Almost every race delivered the same awful outcome. Where once he'd expected to win, Tarrant now rarely expected to finish. At his third attempt to win the London-to-Brighton, he'd squatted miserably in back streets eight times and could manage no better than forty-fourth. In yet another 40-mile world-record attempt, in October, he withdrew, too drained even to walk, after 31 miles. This time, it was an Englishman who triumphed. Slumped feebly at the sidelines, Tarrant looked on as Alan Phillips – wading around a track ankle-deep in rainwater – sliced the record down to 4 hours, 4 minutes and 9 seconds. Gracious as John always was, this was getting close to impossible.

Without running – without even the physical power to compete – Tarrant was well aware he had absolutely nothing. Since Buxton, it was the single thing he'd constructed his entire life around. Work and money had no value. Tarrant had always been the Lamorbey child with the empty locker. He owned no car, no house – not even a bicycle – and there were no material assets he craved. They had a television, which he rarely watched, and half-heartedly he'd occasionally fill in a pools coupon but then never seemed to care about the football results. No one ever doubted the love he had for Edie and his 12-year-old son, but everyone – even Edie – knew where they stood on his list of priorities. 'She had a rough time. No doubt about that,' is the verdict of Derek Davies. Without running, Tarrant had nothing. Somehow, he had to get fit.

Whatever John had would prove very hard to diagnose. When he wasn't running, he felt perfectly normal. The diarrhoea struck only out on the road or the track. There'd been no weight loss or fatigue, and he was manifesting no other consistent symptoms of illness. Ever since he'd refused Maysie's packed lunches all those years ago, he'd taken care over his diet. Now he would be even more careful. Derek Davies remembers him once ripping the cardboard wrapper from a huge block of ice cream and 'eating it like an animal', but all that would have to stop.

Talking to his fellow runners had helped him assemble a list of recommended self-administered remedies. Out went white sugar, in came brown sugar, yoghurt and honey. To his normal diet he added vitamin pills and iron tablets, and, following advice from a top Australian coach, he no longer ate and drank at the same time. He also began to take in much more liquid during races, with the 'corpse reviver' becoming an integral part of his survival kit.

In his own words, he was 'prepared to take a gamble on anything, providing there was no risk to my athletic performance'. None of the doctors he approached seemed too worried, and pharmaceutical drugs filled him with horror. If possible, he'd stick to natural alternatives. 'It appeared to be something I would have to learn to live with,' he wrote. There was also just a possibility it was all inside his head anyway.

The year hadn't been a complete disaster – there'd been strong wins at Exeter and the Isle of Man – but as 1967 dawned, as far as the press was concerned Tarrant was a fading force. Cruelly branded 'an ageing maestro' in one report, his name was now usually preceded in newspapers by the word 'veteran'. At the age of 34 – with a growing reputation as a quitter – he was in danger of becoming one of the circuit's nostalgia acts, eliciting sympathetic sighs for his long struggle but no longer a contender for serious honours. As the winter set in, there was only one date left in his diary which could turn this downward spiral around. November 5th – Bonfire Night – had been earmarked for yet another attempt on the 40-mile world record. The venue would be the Maindy Stadium in Cardiff, and the field would include Alan Phillips, the crack runner from Henley-on-Thames who'd secured the current world record just three weeks before.

For days, the weather had been atrocious. Incessant rain sweeping in off the Bristol Channel had hidden the brown cinder track beneath an enormous lake of muddy water. Throughout the night, stadium staff battled forlornly to brush away puddles which then immediately flowed back. Alone in his bed-and-breakfast room, Tarrant, sleepless, devoured a half-pound block of cheese and listened to the rain lashing the pavements below. He was hoping the cheese would settle his stomach, but, by the sound of it, the race wouldn't be happening anyway.

By dawn the next day, parts of the track stood under a foot of water and a vicious cold wind was slashing through the stadium. The rain, however, had eased, and at 11.30 a.m. the officials felt conditions had improved sufficiently to get the race under way. Wearing two vests and gloves for warmth, the eight combatants inched unenthusiastically to the start. No one was expecting a record – not in this weather – and in his heart all Tarrant really wanted to do was finish. One more failure and he'd probably quit, but for good this time. The next 40 miles would be the most important he'd ever run.

From the start, conditions underfoot were shocking. Although the standing water had drained quickly from the straights, the bends remained a quagmire, and around the entire length of the track the inside lane wore down quickly into a deep rutted furrow. At times, the eight runners found themselves wading through wet ash, and they were lashed by a wind which had veered bitterly round from the east, blowing directly into their faces every time they turned to complete one more of the hundred and sixty allotted laps. For the stationary huddle of timekeepers and seconds there were different hazards. Unable to move, the cold seeped deep into their bones, making it almost impossible to write down the lap times. When one of them sought respite in a canvas toilet tent, there was so much water on the roof that it collapsed on his head.

At the halfway mark, Tarrant was well inside world-record pace, two laps ahead of Phillips and two minutes ahead of his old mate Derek Davies. 'I was there to get him into the pace he needed. I'd no intention of going all the way,' says Davies. At thirty miles, only four runners remained and an eight-minute gap had opened up between Tarrant and his nearest rival. Miraculously, there'd been no hint of complaint from John's stomach. For whatever reason, a priceless physical equilibrium seemed to have been achieved, and Tarrant would do nothing to risk it. Not even his raging thirst could tempt him to succumb to a drink. Later, when the race was finally over, he'd realise that only half a cup of lukewarm tea had passed his lips since the start.

Gradually, the dozen or so frozen spectators began to appreciate that the gaunt man wearing the number 2 on his Salford Harriers vest was in with a chance. Despite the dried red mud which encased his legs, despite his desperate rictus expression, despite his awkward, agonised rolling gait, Tarrant was closing in fast on the record. With just five miles to go, he was still two minutes inside Phillips' time. Across the crackling loudhailer, the event organisers were working themselves into a ferment. A man with a megaphone was babbling crazily to anyone who would listen: 'You are about to see athletic history! You are about to see athletic history!' Knowing he was so close, the three remaining runners stepped courteously aside every time he lapped them. Everyone knew John Tarrant. Everyone knew what this could mean to him. Everyone left inside Maindy on that withering November afternoon was willing him on.

And then – suddenly – it was all over. He'd done it. As he collapsed into the arms of friends and strangers – too weary even to weep – Tarrant's time was confirmed at 4 hours, 3 minutes and 28 seconds. By the narrowest of margins – just 40 seconds – he'd beaten Alan Phillips' record, and for that fragile moment he was the very best there had ever been. He didn't care how long it would last. Every kick, every setback, every slap in the face, every lonely step he'd ever taken: everything had been worth it for this. Every hollow month of these last few aimless years was instantly forgotten. And, as always with John Edward Tarrant in the ecstasy of triumph, the frustrations, the mystery ailments – and the eternally unresolved issues – all withered and shrank to nothing under the onslaught of his self-belief. Never mind 'ageing maestro'. John Tarrant – the ghost runner – was back.

Chapter Seven

Return of the Ghost

1967

Unlikely as it seemed, John Tarrant had developed into a prodigious man of letters. The telephone had never appealed to him (and was much too expensive anyway). Banal conversation had always been a trial and the written word suited him far better. Although he still employed the same clunky Lamorbey syntax – set down in his distinctive childlike longhand – he felt more confident behind a biro, finding it much easier to express those things he found impossible to say well in person. Latterly, his letters – like his conversations – almost always spilled over into expressions of anger and regret. He could also sound pompous, vain and patronising, his views polluted by his many lost years spent fighting the establishment.

If a rival edged him in a race or took one of his titles, they would almost certainly receive unsolicited written congratulations. Following his triumphant record-breaking run in Cardiff, the congratulatory letters had flowed in to Hereford from all corners of Britain, and in every case John sat down and penned a personal reply. The family's kitchen at the TA barracks had become Tarrant's campaign headquarters, and when he wasn't out running with Victor there was a high chance he'd be crouched over a notepad, earnestly orchestrating the next move in his long-running one-man war.

He would never have admitted it at the time, but it hadn't been the same since Jack Crump had slipped off his long list of correspondents. Ever since that very first 'Dear Tarrant' letter, there'd been a frank, almost gladiatorial quality to their fractious exchanges. It had been a terrible shock to hear of Crump's sudden death the previous April. Towards the end, Tarrant had sensed genuine empathy there, and Crump's successor Arthur Gold was showing few signs of continuing the rapprochement. Communication with the new broom was proving blunt and businesslike at best.

Had Tarrant bothered to delve into Gold's pronouncements on the blight of money in sport, he'd have very quickly found out why. No less than Harold Abrahams, or Crump, or any of them, Gold detested the insidious incursion of professionalism. The notion that a former 'pro' boxer might ever represent his country would have appalled him. Instinctively, however, Gold may also have sensed that Tarrant no longer posed any kind of a threat. At 35, he was looking a little old, had drifted away from the marathon and was competing in events which didn't feature at either the Olympics or the Commonwealth Games. What Gold probably hadn't realised was that Tarrant didn't think the authorities could hurt him any more, either.

Towards the end of 1965 – exactly 12 months before his record at 40 miles – he had enjoyed a moment of epiphany. Throughout that year, Tarrant had been demanding to know whether his ban from representing Great Britain extended to him as an individual, whether, in effect, he could simply turn up at a race overseas and compete legally with his fellow runners. By Christmas of 1965, Gold had returned with an answer, albeit the wrong one as far as John Tarrant was concerned.

The IAAF had confirmed to Gold that, under Rule 53 (Subsection 1), Tarrant's boxing past placed him beyond pardon or redemption. Not only was he banned from representing his country, he was also forbidden from competing overseas in any other capacity. Writing in the *Daily Mirror*, Peter Wilson called it 'the final bucket of cold water in [Tarrant's] face'. 'If this is sporting justice,' he thundered, 'the Spanish Inquisition and the Star Chamber were models of enlightened legislation.'

Although Tarrant would later call the news 'a crunching disappointment', he received it with uncharacteristic calm. As Gold had rightly surmised, John's attention was slipping away from piddling distances like 26 miles, and with it had gone his fixation on the acquisition of a Great Britain blazer. Something else had driven his need to clarify Rule 53, something as bold as anything he had ever attempted before. It wouldn't do for Gold to know what it was just yet, but at least Tarrant would know where he stood when the time came.

Ever since the army's abortive team trip to Enschede, John had been intrigued by the prospect of running abroad. His two clandestine trips to Dublin had stirred up the old thrill of those heart-pounding dawn drives perched on Victor's motorcycle. There wasn't a long-distance race in Britain he hadn't run and very few he hadn't won – once, twice or three times. He wasn't so much bored as unsatisfied. He also felt like a prisoner on his own shores.

As early as 1962, he'd discreetly contacted athletes in the United States, wondering if he'd be allowed to run in races over there. Now he knew – officially – that he couldn't, he was suddenly a lot more interested. No one had stopped him getting on the Irish ferry. It therefore seemed unlikely anyone would ever try to pull him off a plane. To be a ghost in Doncaster was one thing. To be a ghost in New York or Durban would be something else entirely.

For some time, one overseas race, above all others, had begun to exert its pull. Since its inception in 1921, the 56-mile Comrades Marathon in South Africa had grown rapidly to become the gold standard of endurance running. No other event in the world attracted more runners, and no course was better designed to strip a man of his will to live. Stretched across the steep green fringes of the Zulu homelands, it exuded a fierce charisma with which few domestic races could compete. Durban to Pietermaritzburg sounded a lot more tempting than London-to-Brighton, and Tarrant wasn't the first British runner to fall under the race's spell.

In 1965, to the surprise of the entire athletics world, the winner had come from outside the usual sporting elite: a tall crop-haired stranger with a northern English accent who'd turned in a record time and taken the South African organisers by complete surprise. Tarrant knew him well. His name was Bernard Gomersall.

For John Tarrant, that was incentive enough. If Gomersall could win the Comrades, then so could he. For a lowly paid caretaker who could barely afford his train fares around Britain, it seemed an improbable goal, but by 1967 the Comrades Marathon had mutated from a mere ambition to an outright, and ultimately all-consuming, obsession. It would continue to be so for the remaining eight years of his life.

As the year started, however, and as Tarrant emerged from his winter's hibernation – light training and rest – there was little evidence that this latest preoccupation would ever graduate beyond idle talk. In every respect, his life seemed locked into a depressingly grey routine: pushing a broom and polishing floors by day; running the hills once his duties were done. For the big spring clean of the barracks, Edie would usually lend a hand, but money was tight and Tarrant was restless. Edie's £1 a week job in the officers' mess had recently been cut. Before leaving Buxton, Tarrant had never held a job for longer than a few months, and he'd been doing this one for almost eight years. A sluggish half-heartedness had infected his performance around the barracks. RSM Jones had long gone, and following a spat over travel expenses Tarrant had quit both the TA and its regimental athletics team.

Slowly, his relationship with his employers was becoming more strained. Never an enthusiastic worker, he now did only the minimum necessary to warrant the pittance he was paid. Even their tied accommodation had lost its lustre. At weekends, there was often closing-time noise from the nearby TA social club – revved engines and slurred banter – which penetrated Tarrant's sleep, leading to angry midnight exchanges.

Once the race season started, however, the mundane frustrations of normal life faded away. In April, he pulled out of a 40-mile track race in Surrey – feeling untypically 'tired and jaded' – but he bounced back quickly, winning handsomely over 40-, 44- and 49-mile distances. Despite the ever-nagging 'stomach trouble' and the irksome diarrhoea, he was in crushing form, with victories in Devon, Lancashire, South Wales and the Isle of Man. At the finishing line of the Liverpool-to-Blackpool – along the town's famous promenade – he'd been violently and very publicly sick, but he'd still turned in a race record, and he now seemed strong enough to win races even when he was losing time at the side of the road.

Fitness was the key. During that summer of 1967, he spent a week running up the mountainous sand-dunes of Merthyr Mawr, near Bridgend in South Wales. Every day, under a blazing sun, Tarrant and the young Welsh runner Lynn Hughes flogged themselves up the sliding sands of the highest dunes in Europe. For the two men, lost in their exertions, it was like being in another world. No cares, no concerns. David Lean had filmed scenes for *Lawrence of Arabia* there. Razor-sharp marram grass sliced at their ankles. Fine white grit filled their plimsolls and stuck to the sweat on their faces. Running uphill was like wading in a tide of dry mud. Running down was sheer childlike joy.

'To me, John was just a gentle giant,' recalls Hughes. 'Always polite. Never a cross word. He was my idol, I suppose. My target, my mentor. When I was starting out in running and got home from race day, the first thing my father always said to me was, "How did you get on against John?"'

Running on the dunes of Merthyr was uplifting, but Tarrant rarely did anything for mere fun. By the autumn – after a hot summer of high-profile victories – John's steadfast fixation on the Comrades Marathon no longer seemed quite so impractical. One crucial victory in particular and it would surely be within his grasp. On 1 October, he was due to run in his fourth London-to-Brighton road race, and traditionally its winner had been sponsored to compete in South Africa. This was how Gomersall had afforded it in 1965, and if Tarrant's guts didn't let him down, there seemed no reason why he shouldn't follow in Bernard's footsteps.

Cresting the dunes in South Wales, it was all he could think about. Seven years before, he'd staked everything on winning a race which he'd then lost to a stranger. So far, his performances in the race to the south coast had been diabolical. Three attempts, three failures, and a shameful forty-fourth place, two humiliating hours behind Bernard Gomersall, barely twelve months ago. Pushing the thorny issue of the international ban from his mind, Tarrant stepped up his daily training to merciless levels, easing off with just one week to go before the race. If fitness and form were the key, then he was ready. Everyone was saying he was this year's favourite. All he had to overcome now was the most excruciating attack of nerves in his life.

For days before the race, he couldn't sleep. Convinced he was coming down with a cold, he guzzled huge doses of vitamins and checked his pulse every morning for signs of the least deviation from his average 46 beats per minute. During gentle evening runs with his son Roger, he felt certain that every ache was an injury and every twinge a tear. Desperate for comfort, he jogged cautiously across to his brother's bungalow, knowing that if anyone could calm him down, Victor could. 'Don't worry, John,' he said. 'Remember you're the man in form and you can bet the others will be worrying like hell about you.'

It helped, but not a lot. By the time Tarrant inched to the start, he was trembling uncontrollably and needed Victor's help to fasten the laces of his running shoes. During the previous night – spent at a youth hostel – he'd woken from a bout of sickness convinced that the clocks were due to change and would not believe otherwise until reassured by the desk sergeant at Westminster Police Station.

At 6 a.m., he'd made his way to the public baths on Great Smith Street, putting his everyday clothes into a numbered kitbag which would be waiting for him at the Brighton Aquarium in six hours' time. Shortly before walking to the start, he'd silently intoned his favourite poem:

> If you think you're beaten, you are.
> If you think you dare not, you don't.
> If you like to win, but you think you can't,
> It is almost certain you won't.

Tarrant wasn't really sure of the author – some Yank, he thought – but whoever had written it, the words seemed aimed at him, and he never entered a race without privately reciting its 16 saccharine lines of uplifting hokum. Looking through the half-light at that day's 60-strong field of world-famous runners, he felt desperate for all the inspiration he could get. As well as Gomersall, there were legends from South Africa, Switzerland, New Zealand, Scotland and Ireland. All these years he'd craved international competition, and here they all were, waiting together for Big Ben to strike 7 a.m. and for the 54-mile race to Brighton to begin.

Almost five hours later, Tarrant was still clinging on in the race of his life. With a three-minute lead over Bernard Gomersall, and with the steepest uphill slog of the course behind him, it seemed inconceivable that he could lose. What only Tarrant knew, however, was that for an hour he'd been fighting the sickening message his bowels were sending. Scarcely five miles from the finish, unable to contain it any longer – and impervious to the wide-eyed horror of the stewards – he was forced to rush from the road to find relief.

For what felt like an eternity, he sorted himself out. Still – incredibly – there was no sign of Gomersall. Swallowing a quinine sulphate tablet to stave off cramp in his thighs, Tarrant hobbled off in the direction of Brighton with the words of that infernal doggerel bouncing around in his head: 'If you think you're beaten, you are . . . if you think you're beaten, you are.' Slowly, his rhythm was returning. The downcast walk became a hopeful jog, which then became a familiar, powerful surge of belief as he sensed the cheering crowd along the seafront, and the finishing tape beyond.

Ahead of him were the men in their black suits and their wives in those ridiculous hats. He could see the portly dignitaries, their chests cluttered with regalia. He could hear the seagulls in comical cackling lines along the flaking painted railings. No one could catch him now. Crossing the line at 5 hours, 41 minutes and 50 seconds, he'd finally won the race which had eluded him for so long. He had also – in the words

Hereford, 1960. John, Edie, son Roger and Victor's Mini.

Private John Tarrant marches to a new record with fellow TAs Ken Flowers (left) and Derek Davies. (courtesy of Ken Flowers)

The all-conquering Hereford TA runners *c.*1961.
Victor is in the front row, second from left; John is in the back row, on the far right.

'He'd always want to hammer you.'
Reinstated and virtually unbeatable
– Tarrant in his pomp.

November 1966, Cardiff. A new world record at 40 miles.

Ned Waring, Tarrant's indefatigable benefactor. (courtesy of the family of Ned Waring)

A ghost in New York, 1967.
(courtesy of Tom Osler)

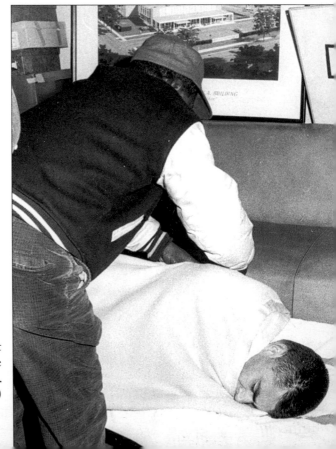

Jet-lagged and weary: Tarrant
on a camp bed hours before
ghosting in the USA.
(courtesy of Tom Osler)

Durban, South Africa, 1968. Tarrant basks in his notoriety.
(courtesy of Independent Newspapers)

Dave Box and Dave Bagshaw,
Tarrant's great long-distance rivals.
(copyright unknown)

Dave Box: the ego of a potentate, the body
of a Greek god. (copyright unknown)

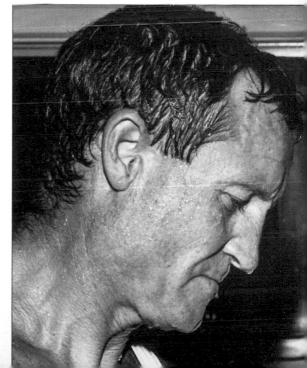

October 1969. John embraces Edie seconds after setting a new world record at 100 miles. (courtesy of *Daily Express*)

Rajendra Chetty. 'You are made in the mettle of great men,' he told John. (courtesy of Rajendra Chetty)

Finishing the Comrades in South Africa in 1968 – the fourth place that never was.

South Africa, 1969.
Running out of steam in the Comrades.
(courtesy of Independent Newspapers)

Posing with the Goldtop Trophy in 1971, only hours after his first massive haemorrhage.

Hereford Football Club, 1974. A gaunt-looking Tarrant runs for the last time. Victor (in the white jumper) keeps time.

of third-placed Bernard Gomersall – 'put the cat firmly back among the pigeons'.

From the beginning, winning had always been the key to Tarrant's simple strategy. Unfortunately, the devil was often in the details he chose not to see. In 1960, he'd naively believed that victory in the AAA Marathon would propel him to the Olympics. No one except him seriously thought this to be true. Blithely, he now assumed that first place in the London-to-Brighton would assure him of the necessary funds to travel to South Africa. Once again, he was catastrophically wrong.

Since 1952, the race he'd just won had been organised by the Road Runners Club (RRC), an organisation dedicated to the needs of those predominantly working-class athletes who preferred the highway to the track. It was the RRC which annually staged ultra-distance world-record events, and it was through the RRC that the disparate bunch of mavericks to which Tarrant belonged had finally acquired a voice.

Without their providing timekeepers and paying for the Cardiff stadium, his 40-mile world-record run simply wouldn't have happened. Here, for once, he thought, was a serious organisation which would put credibility and weight behind his cause. However, the RRC was not quite the free-spirited organisation Tarrant might have wished it to be. Through its affiliation to the Amateur Athletic Association, the RRC's individual members – and the races it staged – were subject to the rules of a higher authority.

On issues of policy, the RRC would bow to the AAA, which would defer to the BAAB, which meant that just one man would ultimately preside over any awkward decisions: Arthur Gold, whose line on John Tarrant deviated not one inch from that of his late predecessor.

Even as he brushed aside the tape in Brighton, Tarrant must

have feared what was coming. In recent years, the RRC's prize for the London-to-Brighton winner had been the cash for a trip to the Comrades Marathon in South Africa the following May. In the anxious months before the race, Tarrant had written to the RRC demanding reassurance that, in the event of his winning, the same largesse would fall to him. If the cat came down among the pigeons (which it now had), would the RRC fund and defend his right to run overseas against the implacable resistance of Gold and the IAAF?

Tarrant was right to be nervous. The RRC was no trade union, and Tarrant's cause – whatever he thought – was only on the distant edge of its vision. Every Christmas, Jack Crump – and later Arthur Gold – would be invited to the House of Commons to join the RRC's officials at their annual dinner. Wearing lounge suits, they'd pick from menus boasting dishes such as 'consommé double en tasse' and 'truite de rivière belle meunière', followed by brandy and cigars, and later (on at least one occasion) a small personal donation from Crump to the RRC for its funds.

Everyone sympathised with John, but no one seriously expected the RRC to take up a gung-ho position which might place such carefully cultivated bonhomie at risk. Even before his victory, the club's officials had been preparing him for disappointment. In a carefully worded letter, the RRC's secretary, Peter Goodsell, had told John that, should the situation arise, the Club would 'put your case most strongly to the [BAAB] Board' as 'they do always have the last word in such cases'.

Following his triumph at Brighton, that situation had arisen, and throughout October John waited anxiously for the RRC's response. Behind the scenes, however, Tarrant was being sold short by the organisation he'd trusted to represent him. Seeking urgent clarification from Gold, the RRC had written:

He and his supporters want him to go to the Comrades next year. This creates a problem. He, as is well known, was a professional boxer in his youth. Some years ago he became known as the ghost runner as he was barred from open competitions. He then re-qualified as an amateur to run. Have the rules been relaxed to allow a former professional to run as an amateur overseas in open competition?

Far from putting Tarrant's case 'most strongly' the RRC's insipid approach to the BAAB had conveyed the impression that they found Tarrant just as irritating as Gold now did. Instead of being portrayed as a worthy case, Tarrant had been cast as a recalcitrant outsider by his own representative organisation. It was not 'we' but 'he', and the RRC's weighted (and inaccurate) use of the word 'professional' suggested distaste akin to that of the establishment's.

Arthur Gold's response was handwritten, terse and unambiguous: 'The IAAF ruled on this two years ago. He is not eligible to run outside GB or in international meetings.' A few days later, Peter Goodsell broke the bad news to Tarrant himself: 'Don't let it worry you John, it just means that you miss out on one or two overseas events.' The Road Runners Club couldn't and wouldn't pay for his trip to South Africa.

Ten years before, Tarrant would have been devastated. In 1967, battle-hardened by rejection, he was better equipped to shrug off the disappointment. Even if he'd known how feebly the RRC had pressed his case, he wouldn't have been surprised. John had long known he was alone in this fight and that relying on third parties was a complete waste of his time. Maybe he'd allowed himself to be patronised for too long. If so, Rule 53 had ended all that. In a weird way, it had set him free.

There was going to be no rule change, no quick fix, no

fairytale release from the ancient curse. He could ingratiate himself all he wanted, but not a damned thing would change. From now on, Tarrant alone would be the arbiter of which races, and which countries, he ran in – not creeps like Arthur Gold. The word around the changing-rooms was that Bernard Gomersall had landed a private sponsor and would be back in Durban in May for a second crack at the Comrades Marathon. It was all the incentive John needed to spread his wings.

For several years, Tarrant had maintained discreet contact with fellow long-distance runners in the United States. Unlike their timorous British counterparts, the officials there seemed positively keen for him to gatecrash their events. Fuelled by his latest setback, Tarrant had quietly reopened the dialogue, enquiring whether he'd be welcome at a 50-mile road race slated for Thanksgiving Day, 23 November, in Poughkeepsie, New York State.

For a disgruntled caretaker who could scarcely afford decent running shoes, it seemed a preposterous notion, but Tarrant's hackles were raised. If they said yes, there would be a way. While he waited for their reply, he headed off to a forty-mile track race in Cardiff – organised by the Road Runners Club – confidently intending to push his own world record below the elusive four-hour barrier.

At the start, all eyes were on Tarrant, but they were on the wrong man. As they had been the year before, conditions were atrocious – sheets of freezing rain – and at 15 miles Tarrant could only watch as Lynn Hughes, his carefree companion on the sand-dunes, swept into the lead. For years, Hughes had idolised John Tarrant. Now he was lapping his friend under saturated November skies, inching stride by stride towards a time which would obliterate the benchmark John had set exactly 364 days before. Grim-faced with fatigue and fury,

Tarrant was unable to maintain his stoic decorum, aiming a string of expletives at the back of the unstoppable Welshman.

It was heartbreaking. Tarrant's precious record had lasted less than a year, and the mythical four-hour barrier was gone to another man. When the watches stopped on Lynn Hughes, he'd swiped almost five minutes from his mentor's old time, an achievement which the deflated Tarrant ranked as highly as Bannister's sub-four-minute mile, not least because of the obstacles Hughes had overcome. Just the day before, the Welshman's doctor had told him he had 'a touch of bronchitis'; Hughes had also recently lost his job, and to pay the ten-shilling (50p) entry fee, he had gone without car tax for a month. 'I just knew I was going to beat it,' he says. 'Everything clicked. I could have run another ten miles.' Against all odds, in filthy conditions, he had crossed the line 23 minutes ahead of his friend and rival.

Twenty-four hours later, a letter arrived at Lynn's home, addressed to 'Lyn Hughes Esq, World 40 Miles Running Champion, Bridgend'. It was John Tarrant's handwritten apology for his spew of invective:

> Please forgive me for my stupid outburst but I do hope you realise how I felt at that very moment. You were running me into the ground and for a brief spell I hated you for it. I wanted more than anything in the world to win and be the first to shatter the four hour barrier to help my case in my bid to represent my country. No praise is too high for your brilliant performance.

It was vintage Tarrant: honest and gracious, laced with anger, self-pity and regret. Although he'd rarely see Lynn Hughes again, the two men had achieved a fleeting closeness which was rare among the peripatetic community of road-runners.

Most ultra-distance events ended with a quick beer and a dash for the train, but since Tarrant invariably foreswore the pint, there were few athletes he could call friends. In Hughes, Tarrant had found a nonconformist with the same contempt as himself for the distant figures who ran their sport.

When approached by Commonwealth Games selectors two years later, Hughes remembers he was asked the question, 'Where does your father work?' to which he replied, 'Who's going to be running this race? My father or me?'

'I wasn't ashamed my father was a miner,' he says. 'I hadn't been to university. I got the feeling that if I'd said my father was a doctor, I'd have been selected . . . I'd always thought John was a fool to tell the authorities about his boxing. Nine out of ten people wouldn't have. He wasn't gaining any advantage by that tiny bit of boxing. Then again, I might have done the same thing: told the truth and then bitterly regretted it.'

Tarrant's disappointment at losing to Hughes was double-edged. Having his fingers prised from a world record so soon was bad enough, but the organisers of the Poughkeepsie road race had now written back, warmly welcoming him to New York State on Thanksgiving Day. It was sickening. With less than one week to go, Tarrant hadn't raised a penny towards the trip. A new world record might have tempted much-needed business sponsors. He couldn't believe anyone would back a loser. And then suddenly – out of absolutely nowhere – came the unlikely figure who would end Tarrant's lifetime run of impossibly bad luck.

John Tarrant didn't know Ned Waring, but Ned Waring knew practically everything about John Edward Tarrant, the ghost runner. He knew every race Tarrant had won and every record he'd set. He knew about his teenage follies as a boxer, and through the national papers he'd followed his struggle to be free of the consequences. Although the two men both lived and worked in Hereford, they had never met, and they moved in very different orbits. Tarrant remained the quintessential anti-establishment outsider with no money. Waring was a well-connected antiques dealer, with five hairdressing salons and a seven-bedroom Victorian mansion.

During the war, he'd spent three years as a British spy in Italy, where he'd been captured by the Germans three times, escaped three times and been shot through the hand once for his troubles. Back in Hereford, he'd been elected to the local council as an independent, earning a reputation as a councillor with a conscience. Knowing what Tarrant had endured deeply affected the older man – Waring was 51 – and in the weeks following John's win in the London-to-Brighton he'd masterminded an extraordinary private campaign on the runner's behalf.

Throughout the autumn, in a series of fiercely argued letters, Waring set out the case for Tarrant's inclusion in the 1968 New Year's Honours List. Describing John as a 'gentleman of the road' who'd been 'hounded for sixteen years', the businessman wrote first to the county's high sheriff and then to both the Minister for Sport, Denis Howell, and the Prime Minister, Harold Wilson, pleading for Tarrant to be taken seriously.

By early November, Downing Street had responded, saying 'the possibility of an honour' would be 'given full consideration'. But there was something about their lukewarm language which didn't convince. Certain that John's rebellious past would compromise his case – even with a Labour government – Waring wondered if there was something more concrete he could do. Two weeks later, he heard about Tarrant's fast-failing battle to raise the funds for the race in New York State – a race that was now just three days away.

On Sunday, 19 November, a disconsolate Tarrant was faced

with an unhappy afternoon of decorating. Before the week was out, he was a ghost runner again, this time on the other side of the Atlantic. Through a mutual friend, Waring had dispatched a £180 cheque to Tarrant's Harold Street home, expressing the hope that the sum would cover both the flight (a huge £142) and any other expenses involved. It was like a storyline from a Dickens novel.

Gleefully abandoning his half-opened paint pots, John dashed to Waring's imposing front door, pouring out his thanks to his benefactor in a giddy state of mystified confusion. Waring urged Tarrant simply to 'treat this trip like a holiday', to run if he got the chance and to do his best 'whatever happens'. More importantly, he showed no interest whatsoever in wanting the money repaid. It was the largest sum Tarrant had ever handled in his life, and it had come without strings.

If he was to take full advantage he would have to move quickly. It was already Monday, and the race started before dawn on Thursday. He'd need to get a smallpox jab, book leave and collect a visa from the American Embassy in Grosvenor Square – all this before the Pan-Am flight to New York on Wednesday afternoon. It was a lot to ask of a man who'd only ever bought train tickets before. But there were other, more pressing reasons for his haste. As John caught the train across to London, a curt letter from Arthur Gold was travelling in the opposite direction, expressing fury that Tarrant was about to defy his lifetime international ban and desperate to prevent such a flagrant public violation of the rules:

> Rumour has reached me that you intend to travel to the USA . . . I have to advise you, John, that you are not permitted to compete in another country without a Certificate of Eligibility under IAAF rules from your own governing body, and that in view of the IAAF ruling on

your case, I am unable to issue such a certificate.

I hasten to write this letter before you become too deeply involved in this affair.

But John didn't open the letter; Edie did. Tipped off that Gold was onto him by his old Fleet Street ally Roy Moor – now at the *Daily Mail* – John had headed for London before the postman arrived. Although Tarrant could honestly swear that he'd never received Gold's missive, the same wasn't true of its contents. He and Edie spoke that night by telephone, and the tone of Gold's warning so badly rattled John that he immediately called Ned Waring offering to refund the £180 and cancel the trip.

'Just enjoy yourself,' said Waring. 'I'm not concerned about the money.' Reassured, Tarrant bid a tearful farewell to Edie and Roger and was driven to Heathrow at the last minute by a friend before flying off into what the *Daily Mirror* dubbed the 'final round of his 16-year battle with the athletic authorities'. Quoting Arthur Gold – 'I think he is unwise' – the newspaper added that Tarrant's patience had run out and that he still wanted the ruling which had outlawed him overturned.

As for what might happen in the United States, Tarrant told reporters, 'The road is a public highway, and if I happen to run along it at the same time as other people, that's pure coincidence.' Edie, meanwhile had other, more proximate worries. Writing to John's father in Buxton to tell him what was happening, she said, 'The papering has been done but I now have no carpet down and it will be quite a long time before I get straight again.'

Edie's living room wasn't the only thing in a state. As his Boeing 707 reached cruising altitude, Tarrant gazed fearfully down through the clouds. These last few days had been too frenetic for clear thinking. Now here he was, alone and 27,000 ft above sea level being offered tea by a beautiful woman wearing a crisp white blouse and a lavender-blue pillbox hat. Apart from those best-forgotten trips to Dublin, he'd never left the country before – hardly ever seen a plane, let alone sat in one.

It would be midwinter dark when he arrived at JFK. What if there was no one waiting for him? Where would he go? How would he get to Poughkeepsie? What if he somehow missed the race or was simply too exhausted to run? What if the officials there pulled him off the road? What if he let everyone down? Victor, Edie, Roger and now Ned Waring – what would they think?

Closing his eyes, soothed by the white noise of the jets, he felt the full force of what he'd done, and his face flushed at the prospect of Gold's reaction when he found out. But Gold already had found out. Tarrant might have dodged his first warning in Hereford, but there was no way he'd move faster than this one. As John dozed uneasily in the skies above Newfoundland, a cable from the BAAB in London was overtaking him on its way to the organisers in Poughkeepsie. Gold would be very surprised indeed if anyone wanted Tarrant to run by the time he'd collected his luggage. With a bit of luck, they might even put him on the first plane back.

Late Wednesday evening, Tarrant emerged raw-eyed into the vaulted arrival hall of John F. Kennedy Airport. There were no phantoms in trilbies to drag him back to England, but there was no sign of any race organisers, either. From what he'd understood, Poughkeepsie was just a few miles from the airport, but when he checked with a tetchy yellow cab driver he was told it was closer to 90. Broke and bone-weary, Tarrant dialled the number on his letter of invitation, only to be told that Gold's telegram had got there before him. Any US athletes who ran in the race with him had been put on notice that their amateur status was in peril. 'We are trying to resolve this without anyone getting hurt,' Tarrant was told, as he recorded in his memoir. 'We want to please you and keep on the right side of the laws.'

Utterly alone amidst the late-night airport clamour – businessmen yelling for cabs, children rushing towards jet-lagged fathers – Tarrant must have felt his willpower sagging. This thing he'd carried around with him since Tommy Burton's wretched fight nights – it was worse than a millstone, it was a virus. John knew what it said in the rulebook: 'An athlete shall have ceased to be an amateur by . . . entering, or allowing himself to be entered in, any athletic competition knowing that it is not confined to amateurs.' Simply to share the road with Tarrant would render an athlete vulnerable to infection.

Tarrant had never taken a penny from athletics. All he'd ever wanted was the respect and recognition of his peers. Now every athlete in America would fear him, regarding him not as a comrade but as a contaminant. Men like Gold, they were beneath contempt. He'd said it since 1956. The world was an insane place run by hypocrites, and now here he was in New York, with the time near midnight. Gathering his few belongings, he leapt into a taxi and headed for Manhattan.

By the time he arrived in Poughkeepsie – having hopped a train north from Grand Central Station – it had been 27 hours since Tarrant had last slept. It would be the same again before he finally closed his eyes on the plane back home. After rattling the locked doors of his YMCA accommodation, he stretched out sleepless on a bunk bed for two hours until a 5 a.m. wake-up call summoned him – and his fellow runners – across the deserted road to an all-night diner for strong coffee and hash browns.

'I went to that race having no idea he was going to be there,' remembers one of the runners, Tom Osler. 'We were all aware of John and his situation. We all knew that if he came he was not going to be allowed to run officially and there could be absolutely no mention of anything in the papers because if it got out it could threaten the amateur status of the other runners. And that's what happened. Tarrant came and went before anyone knew he'd been and gone.'

Much to his relief, Tarrant wasn't shunned by his fellow runners. Whatever virus he was carrying, no one in Poughkeepsie seemed too concerned about it. Not that the cafe seemed thick with opposition. Looking around – with frozen sleet sliding down the window outside – John counted no more than a dozen runners. He'd come a long way, and spent a lot of someone else's money, to circle a damp, decaying town on the Hudson River with just a handful of strangers. He'd also come a long way to be invisible.

Just as in the old days, Tarrant had accepted that however well he ran his prowess would never be formally acknowledged. To placate the jumpy American organisers, he'd volunteered to run as a ghost, and would start a few yards back from the official competitors. Even if he won, the results would never disclose his presence. 'At that time, the US amateur authorities had life or death over the runners,' recalls Osler. 'They were suspending runners left, right and centre, and we were really scared about the threat to our status in having him there.'

In the pre-dawn darkness, watched only by the early-shift waitresses from the roadside diner, the race began. Wearing gloves and a bobble hat to ward off the icy cold, Tarrant bounced easily along glassy, wet streets illuminated by the pinks and purples of reflected neon. After 40 miles – and 30 hours without sleep – it was just him and Tom Osler up front, chatting warmly together as Poughkeepsie woke up and the roads began to clutter with honking trucks. Five miles from the finish line, however, Tarrant's week of shocks and exertions finally betrayed him. Although his stomach had behaved, the rest of his body had become weary, and Osler wasn't to be caught. 'I only beat him because of the circumstances,' admits Osler. 'He was a much better 50-miler than me.'

In the dazed aftermath, Tarrant snatched a few hours sleep before being led to a post-race reception, still wearing his shorts and still streaked with dirt. As in Liverpool a decade earlier, he entered to rapturous applause – 'just like an earthquake', he remembered – from his fellow runners. Shyly, he moved among them, amazed to learn that the story of his fight had travelled so far, adding clandestine frisson to an otherwise low-key event. 'No one there could see any logic in the ban . . . for a youthful indiscretion so many years ago,' he wrote.

Amongst the hubbub, there were numerous memorable kindnesses. Someone slipped him ten dollars towards his expenses. A handful of travel books was pressed on him to take home for Roger. Despite his exhaustion, Tarrant felt energised – and moved – by Poughkeepsie's spontaneous embrace, and in a letter to Tom Osler a few days later, he would call it 'the greatest thing in athletics to happen to me'.

To the journalists who bought Tarrant a cup of tea 36 hours later at Hereford railway station, he would simply say that 'if the athletics board now decide to bar me, at least they'll never rub the memory of that away'.

As a race, the Poughkeepsie 50 had been a non-event. As an experience, it marked a critical turning point in John Tarrant's tortured life. Despite Arthur Gold's threats, there'd been no official retribution. No one had been banned and no one had policed the IAAF ruling. In Poughkeepsie, Tarrant had rediscovered the potency of the ghost and felt the liberating rush that came from running when and where he chose, fearless of the consequences.

The tongue-tied boy from a children's home had travelled alone to another continent. He'd hacked his way through the so-called New York jungle and survived. Despite his insane 48-hour schedule, he'd run with distinction against strangers in a strange town. Everything he'd experienced now swung his compass determinedly towards the Comrades Marathon in South Africa the following May. 'I am preparing myself in the hope that I can make it there,' he confided to Osler. The only thing that was still missing was the money.

Two weeks later, Tarrant was unexpectedly summoned to the antique-festooned home of his mysterious Hereford benefactor Ned Waring. It was a meeting John had secretly been dreading. There'd been mitigating circumstances, but his second-place finish in America had felt like a meagre return on Waring's £180 investment, and although the councillor had expressed satisfaction on the phone (Tarrant had called him post-race from Poughkeepsie), he might not be so sanguine in person. Nervously, John knotted his tie, buttoned his cardigan and trotted round to see Ned fearing the worst.

Far from dampening Waring's interest, Tarrant's novel American escapade appeared merely to have enlivened it. The former war hero was so tickled that he now wanted to get John to the Comrades Marathon in six months' time. At a cost of £400, it was beyond even Waring's purse, but if Tarrant was interested – and he naturally was – Waring offered to mastermind a public appeal to raise the cash. He would also write personally to the race organisers in South Africa seeking permission for Tarrant to run as an official competitor. Should the appeal fall short, Waring promised to step in with his own cash.

It was an extraordinary offer, born entirely of the businessman's disgust at the treatment Tarrant had sustained and his admiration for the way John had resisted it. No financial or political gain would ever flow from his support, and, far from being a self-publicist, Waring appears to have actively preferred the shadows, leaving the glory to the man he now championed. On a handshake, the deal was sealed, and both men set out to deliver their half of the bargain: Waring to find the money, Tarrant to galvanise every fibre of his being for his crack at the Comrades.

Never before had he been so consumed. Never before had he devised a regime so painful in its ferocity. Between mid-December and May, he would not miss a single day's training. To prepare for Natal's famously brutal gradients, he'd spend hours sprinting alone up soul-sapping hills – a 220-yard burst in 40 seconds followed by a 440-yard sprint in 90. At the top, there'd be no rests. Even when his pulse thumped and his lungs could scarcely function, Tarrant would turn round for the soothing jog downhill before pushing himself back to the summit. No quarter given. No weakness shown. Night after night, the same routine. Not one uphill sprint, but forty, followed by sixty-mile runs at the weekend, until he was satisfied no corner had been cut. By the end of 1968, he'd run 3,868 miles, the highest annual total in his life so far.

Waring, meanwhile, was beginning to learn what it felt like to be John Tarrant. Despite his eloquent appeal on John's behalf, the Comrades Marathon committee in Durban flatly rejected Tarrant's application to race, news of his stigma having spread from the United Kingdom to the southern hemisphere via the United States.

'I am sure it is realised that we cannot flout the authorities . . . if John insists on running he will embarrass the organisers.' Not only that, warned Comrades organising chairman Bert Bendzulla, but if Tarrant competed as a gatecrasher, he would not be permitted refreshments during the race and would be prevented from crossing the finish line. 'Candidly, we would rather that he did not run.'

Thankfully, Waring's efforts to raise money were doing

rather better than his personal entreaties to the paranoid South African athletics establishment. By Christmas – operating from a room above his Hereford bric-a-brac shop – he had sent more than 2,000 flyers for the John Tarrant Appeal Fund to businesses, sportsmen and well-wishers, seeking their immediate help for 'an exceptionally fine athlete of undisputable world class'. Listing every one of Tarrant's key wins and achievements, the flyer concluded with Waring exhorting 'all who value Britain's sporting prestige to send me what they can afford'.

Within days, the cheques, coins and notes began flooding in. Two pounds from Edie's uncle. Six pounds from the Tabard Inn in High Town. Six pounds from the British Legion. Five pounds from West Country Carpets. There was money from hair salons and shoe shops, ironmongers and estate agents, and although Tarrant didn't drink, there were whip-rounds at more than 20 Hereford pubs. From the local cider-makers Bulmers came five pounds' 'backing to an outstanding athlete'. There was even a cheque from the Hereford Young Conservatives. By April 1968, more than 300 contributions had been received, many of them from friends and former rivals who were pouring out of Tarrant's past to help: Ted Hockenhull from his Buxton boxing days; Joe Lancaster from the Salford Harriers; Billy Morton from Dublin; even Arthur Keily – the bane of Tarrant's first forays – had happily dipped his hand in his pocket.

Every penny donated was carefully noted – every letter kept and personally acknowledged – and gradually the total crept towards £400. For Tarrant, it was a magical endorsement of what he had always believed: that in the eyes of ordinary people – the ones who understood the value of common sense – he was the victim of a terrible unfairness. But not quite everyone was as happy with the appeal as Waring and Tarrant were. And one person in particular was indignant.

Throughout Tarrant's years of struggle, Bernard Gomersall

had been the golden boy of ultra-distance. Given their backgrounds, the two men should have been close. Both had connections with the North: Gomersall was a straight-talking Yorkshireman and lived in Leeds; Tarrant's formative years had been in Derbyshire. Both were married with a young child. Each had his own idiosyncratic, awkward style of running, and each had been smitten by the joys of the open road. 'It didn't cost you anything,' says Bernard. 'Training was free and it started at your back door.' Both men were also intensely competitive and had developed a fascination with the same race: the Comrades Marathon. But there were differences, too, and the Comrades would force them out into the open.

Unlike Tarrant, Gomersall did not labour under the legacy of a ban and was liked by the athletics establishment. Unlike Tarrant, he refused to compromise his family life and had carefully limited his racing activities accordingly. Gomersall was also – by instinct – a conformist, and, whilst he publicly abhorred what had happened to John, it was an endorsement which had limits, just as the ghost's growing sense of persecution had none. 'Off the track, he'd never leave it alone,' remembers Gomersall, 'moaning about officials all the time. He'd be saying, "Now where do I go from here?" He was a proper pain in the neck, to be honest.'

For almost ten years, the two men had maintained a harmonious sporting rivalry, but as 1967 drew to a close an envelope fell through Gomersall's letter box in Leeds which would drive them violently apart.

The Yorkshireman had never made any secret of his plans to return to South Africa. He'd won the Comrades Marathon in 1965 and had always intended to go back. ('I got a clock. The winner today gets £150,000.') Thanks to his own private benefactor, he already had the cash for the trip, and, unlike

Tarrant, he had the absolute backing of Arthur Gold and the BAAB. He was, in effect, Britain's official entrant, and the news – via Ned Waring's mailshot – that Tarrant was planning an unofficial rival bid had horribly unsettled him.

'There were mixed emotions,' he remembers. 'Much as I sympathised with him, I could see the friction John's presence was going to cause out there.' Politely, he declined the invitation to contribute to John's fund, pointing out that 'as a member of a club affiliated to the BAAB, I cannot support an action which is a direct contravention of [the International Federation's] ruling'.

Tarrant was enraged, dashing off a poisonous rant (which Bernard promptly destroyed) accusing him of 'selfish and unsporting behaviour'. Both accusations were unfair. Gomersall's anxiety stemmed solely from the rule which forbade amateurs from running with so-called 'professionals', the same stick with which Arthur Gold had recently tried to beat the Americans.

Although Tarrant had been free to run in Britain for ten years, his international status remained unchanged. Overseas he was a pariah – a non-person – whose presence was to be discouraged at all costs. If Tarrant turned up in Durban, and if Gomersall ran alongside him, then the Leeds man – and technically everyone else in the field – might be looking at a lifetime ban. Registering his feelings was hardly unsporting. It was an entirely reasonable act of self-preservation.

Furiously, Bernard fired back his own riposte to Hereford. He also contacted the Road Runners Club seeking a candid assessment of the risk. Confidentially, Gomersall was reassured that he had nothing to fear:

> Dear Bernard . . . it is certain that he [Tarrant] will never run outside this country. In fact you can take it from me

> [Peter Goodsell, secretary of the RRC] that he is very lucky
> to be running at all, although he'll never understand this.
> Hope this sets your mind at rest.

Even the BAAB had never articulated their distaste for Tarrant's behaviour more unambiguously. A chasm had opened up between the ghost runner and almost every representative body in British athletics. Even once supportive runners were growing weary of his relentless grumbling, and, as if to highlight the widening gulf, Tarrant's response to Gomersall provided a masterclass in paranoid rancour:

> The alarming apathy among responsible British officials is
> the reason why John Tarrant is still in the same predicament
> after sixteen years. The truth will always remain invincible.
> The BAAB, the AAA, the RRC, are sadly lacking real men
> of real courage to fight for a JUST cause. Bernard, the truth
> is born to victory and I will never give up fighting for my
> RIGHTS. I am hoping that I will eventually compete in the
> Comrades with the official blessing of everyone. If not, I
> hope I will have the chance to prove myself in ghosting the
> race. No MAN worth his salt would object.

It was the most revealing, and tragic, letter Tarrant had ever written, laying bare his sense of isolation and exposing the fragile ego beneath. The fatal flaw Victor had identified at Lamorbey – his absolute lack of cunning – had rendered him alienated and alone. In America, he'd felt refreshed. In Britain, there was a rotten sourness which hung over everything and from which he could find no escape. If he could only get there, South Africa would surely be better than this.

By early May 1968 – less than four weeks before the race –

Waring's appeal was beached on £337 and the fund was closed. Having already paid for 2,000 stamps out of his own pocket, Waring wasn't going to quibble about making up the £67 difference. A promise was a promise, and despite the unremitting chorus of discouraging noises from both South Africa and London, Tarrant was in too deep to be denied.

Sadly resigned to running as a ghost, he'd booked his entire two weeks' annual leave, and Ned Waring had handed over a return ticket to Durban. Although nervous, John felt optimistic and fit. It was the journey more than anything he was dreading. A few weeks earlier, he'd easily won the Exeter-to-Plymouth 44-mile race for the fourth time, and for days goodwill letters and telegrams had been pouring into his home, 'some from people I've never met and probably never will meet', he said. 'All I can do now is win the race for them.'

On Friday, 24 May, he walked down to Hereford railway station to catch the 10.55 a.m. train to London airport. Edie was there to wave him off, alongside the indispensably optimistic Ned Waring, and for the local paper's photographer Tarrant showed off the porcelain Hereford bull he'd be presenting to the Mayor of Durban when he arrived. In his outside jacket pocket was a Union Jack on a stick. In the inside pocket was a letter from his brother Victor which John would cherish for the remainder of his life:

> I know that if your guts don't let you down, you can win. You are the finest ultra-distance runner in the world, but I realise that you cannot run to enjoy the race and that only winning will compensate you for all your dedication. If only it was in England so that I could help you, and give you what little help I do give you on your big races. Please if all goes well, and you pull it off, do not rant and rave at all about you. Please take your win, like you take your

defeats, like a gentleman and a sportsman. Please try it my
way this time, and as you win think of me . . . and smile,
and keep smiling, for you will have a lot to smile about.
Good luck, John. Good luck. Vic.

Only Victor really knew him inside out. As the countryside
slithered by, vivid with fresh summer promise, Tarrant fell back
against his seat and retreated into his memories. There'd been
another silent train journey once, the journey when everything
had started and ended all at the same time. Paddington to
Sidcup. Victor and John. Jack and his beloved, fast-fading wife.
It was funny, this journey really wasn't that much different
from the first. He'd not been sure where he was going then.
And he'd absolutely no idea what would happen when he got
there now.

Chapter Eight

A Man Apart

1968

He had known nothing quite like it in his life. Beneath him, the Mediterranean Sea sparkled like spun silver, cutting hard to the endless dappled desert sand as the plane flew over the North African coast. At Addis Ababa, where the jet stopped for refuelling, sweetly alien fragrances had rushed the cabin, and somewhere above Kenya, after the pilot had announced they were crossing the equator, Tarrant peered earthwards, trying hard to imagine an extravagant Eden of green space and creatures running free.

Six months before, he'd dropped towards New York in Stygian winter smog. Now, as the plane banked over the Indian Ocean, he could finally make out the shining mass of Durban, hunched tight between undulating hills and the sea, where row upon unbroken row of white rolling waves stretched north and south before fading into the haze of seemingly infinite space. It was a relief to be landing. Somewhere above Tanzania, they'd been strapped into their seats as the turbulent mischief of a dozen bulbous thunderheads had shuddered through the wings. Although he'd long ago come to terms with the privations of solitude, 6,000 miles had drained him of any residual curiosity about long-distance travel. If there'd been other ways of diluting the monotony, he'd have welcomed them, but John didn't read and there was no in-flight entertainment, so he thought of nothing but the challenge ahead.

Sometimes, it seemed as if his entire life had been conducted at such a terrible rush: always trying to catch up; always trying to reach the time, or place, where he could function without his past pulling him to earth. It was rare for him to sit still for so long – with no ready alternative to introspection – and by the time his plane landed, Tarrant had persuaded himself that South Africa would be different. He could already feel the sunlight warming his lap through the tiny window, stirring the ever-reliable heartbeat of his optimism. Here, for the first time – at the age of 36 – he felt certain he would find that elusive something he'd been floundering towards since he was a child.

From first breath, he was seduced by his new world. It was autumn in Durban, and the air drooped with unseasonal heat, tolerable by day, as the wind blew in across the ocean, but sticky and humid at night, rarely dropping below 24°C, and breathless in the cheap back-street hotel Tarrant had found for the duration of his week-long stay. Unable to sleep, he slipped out into the city streets, hoping exercise would still his restless muscles.

Along Victoria Embankment – under a cool row of palm trees – he looked out across the vast, clanging harbour with its interconnecting maze of railways and warehouses. By Dairy Beach, he strode out on the warm sand, astonished by the constancy of the ocean's static hum, hypnotised by the fulminating hiss of breaking surf, which sprayed and cooled him with fine specks of salt water.

No one was surprised to see a strange white man running alone through Durban. With less than a week to go before the Comrades Marathon, the city was filling up with intense, solitary runners. Somewhere out there, thought Tarrant, would be Bernard Gomersall, who – if the rumours were true – had preceded John by a week and was already fully acclimatised to the hot conditions. Tarrant envied him. Nothing back home could have prepared him for this swelter.

As the days ticked by, John's weight dropped by 5 lb, a fall he monitored on his thrice-daily trips to the scales and which he blamed on the claggy air and his untypical profusions of sweat. Rather than weaken himself unnecessarily, Tarrant eased back on the training and rested up during the afternoon heat. According to the local weathermen, the day of the Comrades was going to be even hotter than this.

In Durban, white people talked about little apart from the race. As far as the indigenous black and immigrant Indian populations were concerned, however, the Comrades simply did not exist. Organised for whites by whites, it was an international event in which they could play no part. By 1968, when John Tarrant was pulling on his running shoes and heading for the (whites only) beach, racial segregation had been in force for two decades, and apartheid – meaning literally 'separateness' – had perfected its perfidious form of institutionalised racism.

In South Africa, it meant the 1960s were only swinging if your skin was white. If it was anything else, you were the citizen of an underworld. Separate schools, separate buses, separate hospitals, separate park benches and separate sporting events. For young working-class men from northern England, life around Durban offered an unsettling peek into a society going in the opposite direction from their own, and when Gomersall had first run the Comrades three years before, he'd been deeply shocked by what he found. 'One of my closest rivals had always been the American black runner Ted Corbitt, and whilst he could run in the London-to-Brighton he was not allowed to run in the Comrades in South Africa.

'Before I came down, the Road Runners Club had told me not to get involved in politics, but you couldn't help but see things,' says Gomersall. 'The white athletes down there had the weather, the money and the time. Mostly they had "boys", too – blacks to do their chores, gardeners and helpers and cleaners. I was once asked how many servants I had and I said, "One. My wife." I was a country yokel in the middle of something I'd no previous idea about.'

Whatever Tarrant's views were, he wasn't for sharing them. Throughout his life he'd known how it felt to be marginalised, but he'd always dodged political arguments, and in Durban he'd keep his mouth shut and his eyes on the pavement. In two years, he would make his own idiosyncratic stand alongside South Africa's disempowered majority, but this wasn't the right moment to be ruffling any more feathers. According to unnamed sources in the newspapers, his 'pig-headed insistence' on travelling to Durban had already infuriated the nation's senior athletics officials.

'I disapprove most strongly and appeal to him not to run,' pleaded Herman Delvin, the Comrades race secretary. 'Rules are rules and he should be stopped at the gates,' demanded Bob Calder, chief of the Natal Amateur Athletic Association. It was even being said that 'several other veteran runners' were keen for Tarrant to disappear, although the Durban papers never named them, and Tarrant – entrenched in his clammy hotel room – very much doubted whether they existed.

For months, he'd heard nothing from Arthur Gold, but this sudden chorus of hostility bore the hallmark of London string-pulling. Back home, Tarrant had made no attempt to conceal his plans – his very public fund-raising had seen to that – and it seemed inconceivable to John that Gold hadn't leaned on his South African counterparts.

For once, it was even more complicated than Tarrant could comprehend. The bushy-browed man lying alone in his hotel had strayed into a minefield of international sensitivities. Apartheid had made South Africa the reviled outcast of world affairs, its citizens excluded from almost every form of civilised communal global activity. No Olympic Games since 1960. No World Cups. No Commonwealth Games. Not even the raw meat of Test Match rugby. For a fiercely masculine, hugely competitive society, the resulting vacuum imbued every home-grown South African sporting event with an intensity out of all proportion to its size.

By 1968, the Comrades was no longer just a world-famous 56-mile road race; it was the annual cue for a mass expulsion of stored national adrenalin. 'The Comrades had become our Everest, our private Olympics,' says Durban journalist Ronnie Borain. 'It was the thing people here most aspired to, and even though we were in disgrace as a sporting nation, everything about it was on show, and it had to be right.'

Having the outlawed John Tarrant in Durban – wantonly threatening to flout international rules – was publicity the ultra-conservative South African athletics chiefs could badly do without. To make matters worse, the same two names kept being touted as race favourites and both of them were Brits. Bernard Gomersall was one. John Tarrant was another. It was intolerable. Any scenario in which Tarrant crossed the line first was simply unimaginable. If he couldn't be escorted from the road, it would be far better if he lost. 'We knew who he was. His name and ability came before him,' says Comrades official Mick Winn. 'But if you had a guy like him coming first, it would have brought a whole lot of concern and would have felt very uncomfortable. Knowing how good he was, this was a very real possibility.'

Unless Tarrant could be stopped, it wouldn't only be South

Africa's sporting probity which went under the microscope; the very essence of its sporting manhood would be on trial as well. Mesmerised into sleep by the drone of the ceiling fan, his alarm triggered for his final dawn training run, John Tarrant knew nothing of these Byzantine complexities. With just 36 hours left before the race, he felt still and he felt ready. No one would have the courage to prevent him running – he felt absolutely sure of that.

It didn't matter that these deeper currents eluded him. For years, he had imagined himself running this race, and here at last, around the streets of Durban – where his face had quickly become known – he had finally felt the heft of its importance. Every radio babbled with speculation and race gossip. Every television news programme lined up veterans and pundits to pore over weather forecasts and form books. For days, the local newspapers had been filling their pages with Comrades tittle-tattle, feasting on the glut of shops wanting to advertise their weekend offers on beer and beef and barbecues.

During the London-to-Brighton he'd seen little but cows and sheep and maybe the occasional lady steward with a wet sponge. If the warm weather held here, thousands would picnic along the route. It was thrilling for Tarrant to be a part of this ballyhoo. Under a smouldering, posed photograph – recumbent under palm trees in his running shorts – his story had been spread across a full page in Durban's *Daily News* ('I don't want to upset anyone,' he'd said). He'd even delivered his porcelain bull to the local Town Hall, apologising profusely for the tail, which had broken off during the long journey from the Welsh borders.

With one full day left before the race, chauffeured by a local journalist, Tarrant left Durban for the first time, following the route he would shortly be running. Snaking west out through the city's spreading concrete tentacles – past whistle-blowing policemen in pith helmets – the road climbed without respite for 20 miles, breaking out into the distinctive rolling hilltop crests of KwaZulu Natal at Bothas Ridge, where today he'd have found roadside craft centres selling 'zulu hammocks' to tourists eating calamari and chips sluiced down by the local Hansa beer.

More than 40 years ago, up on the high plateau – the Zulus' so-called Valley of a Thousand Hills – he found a welcome echo of Herefordshire. Fields dotted with cattle. Rain-bloated rivers sliding through deep green clefts beneath skies peppered with dumpling clouds. Only the rust-coloured earth and the black women in vivid floral wraps carrying improbable loads on their heads spoke of Africa. If he could master the heat, these landscapes were comfortingly familiar, even if the names along the route – as yet – were not.

Cowies Hill. Fields Hill. Inchanga. Cato Ridge. Harrison Flats. Polly Shortts. In South Africa, the physical iconography of the Comrades was known even to those who'd never run it. Since the very first race between Durban and Pietermaritzburg in 1921 – in memory of South Africa's First World War dead – the course had amply delivered on its wish to 'celebrate mankind's spirit over adversity'. Every inch of the route had its legends. There were stories of runners being carried up to the top of the last killer hill, Polly Shortts, some 45 miles out of Durban, and even in a car Tarrant could sense the damage it might do. Five steadily grinding uphill miles. The kind of miles which eat silently into an athlete's last crumbs of resistance, the sinews finally failing under the piercing eye of a crowned eagle floating high overhead on the thermals.

Assuming he'd make it this far, Tarrant would have just ten downhill miles to go. Suddenly, he'd be in a 10-mile dash, not a 56-mile epic, and knowing that would surely push away every pain as the rooftops of Pietermaritzburg loomed and the crowds thickened again after the loneliness of the mid-race wilderness and the only sound seemed to be the hard banging of his bruised and swollen feet.

That evening – inspired by what he'd seen – Tarrant put in his last five-mile training jog in a state of high excitement. Looping around Durban's crumbling art deco hotels, underneath fruit-heavy coconut trees, he strode out along the North Shore, deserted but for a few twilight surfers. A 'tremendous feeling of power' had come over him – 'a magnificent feeling of well-being'. He could do no more.

The following morning, he arose at 5 a.m., picked at a light breakfast, and watched from his hotel window as first light revealed warm, still skies. Although Tarrant had travelled alone, he'd been joined on the day by a former Salford Harrier working in Johannesburg, Dennis Clayton, whose job would be to ensure a steady supply of liquid refreshments. 'It's going to be your day, John,' he whispered to Tarrant, by now quivering with apprehension. 'They won't be able to live with you on a course like that. But for God's sake don't get carried away and run too fast.'

With barely a minute to go, John stepped out into the Durban sunshine and walked to the starting line. Along the kerbside, early risers – many still in their pyjamas – cheered the man with no number as he approached the bouncing nerve-scrambled mass of 640 runners. Never before had he run with so many people. A head above the rest he could make out Bernard Gomersall's familiar tight-cropped scalp. No man had ever run this race faster than the Yorkshireman. Whatever bitterness had passed between them was over now. All that really mattered was here. There were warm handshakes from strangers, respectful nods from local co-favourites Jackie

Mekler and Gordon Baker, and indifferent scowls from white-shirted officials realising that he'd left them no time for reprisals and that the ghost was intent upon spoiling their day.

Looking around him, John noticed that he wasn't the only runner without a number. There were a handful of anonymous black and Indian athletes too, huddled apart, bashfully awaiting the signal to get going. For the first time in his life, Tarrant had unofficial company. The organisers referred to them with euphemistic disdain as 'non-European runners'. John Tarrant had become a ghost in a nation of ghosts.

At precisely 6 a.m., the 1968 Comrades Marathon was under way, the field bunching through the city's scrappy outskirts before joining the Jan Smuts Highway, and the start of the elongated climb up to the sanctuary of the plateau beyond. Twenty-five years before, Italian POWs had laboured to make this road. Up Westville Hill, beyond the 45th Cutting – alongside a phalanx of acacia and banana trees – Tarrant strode forward, egged on by crowds five deep who were seemingly delighted that the British upstart was performing so well.

Behind Tarrant's locked frown of pain, however, he already had growing reasons for concern. Despite feeling equal to the leading group of Mekler, Baker and Gomersall, there had been no sign of his second, Dennis Clayton, and after almost 20 miles – in what had become a cruelly hot day – Tarrant had been unable to get a drink. Fearful that other people's refreshments might upset his temperamental stomach, he was beginning to wilt at the very moment his rivals were poised to stretch out the field. On the outskirts of Kloof, fearing that his race might already be over, he was approached by a well-spoken young Englishman on a motorcycle. 'You must be John Tarrant,' he said. For the second time in his life, a man on two wheels was about to play a pivotal part in John's story.

Bombastic, opinionated and mildly eccentric – a quintessential expat – Colin Shaw had come out to South Africa in 1960. ('Before that, I'd been hoping there was a place for me in my dad's garage in Rhyl, but it didn't work out that way.') With no particular skills, other than a few years in the RAF, he'd drifted between Johannesburg and Durban, where in 1968 he had a wife, two daughters and a job as a rep with a paint company. Shaw had never run, and had no interest in running, but the prominent newspaper articles about a bitter Englishman they called 'the ghost' had touched him. 'I had these old values. I felt terribly sorry for him,' he recalls.

On a whim, Shaw had pulled on his cloth cap and motorcycled to a key vantage point, hoping for a glimpse of the runner everyone was talking about. As the leading bunch approached, Colin could clearly see the man with no number, wearing a white handkerchief knotted around his neck and a look of the utmost discomfort. Stepping out from the crowd, Shaw skipped clumsily alongside Tarrant in his polished brown salesman's shoes, introduced himself and asked what he could do to help. After a few seconds, Tarrant had barked his instructions and Shaw was back on his motorcycle ready to carry them out.

'I'd never been a second before,' explains Colin. 'It was uncharted, virgin territory. I had no script and I had no map, but we quickly worked out a system where he'd tell me what food and drink he needed, I'd get on my bike and sort it out and then I'd meet him at an agreed spot further along the route.' Although Dennis Clayton finally turned up, pleading a broken-down car ('What do you think I am? A bloody camel?' Tarrant fumed), it was Colin Shaw whose two-wheeled mobility was keeping Tarrant in the race.

After 30 miles, however, the leading cluster had broken up and John seemed incapable of closing the gap. Up the infamous Polly Shortts hill – with Pietermaritzburg in his sights – he could summon no magical kick, no game-changing surge of fresh energy. As he entered the city's arena for the finishing lap – in front of a thousand-strong crowd – he was lying fourth, and every spectator rose from their seats to greet him. 'The loudest applause I have ever received,' he would later write. From the official loudspeakers, however, there was nothing but static.

Refusing him even the dignity of a public name-check, the race announcer switched off his microphone until the fifth finisher – one of the official runners – came into view. As far as the Comrades organisers were concerned, Tarrant's run had never happened. As far as the official records were concerned, he'd not even been there. Almost fifty years later, his fourth-place finish has still never been recognised, long after women, blacks and professionals have been welcomed back into the Comrades fold. The first six runners home that day were awarded a gold medal – one of the most cherished honours in long-distance running – but John was not counted among them. And, for different reasons, nor was Bernard Gomersall.

Twenty minutes after Tarrant's ovation had faded away, Bernard crumpled over the finishing line, eighteen pounds lighter than when he'd started six hours and thirty-eight minutes before. 'I have terrible memories of that race,' he says. 'I just fried.' It was sad, but Bernard had felt for some time, he might be near the end. Eighth place in the Comrades (the records would show seventh once Tarrant's name was airbrushed out) felt like proof. Later that year, at the age of 36, he called time on his brilliant career in top-flight athletics. 'I had a new job. I travelled more.' As a millennium treat in 2000, he returned one more time to the Comrades route and travelled its length ruefully in a car. 'I thought, "Bloody hell, I didn't run this, did I?" The hills were enormous.'

If John Tarrant (also 36) harboured similar thoughts, they were quickly swept aside. Away from the official rancour, there'd been widespread respect for what Tarrant had achieved. In baking conditions, he'd recorded a time which would have won many of the previous races between the two cities. On the day, he'd been unlucky to come up against a South African giant like Jackie Mekler, and – without a credited second – Tarrant's feat had been near miraculous. Along the way, he'd also been touched by countless spontaneous kindnesses. For the final 15 miles, he'd been shadowed by a South African spectator carrying a bucket and sponge to help keep him cool. There'd been that odd man on his motorcycle, and at the end – despite his physical distress – the unceasing knuckle-crushing handshakes from well-wishers had more than neutralised the acid taste left by South African officialdom.

One more chance encounter would leave its mark on Tarrant before he flew back to England. In Johannesburg – at a farewell party for Bernard Gomersall – he'd been introduced to a lifelong hero, the 62-year-old South African ultra-distance runner Wally Hayward. Although separated by age, the two men had much in common. In 1953 – barely three years before Tarrant's nightmare began – Hayward had been branded a professional following a piffling dispute over travelling expenses to England.

Despite being the holder of the world track record at 100 miles, Hayward had been barred from overseas competition, and instead had feasted himself domestically with five Comrades victories, which included a course record set when he was forty-five years old. Tarrant had heard nothing like it before. If there were any lingering concerns that he was too old, this uplifting evening with Wally Hayward had removed them. If there had been any private sadness that this might be John's solitary excursion to South Africa, then that was gone too.

On his homeward plane, Tarrant was already planning how he could get back to Durban the following year, already

rehearsing just how he'd sell it to Edie. In 1969, the Comrades
would be staged on the supposedly easier downhill route from
Pietermaritzburg back to the coast, and it would surely be
madness not to take advantage. But for the heat and his
inexperience – and Dennis Clayton's vanishing act – he might
even have won it at his first crack. His unexplained stomach
problems had gone away, and Edie would know how unhappy
he'd be if she stood in his way. Just one more try. That's all he'd
be asking for. Assuming he could raise the cash, and that wasn't
going to be easy. But then it never was. And soon after he
returned from Durban, Tarrant's perennially ruinous finances
got even worse.

For years, Tarrant had cut a forlorn figure around the Territorial
Army's base in Harold Street. Not since the heady early days
– when the all-conquering TA running team were silver-
spooned by doting officers – had his job felt like anything more
than underpaid drudgery. Mopping out toilets or putting a
shine on the regimental brasses didn't inspire Tarrant at the
best of times, and the best of times were long gone. In their
place were fiery spats with uniformed and civilian superiors
worn down by his attitude and no longer prepared to allow his
job to play second fiddle to his running.

Summoned to explain his late return from Durban (he'd
resurfaced two days after the agreed date), Tarrant blamed a
nosebleed which had prevented him from flying. In a separate
incident – evoking memories of Jack Crump – he'd reacted
furiously when a senior officer addressed him as 'Tarrant' and
not 'Mr Tarrant' or 'John'. Rumours were spreading that he
was about to be replaced. There was even talk of him hiring a
solicitor to defend his position, but by September it was too
late. After his longest-ever period of full employment, Tarrant
had lost his job and with it the tied army accommodation that

had been his family home for almost ten years. For anyone else, it would have been a crisis. No money, no house and no work. But John Tarrant wasn't giving much time to his career prospects.

Ever since his return from South Africa, he'd talked – and thought – constantly about going back. Striding out in the high altitudes of Johannesburg appeared to have turbocharged his metabolism, and he was running faster in training than ever before. In September, he won the Liverpool-to-Blackpool, despite getting lost and running two miles more than required. In late October – overcoming an unwelcome return of his stomach trouble – he comfortably held on to his cherished London-to-Brighton title.

In his 37th year, it seemed he was still a dominant force in ultra-distance running, and to anyone who would listen he told stories about Durban and the Comrades, laced with winsome memories of the sunshine and the ocean surf. Losing his job wasn't a problem; it was the final key to the puzzle of his life. If he could bring Edie round, then everything would come good. The three of them could emigrate to South Africa – turning their backs on the stinking, cankerous hypocrisy of British athletics – and start all over again. It didn't matter that South Africa's officials wanted nothing to do with him either. Better to be unwanted and hot than unwanted and frozen half to death.

Whatever private misgivings she had, Edie was in no position to resist. Although John briefly found work as a storeman – and Hereford Council provided them with a flat – she had never been a match for his whirlwind obsessions, and long experience (dating back to their honeymoon) had taught her not to try. With luck, this one might eventually blow itself out. But by the autumn of 1968, the signs were not good. Tarrant's emigration plans had leaked into the South African newspapers, and since his sacking he'd been writing feverishly to Colin Shaw in Natal, asking where he might work and what jobs he might be qualified for.

Thrilled to be helping the ghost, Shaw had contacted prospective employers and was urging Tarrant to travel alone ahead of Edie and Roger to secure a job and suitable housing. 'The weather is beautiful,' he added impishly at the bottom of one of his airmail letters. High summer had arrived in the southern hemisphere, and that knowledge deepened Tarrant's seasonally affected mood of Yuletide despair. Knowing what he wanted wasn't making it happen any more quickly. Less than five months remained until the 1969 Comrades, and he still hadn't got a bean to his name. As the New Year began, the clammy grip of financial panic prompted the urgent contemplation of drastic measures in the Tarrant household.

Most working runners had, at some time, needed to flog their silver trophies, sometimes for food, sometimes for a rail ticket to a race. So far, Tarrant had clung on to every one. In his 12 years of top-flight running, he'd accumulated a mountain of them, but now he could see no alternative. It was regrettable, but they'd have to be sold. The Tarrants' new first-floor council flat was tiny, and it took three glass-fronted cabinets to house a collection which was probably worth – in their terms – a small fortune.

Tarrant had never done it for the prizes. Edie should flog the lot of them. There'd be no room for them in South Africa anyway. But his wife wasn't having it. Every time she cleaned those glistening pots, she held the proof in her hands that everything had been worth the struggle. Over her dead body were they being sold for a plane ticket. Somehow there had to be another way.

As always, Victor was ready to help. Quietly, he'd already

been bailing his brother out for years. A fiver here, a tenner there. Throughout the winter months, the former chef had made dozens of chocolate eggs, which he'd then sold at Easter for five shillings each. Anything to keep John running. He'd even taken on holiday jobs – working as a civilian chef at army camps – to pay back Ned Waring for the cash he'd given John in previous years. 'Ned didn't ask for the money and I had a job to force it on him,' stresses Vic. 'I probably paid back £300 in all, which was a lot of money then, and it took some getting, but it was freelance work and I was well paid . . . John knew I was doing it. I was his cushion. He paid none of it.'

While his brother trained, Victor spent his evenings tapping out begging letters to local businessmen on his typewriter. But Victor was not a salesman, and cold-calling for donations didn't come easy. With barely a fortnight to go, the campaign pot was virtually empty, and it would again require Ned Waring's entrepreneurial flair to galvanise their faltering efforts. Following John's trip the previous May, the Hereford businessman had received more than 300 letters from South Africans applauding his efforts on Tarrant's behalf. That alone had made it worthwhile.

He understood why John felt bashful about coming back for more – and maybe this time they'd left it too late – but Waring had no mystery agenda and wanted only to help a man he pitied. It was also a perverse kind of fun. Hearing of the trouble they were in, he gladly offered to help. In the few days that remained, he'd do what he could to get Tarrant to the 1969 Comrades.

Within a week, the three of them – Edie, Vic and Ned – had raised £200, half of it from a local cider-maker, the rest from the people who drank it. Around the pubs of Hereford, everyone knew the story of the ghost runner. A few bob in a tin was the least they could do for the poor sod. There'd even been one eccentric offer from a local teacher to drive John the length of Africa. Tarrant, meanwhile, had discovered that a one-way ticket to Durban would cost £167. If that was all they could afford, he'd have no option but to stay in South Africa after the race, find a job and either wait for Edie and Roger to join him or work until he'd saved enough money to fly home.

There was another option – Tarrant could have abandoned his plans – but that wasn't up for discussion. Around the small square table in their kitchen, the couple argued in whispers about what was best. All her married life, Edie had carried out what she believed were her duties as a loving, faithful wife. Until now, she'd asked for nothing. It had only ever been what John wanted that mattered. Finally, and very painfully, it was time for her to say no.

The previous summer – as she did every year – Edie had travelled back to Buxton. She'd strolled happily in the Pavilion Gardens, enjoyed tea and gossip with Jack and Maysie, and caught up with the family and friends she'd been torn from ten years before. It had been comforting to shop in Potters, the town's timeless outfitters, where her father had once sold string vests. It had been soothing to see the fells as the train rolled sleepily through the Peak District. Living in Hereford couldn't come close to this. Living in South Africa – for her – was never going to happen.

'I couldn't go,' she says. 'I said I was sorry, but I wasn't coming. To be honest, I was mad about it in lots of ways. It was wishful thinking on his part to think I'd even consider it, but I never weakened because I already wished I was still in Buxton. I'd come to Hereford and regretted it. I always wished I'd stayed at home.' John would be at liberty to go – and free to stay out there if that was required – but his wife and son would never be joining him.

If they were ties, Tarrant had been released from them. Edie had given her tacit blessing, and since he'd already lost his latest job, he was ready to go. With four days remaining, Waring lent him the £200 he would need to survive while he looked for work in Durban. Colin Shaw was on standby to meet him at the airport in South Africa. Edie and Roger were preparing to say goodbye to a husband and father who might not be back for months, and quite possibly longer.

Five years later – as he lay dying – Tarrant would claim that Edie had always 'fully realised the implication of what I was doing'. But this was merely hindsight aimed at the raised eyebrows of posterity. Tarrant was walking out on his family indefinitely so he could run 56 miles along a road in Natal. His wife was being left in a town she loathed, with no visible source of income, and a lonely 15-year-old who had failed his 11-plus and was struggling badly at school.

All serious athletes will say that running is a form of addiction, but in John Tarrant's case there now seemed to be no price he wouldn't pay, no continent he wouldn't cross to flood his being with the drug of his choice. If there is a line between obsession and something darker, he had crossed it by the time his plane set off for Johannesburg at 8.15 p.m. on 27 May 1969.

For almost a year, there had been silence from Arthur Gold and the British athletics authorities. It wasn't that surprising. Tarrant had long abandoned his quest for a British international vest, and his ghosting activities overseas, whilst irritating, were of minor concern. If Tarrant approached them for a formal permit to run in the Comrades – which he didn't – they would politely show him the door. Although the reasons for his ban seemed lost in time (wasn't he a pro boxing champion at one time?) the antediluvian international rules hadn't budged one millimetre. As soon as he left British soil, those ancient transgressions in Buxton ensured his presence in an overseas event remained illegal. And just like they had been the year before, the South African athletics authorities were praying that he wouldn't come.

The 800 official runners entered for the 1969 Comrades had even been warned that merely by running alongside Tarrant they would be at risk of disqualification. 'Tell him to hop it,' advised that year's race booklet, appending the view that unofficial runners – whether black, white or female – were 'immature citizens more concerned with self-glory than with sound basic principle'. It was the sort of vile claptrap Tarrant had been hearing since Victor had run down a steward on his motorbike in 1957. Much as they'd like to, no one was going to stop him, and by 29 May, just two days before the race, Tarrant was back in Durban, thrilled to be training in the sunshine, happy to be in a city which talked of little else but running.

'You were royalty if you'd run the Comrades back then,' says Bernard Gomersall, who that year would be staying in Leeds. 'If people there knew you'd won it, it was like drawing a curtain of astonishment back on people's faces. I could easily understand John's obsession. It was a race like no other. All the time in Durban, it was Comrades, Comrades, Comrades. Had I been able to stay, or go back, I'd have run it as often as I could.'

Within hours of arriving, Tarrant himself had enjoyed his own first-ever 'royalty' moment. Introduced by Colin Shaw to the director of a pest-control company, he'd been offered a lucrative job as a rat-catcher – on a one-month trial – complete with rent-free house and company car. It was an absurd proposition – John didn't even have a driving licence – and to Shaw's intense annoyance, Tarrant turned it down within 48 hours. 'Everyone had him down as one of the favourites. They wanted him for his name and the publicity it might bring,' says Shaw, 'but he was frightened of the job. He had absolutely no skills. It would have been too big for him.'

Colin had never known a man of so many perplexing contrasts. Tarrant could be simultaneously affable and brooding, impeccably polite and forbidding, seething with deep fury and yet quietly spoken and often difficult to understand. 'There was even a very slight speech impediment, I think.' To Shaw, it seemed perverse that this serious man was so unserious about work. All he appeared capable of thinking about was the race. Getting a job – getting home – these things could wait. Before leaving Britain, he'd told newspaper reporters, 'Beggars can't be choosers . . . I'll hitchhike home if I have to.'

Tarrant liked and needed Colin. But he couldn't expect him to understand. Only Victor had ever really understood these things. Tarrant had always been the Lamorbey kid with the empty locker. He didn't need a car or a house or the things people put in them. Being able to run and to run with the best, these were still the only commodities with any value. Watching the sun sink as he ran alongside the Bay of Plenty, feeling the intricate wiring of his bone and tissue generating power without pain – what could better this? Anyone could poison rats, but there was only one ghost runner, and tomorrow he would mount his second assault on the only race that mattered.

From the outset, he would have Colin Shaw as his second. The night before, they'd motorcycled the route together, looping down at dusk from Pietermaritzburg to Durban, braking hard on the long downhill dual carriageway into the city. Feeling nerveless, Tarrant had enjoyed a robust evening meal – a steak dinner paid for by the still-hopeful pest-control man – before retreating alone to his hotel room to make his last-minute checks, carefully labelling his drinking bottles ('baby's plastic feeding bottles,' he revealed later, 'so I could drink without actually having to stop') then filling each with his famous 'corpse reviver'.

As dawn arrived, chilly and still, Tarrant, numberless as always, made his way through the half-light to the start. There'd been no scares in his training; he felt optimistic. And the waiting pack of athletes – none of whom told him to 'hop it' – opened up to allow him to reach the front line of runners. 'There is no sport with a higher standard of sportsmanship,' concluded Tarrant, who sprang straight into the lead, finding the pace slow and the cool, limpid conditions much to his liking.

'He looked incredible. He was running so brilliantly,' recalls Shaw. 'I remember telling him very early that he was going too fast, but he said, "They're not going to catch me today, Colin," and at that stage it was hard to see how anyone would.' Rarely had he felt so strong or so utterly in command of his rhythm. 'I was feeling relaxed, running beautifully, fully confident,' he remembered. 'It was going to be my day.'

But after just 15 miles, Tarrant felt the dreaded heaving in his stomach and was forced to dash from the road. At 20 miles and 25 miles, the same. 'When he got to the halfway mark, he simply wasn't the man who'd started,' remembers Shaw, who knew nothing about John's fragile guts and was shocked by the swift deterioration in his runner. At Drummond – despite setting a record time for the first 28 miles – Tarrant's commanding lead had disappeared, and the trailing pack thundered past the now-shattered figure of the ghost.

'I'll never forget the look on John's face at that moment,' says Colin. 'It was truly awful. He was knackered. His hands were on his knees. He looked over his shoulder and the runners who'd been floundering behind him swept by and were gone.' The next few hours would be amongst the most painful, and humiliating, of Tarrant's life.

Pale, weak and sweating – with Colin Shaw hovering at his side – Tarrant slowly battled on towards Durban. When he couldn't run, he walked, and when he couldn't walk, Shaw massaged his weary limbs at the side of the road. Another five attacks of 'stomach trouble' forced him staggering into the bushes, and each time he fell further behind. Occasionally, one of the passing runners would offer to jog with him – hoping this might cajole him back into his stride – but Tarrant always waved them away. He wasn't worth the risk. He had the virus. If they'd been seen, they'd have been disqualified.

Around the suburbs of Pinetown, just as the coastline came into focus, Tarrant's race looked run. 'He was virtually freezing up,' says Shaw. 'His hands were on his haunches. He just couldn't give any more and wanted to pull out. I got hold of him and I was screaming at him, "This is bullshit. This is bullshit . . . you've got people back home . . . you've come all this way." I was screaming names at him. "Edie, Victor, Roger . . . you can't just bloody sit there."'

Somehow, through the fog of disappointment, Shaw struck home. John had come so far. There was too much at stake. Lumbering to his feet – 'all bent, like a broken camel', as Shaw recalls – Tarrant asked his second to find him a sugary drink and then hared off downhill towards the finishing line, still 15 miles away. Ten miles later, and Tarrant was storming back up through the field. Alongside him on his motorbike, Shaw was clocking nine, then ten, then eleven miles per hour, as dozens of exhausted stragglers stepped aside to let this blank-eyed phenomenon through.

'At the end, he'd run his bloody arse off and the announcer still didn't mention his name on the tannoy, even though the crowd were going mad,' fumes Shaw. 'I was really bloody hurt by that. Considering the state of him . . . to even finish it was a miracle. Bloody hell, they should have given him an MBE not a Comrades medal. He was 28th in the end, but he'd been stuffed. Christ. The poor guy couldn't even straighten his body at one point.'

In the deflated hinterland of defeat, it would not be his bruised stomach or his road-battered knees, nor even the familiar turned backs, which gave Tarrant the most pain. With a record time of 5 hours, 45 minutes and 35 seconds, a newcomer had torn apart the race Tarrant had left his family for. Dave Bagshaw, 25 years old and an articulate Sheffield-born graduate of the London School of Economics, looked poised to dominate ultra-distance running for years to come.

In Durban 12 months before, Bagshaw had borrowed a scooter and carried Bernard Gomersall's drinks. From the sidelines, he'd watched Tarrant with awe and fascination. Now, just a year later, he'd crushed a world-class field and ripped six minutes off the record. Another new kid on Tarrant's block. Although Durban was buzzing about the ghost's final flourish, the older man had finished more than an hour behind his rival. It was comforting to hear the crowd roar, but the sympathy vote hadn't helped Tarrant against Keily or Phillips or Gomersall, and it wouldn't help him now against Bagshaw, with his confident good looks and his peerlessly sleek style of running.

Alone and near-destitute in a South African city on the doorstep of winter, Tarrant's wilful pursuit of victory in the Comrades suddenly felt like the misguided obsession of a man closing in on 40. Never in his life had Hereford felt so attractive, or so very far away.

Since arriving in Durban, Tarrant had been living with Colin Shaw and his family, but soon after his catastrophe in the Comrades, he moved out. They'd team up again for races, but the two men had little in common and Tarrant was an awkward house guest, ill at ease around strangers. Solitude would be the best palliative for his current state of mind, and a spartan cell in the Durban YMCA would provide adequate shelter for his meditations. He had much to ponder. If he was to build a life which might lure Edie out of England, he needed work, but Tarrant's curriculum vitae was wafer-thin and four weeks of street-pounding had failed to unearth a job. In Durban, the menial graft he was used to was usually done only by black Africans. Everything else seemed to need either a driving licence or a working grasp of Afrikaans, and Tarrant had neither.

Just for once, luck was on Tarrant's side. During an interview with the South African Railways, he'd been recognised as 'the ghost runner from England' by a civil servant prepared to overlook the candidate's woeful lack of skills and offer Tarrant a job as a trainee forklift truck driver on the Durban docks. At 48 hours a week, he'd be working harder – and earning more money – than ever before in his life. As a railway employee, he'd also be allowed to live in a single man's hostel – the ER Carney Hostel for railway workers – perched high above the fumes of the dock road, its windows rattled at night by the percussion of freight trains slipping south towards Cape Town from Johannesburg. For most of the next 18 months, this unprepossessing backwater would be his home.

In the decades since Tarrant was there, very little about the ER Carney Hostel has changed, apart from its name. Although black residents now mingle with white, it still resembles a large English secondary school, and its red-brick accommodation – while comfortable – aspires to little more than basic. From a boxy single room, John's view embraced a dusty knot of hilly streets and abandoned industrial buildings choked with litter and flowering bindweed.

A utilitarian refectory offered simple cooked meals, which Tarrant rarely ate, and the pattern of his shifts – and his running – meant there were few people there whom he ever knew or spoke to. Not since the children's home in Kent had his lifestyle been so utterly bereft of joy. No friends. No comforts. No luxuries. He had found the perfect place for lonely introspection during the long, sleepless nights of a Durban summer (or the distinctly chillier ones of winter), somewhere to run over and over his life story as the trains clanked, the dogs howled and the lorries roared at the distant traffic lights.

Every day at 6.15 a.m., he set off on his run to the dock gates, down the steep hill past Trixie's Superette, left onto Maydon Road, already thick with the soup of trucks and cars and squealing mopeds piled high with crates. Street vendors wheeled roadside barbecues into place, heavy with golden corncobs and green bananas. Mountains of cement were stacked up by railway sidings. Piles of fruit lay rotting everywhere, and indifferent rats scuttled constantly out of manholes, sometimes dodging the traffic and sometimes not. Past the yacht club and the hangar-like sugar warehouses and Maydon Wharf tearooms he'd swing out sharply in front of downtown Durban – where the 'outies' would already be slurping gin out of bottles in paper bags – and then round into the vast docks complex itself.

In the Territorial Army, although nominally a 'driver', Tarrant had been kept well away from lorries and trucks. One glimpse of his expression of bewildered confusion behind the wheel of a vehicle was usually enough. Clearly, he hadn't shared this indisposition with the South African Railways, whose trains he would now be filling and emptying from the seat of a forklift truck.

Unsurprisingly, there were teething problems. When told it was safer to reverse a fully loaded truck down a ramp, Tarrant insisted he could do it going forwards, only to topple the vehicle over on several occasions before finally accepting defeat. There were rumours of 45-gallon barrels of paint being punctured by the prongs of his hoist and of crates disappearing into the sea, but Tarrant's willing demeanour invited forgiveness. For the first time, he had a job which inspired him, and with it came a pleasing sense of purpose. Every morning, he ran to work with a smile, and it rarely left his face.

As the summer returned, he could work bare-chested in shorts, by now spinning confidently around wharfs rich with the stink of diesel and rotting cargo. As the ships rolled in and the cranes gutted their holds, Tarrant would scuttle back and forth, laden with crates and bales, stacking goods into holding warehouses or directly onto the trains quivering in the rising heat. At lunchtimes, he'd cut quickly through city-centre back streets on foot to spend his free hour running on the beach. A quick dip in the surf, then back to work until the dusk fell and the immense floodlights blinked on to keep the docks constantly moving and the cranes wheeling overhead.

In the ebbing day, he'd watch as a cruise liner, its portholes ablaze with reflected light, eased out of the harbour on its way to Madagascar or Bombay. Passengers, dazzled by the final gasp of the sun, waved hopefully at the receding quay, and as the clock nudged up to 4.45 p.m., John prepared himself keenly for the eight-mile run back to the hostel, happy in the knowledge that, finally, he'd no longer be running alone. Waiting for him at the dock gates – bristling with furious impatience – was the man who would transform Tarrant's life in South Africa, the only man, apart from Victor, with whom he ever truly felt at ease.

It was hard not to notice Dave Box. With the curmudgeonly ego of a potentate and the body of a Greek god, he wasn't a man who slipped people's attention easily. In his youth, he'd been a bodybuilder and built up his chest from 38 to 44 inches. It was even said he could pick up a penny in the hard clench of his pectorals. Box was a strutting pitbull of a man, with a boxer's nose and a short, immensely powerful frame that brooked no arguments. In his late 70s – his hair knotted back in a Nelsonian pigtail – he could still be seen pedalling the length of the Comrades, barely out of breath, never happier than when overtaking cyclists a fraction of his venerable age. In his 80s, on Mediterranean holidays, he'd think nothing of hiring a mountain bike and heading for the Turkish hills in the heat of August.

Born in Cirencester, Box was a trainee architect when he shipped out to Rhodesia in 1958 'because it was warm'. Political upheavals drove him south to Durban and a bungalow home within earshot of the ocean's roar. Never once was he tempted back to Britain, and nor was his indomitable wife Adrie, whose competitive fires burned as fiercely as her husband's, even if the game was bridge and the only thing at stake was pride. At the age of 36, Box took up running with the single goal of winning the Comrades. As a daily reminder, he pinned up a plaque in his bedroom – 'Win The Comrades' – and yet so far he'd failed to live up to it.

Jogging on the spot at the dock gates, glancing irritably at his watch, Box, as always, was itching to get running. Tarrant wasn't the cheeriest of partners, but Box doubted whether nature could have designed a better companion. Broadly the same age – Box was two years older – the men shared a contempt for discomfort and an aversion to losing that bordered on the pathological.

Although Box was outgoing and Tarrant was reclusive, their differing personalities were built on the same flinty bedrock. Tarrant's abrasive disregard of authority was legendary, and in the small pond of Durban athletics Box was an acquired taste that not everyone acquired. 'They were very similar characters,' remembers Dave Bagshaw, also living in Durban at that time. 'Both lacked diplomacy. If you asked Box a question, you'd get a straight answer. I'd a lot of admiration for that, but I know people found him difficult.'

Setting their watches, the two men turned south along the Esplanade with scarcely a word: past the Vasco da Gama clock with its four faces each displaying a different time, alongside the bereft-looking statue of Dick King on his horse and then through the thunderous dust of the dock road (what Colin Shaw called their 'hell run'), taking care on the ruined pavement and keeping a watchful eye on the rampaging trucks. To even the most indifferent observer, Box would have appeared the smoother athlete, a man who always ran as if the pavement were burning hot – arms bent loosely at his side, back straight, eyes forward and alert – more of a tiptoe than a run. Tarrant, on the other hand, was, in Box's words, a 'terribly awkward runner . . . legs OK . . . body and arms strange . . . not smooth at all'.

It didn't matter. In the crowded noise of Durban, they had somehow found each other. After the Comrades a month or so before – in which Box had managed second place – Tarrant had wearily tracked Box down to congratulate him. Now they were friends, and every night after Dave had finished at his Durban practice, the two men would risk the rush-hour fumes to run home, parting company at Tarrant's hostel, from where Box would run alone across to his family in the leafy white enclave of The Bluff.

Tarrant was as settled as he'd ever been. Everything about Durban life filled him with joy. He had a friend. The sun shone, people smiled and life was cheap. For the first time, he'd opened a bank account and was saving money. Even when the docks needed him at the weekends, he could still find time to run 150 miles a week, and almost every day there was a letter from Edie, to which he always replied the same day, peppering his news with kisses and declarations of love. By the middle of

1969, Tarrant had every reason to ensure his letters were unflinching in their devotion. After three months in South Africa, he had decided he would not be going home.

It was no more than Edie had expected: all that talk of emigration; the one-way ticket; John's unrequited love affair with the Comrades. There'd always been a hollow vagueness about his plans, and now she knew why. One more try at the Comrades the following May, he was saying, and then – he promised – he'd be on the first plane back. It was helpful that John could finally afford to send her some money – she'd been 'struggling like hell' cleaning offices and shops – and his letters moved her deeply, but although she would never tell him, nothing had ever wounded her quite like this.

Instead, she wrote offering her unwavering support. She understood why it made financial sense for him not to come home. She could see that, for once, he'd be properly acclimatised. It had never been in her nature to make him feel bad about what he loved. Whatever she – and their son Roger – thought privately, she was not about to criticise him now. 'He knew what sacrifices I was making. He already felt guilty enough,' she says.

Tarrant poured his relief into his letters. 'Half of my success belongs to you my darling, the backroom girl with a heart of gold . . . the destiny of one's life is strange but somehow I feel all will come right for us in the end . . . my own true angel, I LOVE you with all my heart, more than I could ever express in words . . . I love and admire you more than anybody on this earth . . . I yearn to see you and Roger but I know in my heart I will be very disappointed if I don't have one more crack.'

It was all true, but he was telling only half the story. There was no mention of the aching blue skies or the sand so hot it couldn't be stepped on. He didn't tell her about the columns of bottle-nosed dolphins which swam alongside him as he ran by the shore, or the thrill of seeing a solitary humpback whale as it burrowed south in the icy Agulhas current. Much as he liked to claim his life was 'all work, running and bed', Tarrant drew a veil of silence over the warm summer winds, the weaver birds zipping to and from their nest balls and that last swim of the day around the time Edie was mopping an office floor after the workers had gone. 'Work wouldn't have been that tough for John, to be honest,' reckons Dave Box. 'In those days, there'd have been very little cracking of the whip.'

What would have been even more hurtful for Edie had she been able to see it for herself was Tarrant's gradual absorption into the family life of this new friend. For such fiercely restless men, the eight-mile run back from the city centre had soon proved unsatisfying. Most evenings now, they'd double that, weaving their way towards the colonial suburbs of The Bluff, watched by somnolent monkeys and the occasional distracted ibis, before pulling up at Box's home on Hill Head Road for tea and refreshments with Adrie and the Boxes' three young daughters.

On Sunday mornings, Tarrant would run from his hostel in Clairwood to Box's home, arriving just after dawn for a routine 40-mile stretch, followed by lunch and a 12-mile jog to warm down before a family trip to Ansty Beach – John, Dave, Adrie and the girls watching lissom teenagers on surfboards and fishermen casting for shad.

Never in Britain had he done these things. Only here on The Bluff – with its arching ocean skyline and its comical hornbills – could he finally sit on a beach and let the sand run idly through his fingers. 'We practically adopted him,' says Dave. 'He had no other social life. No drink. No women. Me and Adrie were the only people who took him out. He was part of the family.' For a day out, they'd all squeeze into Dave's estate car and drive south to Port Edward beach resort, Dave and

Adrie up front bickering over the directions, John talking incessantly about his ban, Adrie catching her husband's attention with a raised eyebrow ('Oh God, can't he talk about anything else?'). 'He could be very hard work,' she admits. 'I got more tired of him more easily than Dave.'

Everything Tarrant did, everywhere he went, was an adventure. In early August, he hitched a lift to Swaziland, travelling 400 miles across the African savannah to take part in a high-mountain marathon. It was the first race in his life in which black runners outnumbered white ones, and the first time since he'd left England that he'd seen black runners with numbers on their vests. There was no policy of racial segregation in Swaziland, and the only ghost in the marathon was a white one, whose narrow victory and record time would never be acknowledged by the apologetic organisers. History would show that the race had been won by a 20-year-old Swazilander called Dlamins – and legend would always insist that Dlamins had never raced before in his life.

Heading south back to Durban, Tarrant felt again the guilty exhilaration of his new horizons. Far to the west, he could see the folds of the Drakensberg Mountains rising sharply from the plain. Everywhere he looked, the landscape seemed dotted with game, and although the air was still raw, the empty sky held the sharpness of an English spring morning. How bizarre that his ban should have followed him here, to a landlocked kingdom in southern Africa. How could this life possibly be connected to the life of that skeletal boy who turned out for Tommy Burton's fight nights? Edie should be here. Roger should be here. Whose fault was it that they weren't? Mostly, these days, he felt only contempt when he looked back at what had happened to him. But sometimes – such as mornings like this – he softened. Since leaving Hereford, his eyes had been opened. There'd been a joy about the Swazilanders – and a flowing grace – which he would never forget, and which he'd not yet seen in the cowed eyes of Durban's black majority.

As September loomed – contented though he was – Tarrant's old restlessness began to stir. In four weeks' time, under the street lights on Westminster Bridge, the starter would be firing his gun on the annual London-to-Brighton road race, the race Tarrant had won in 1967 and 1968. Infuriatingly, Dave Box – and Comrades record-holder Dave Bagshaw – had already got their air tickets. Without Ned Waring to help, it looked unlikely that Tarrant would be competing for his hat-trick. Work was steady – 13 hours a day with overtime – but raising £300 so quickly looked impossible.

Fund-raising letters sent to Durban newspapers had met with cold indifference. A forlorn appeal to Arthur Gold at the BAAB had earned Victor a frosty and unequivocal no. Even the Road Runners Club had refused to make a contribution, fearing the consequences of assisting Tarrant's return from 'an athletically illegal escapade'. Not for the first time, Tarrant was frantic and stuck, and to make matters worse he had another compelling reason to get home.

Starting at midnight on 25 October – by invitation only – around 15 crack runners would run (or try to run) 400 laps of a track at Walton-on-Thames in less than 12 hours, 46 minutes and 34 seconds – a 100-mile world record attempt. Tarrant simply couldn't see how they could run it without him. No record intrigued him more or came close to its monstrous demands on mind and sinew. Only a handful of men had what was needed to take it on, and, in his mind, he was one of them. The previous year, Dave Box had sliced six minutes off the record, only to be denied by a flaw in the official timekeeping. Box had his air ticket. Box would be in England. Box would be at Walton-on-

Thames. Somehow or other, Tarrant would be there too.

After a marathon in Durban – which he won, unofficially – Tarrant had been approached by two young runners who'd heard about his faltering campaign to get back to England. The men were twins – James and Gerald Delport from Pietermaritzburg – and they were curious to know more about his story. Never happier than when talking about himself, Tarrant obliged. Although an airline company had offered to lend him the ticket money, he'd failed to find anyone willing to act as his guarantor. Without hesitation, the Delports offered to help out. 'We were young,' says James Delport. 'We were sympathetic. We were probably naive, but we both had teaching jobs, and we didn't think it through.' Two weeks later, Tarrant was in a taxi to the airport, trying hard not to think about his new £300 debt. In his pocket was his air ticket. A return ticket for one. Whatever happened in England, he was coming straight back to Durban. Alone.

Tarrant had cut it ludicrously fine – too fine – and there'd be no glorious hat-trick in the London-to-Brighton. Two days after his return – on a windless late September morning – he led for twenty miles before dropping back and then withdrawing (at Victor's insistence) to conserve his energy for the hundred-mile track race in four weeks' time. Although he'd set out to 'wipe the floor' with Dave Bagshaw, the younger man ran him shoulder to shoulder before Tarrant finally wilted and then stopped running altogether.

No matter. At least now Tarrant could get back up to Hereford to see Edie, Vic and Roger, who, at fifteen, was running sub-six-minute miles and eager to show his father what he could do. Edie had baked a 'Welcome Home' fruitcake, and everyone noted how tanned – and relaxed – John seemed. On the outside, at least, these three months in Durban had changed him. He seemed mellower and more self-confident, as if, finally, he had untangled the skein of his unhappiness.

Maybe it helped that John had Dave Box around to stay. A few weeks before the 100-mile race, his friend from The Bluff had squeezed into the Tarrant's Hereford flat, and the two runners were putting in 40 to 50 miles a day, flat out under the damp October clouds, with no quarter given, even in training. 'One day I tripped on a kerb and tore my thigh muscles,' says Box. 'John took me to the football masseur in Hereford, and she was an absolute butcher, and I said it was making it worse not better, so I took a few days off.'

As the day of the race approached, Tarrant's unrecognisable calm intensified. Instead of the usual jitters, he felt the soothing certainty that he would do well. His father, Jack, his stepmother, Maysie, and their children, David and Elizabeth, were travelling down from Buxton. Edie and Roger had promised to be there, and of course Victor would be his second throughout the ordeal. Over the years, Jack Tarrant had seen precious little of his eldest son's running. There'd been a road race in Stoke where he'd tagged along on a bicycle, carrying his son's drinks. But that was all. They'd lost touch over the years. These days, it was Edie who kept his family up to date with his news. It would be good to see the old man again, with his comical moustache, his corny patter and his knee-length herringbone coat.

A few hours before midnight on Saturday, 25 October, the Tarrant family, 16 other ultra-distance runners and 25 timekeepers began to converge on the dismal Stompond Lane track at Walton-on-Thames. Tarrant himself arrived around 10 p.m., having slept most of the day before catching the train cross-country with Edie. More than anything, he wanted to win this for her. Standing next to him, she looked tired and pale. Durban was easier for him than life alone in Britain was for her, and he owed his wife one moment in the sunshine.

Washing down thick jam sandwiches with honey-sweetened tea, Tarrant still harboured no doubts about making that happen. As the floodlights sprang on around the 440 yards of cinder, every one of his fellow athletes could sense the change in him.

'He seemed to be going into it with more determination and certainty,' recalls Peter Bennett, who would pull out after just 20 miles. 'You had that feeling he was more organised than usual. He had a lot more people surrounding him, and he seemed to have a premonition that he would win.' Noel Henry, the dazzling Irish runner who'd paced Tarrant years before in Dublin, was struck by his 'supremely fit and bronzed' appearance. Not only did he intend to win, he'd confided to Henry, but he would also crush Wally Hayward's 16-year-old world record.

Apart from chilled clusters of family members – and a healthy turnout from Fleet Street – there were very few spectators, and as midnight approached everyone became aware of a fast-falling silence around the deserted stadium. Other than Dave Box, hardly any of these men had ever run 100 miles. John Tarrant had never run 100 miles. Most had run no further than 50. If they were to finish the race, they would each need to run 400 times around this rain-softened track.

A new world record would require 100 consecutive miles run at an average of around 7 minutes and 30 seconds per mile. That meant starting at midnight and finishing at noon, running through the night and the dawn and deep into the next day. Privately, very few of the lean, muscular figures stripping down to their shorts thought they – or anyone else – had a chance. It was a glorious form of madness. But it was madness just the same.

'You knew you were going into a bearpit and you were going to be tested,' says Bennett. 'The people around you were the hard men of the sport. Everyone was feeling nervous. Everyone wanted to do well. Everyone wanted everyone else to do well. There was a community, a fellow-feeling, amongst that breed of runners, and, as far as we were concerned, this was the ultimate sporting event of its time.'

On the stroke of twelve – with a pistol shot from Mr J.W. May and a burst of partisan yelling – the race started and each man locked himself into his stride. Tarrant's plan – masterminded by Victor – was to run each lap at around 1 minute and 45 seconds, regardless of what was happening around him. Over 100 miles, there would be withdrawals and surges, and it would be foolish to get drawn into exhausting subplots. If he could stick to the agreed pace – and if he could fight his racing instincts – the record would be Tarrant's.

After 20 miles, Bennett had 'run out of steam' and was watching from the sidelines. At 25 miles, Tarrant was 5 minutes off the pace but running strongly. At 40 miles, he'd pulled himself into the lead, with Dave Box somewhere behind him in second place. It was just as Victor had promised. If he could stay disciplined, the result would look after itself. But what neither of them had accounted for was Tarrant's fickle stomach, and, approaching the halfway point – still two hours away from sunrise – illness and nausea struck.

Desperate to vomit but unable to, John could do nothing as Box overtook him and established a comfortable one-lap lead. Two miles later, Tarrant fell to his knees and was violently sick at the trackside. Coming alongside, Noel Henry – who was suffering from agonising hamstrings and could barely walk – helped John to his feet and for two laps they jogged slowly together until Tarrant had revived. A few laps later, and Henry's race was over. When he returned to join the spectators after a shower, it was to witness one of the greatest sporting epics ever seen.

There was now a one-mile gap – four laps of the track –

between Tarrant and Box, and even with forty-five miles still to run, Tarrant felt his chances of victory had gone. No matter how hard he pushed – or how loud his son was shouting – he seemed incapable of upping his pace. What were those platitudes Box was always gushing? You're never as tired as you think you are? There's always something left? For Box maybe, but not for him. Look at the irascible little bugger go. Steaming ahead like a pocket battleship, he was. No catching him now, he didn't suppose, but, whatever happened, John Tarrant would finish. He wasn't letting all these people down. Not Edie. Not Jack. Not Roger. Head down. Keep on going. There's always something left.

As daylight bled weakly across the track – nearly delirious and entirely lost in random thought – Tarrant had unknowingly rediscovered his speed, and lap by lap he was gaining fast on Dave Box.

'If you keep this up you can break the UK record,' screamed Victor as his brother trudged by.

'Bugger that. I want the world record,' came John's reply.

Coming up to 70 miles, he was running in Box's shadow. He could feel the heat of Box's tanned body, just as Box could hear the laboured breathing of Tarrant behind. Suddenly, the two men were no longer in a marathon; they were in a sprint.

Taking off like a whippet, Box surged forward, desperate to hold Tarrant off and break his charge. 'I hated being overtaken,' he says. 'I couldn't stand it.' From the sidelines, Adrie was screaming at him to slow down. Victor's head fell into his hands as Tarrant responded and pushed back past Box, running dementedly clear until – one lap later – Box came back and recaptured the lead. For lap after lap, the gap between them opened and closed as each tried to outsprint and crush the other. Just four people remained on the track, but only these two had any chance at the record. After eight hours of non-stop running, what they were doing seemed maniacal but miraculous. However it ended, no one would forget what they were seeing.

At the three-quarter mark – with 75 miles run – Box's iron spirit was finally broken and his friend took a lead he would not surrender for another three hours. Despite cramp and mild delirium – 'the brain tires long before the body,' he would write later – Tarrant kept on going in bright autumn sunshine. With just a few laps to go, the crowd began to chatter and swell. Few of them had slept and until now – for most of them – it had been a cold and boring night. Abandoned flasks and plastic beakers littered the trackside. Every one of the runners who'd staggered out of the race had stayed behind to see what would happen. Without exception, they were bellowing and clapping Tarrant towards victory.

And then, finally, it was his. After running for 12 hours, 31 minutes and 10 seconds, he was there. Tarrant had completed 100 miles more than 15 minutes faster than anyone in history. For the second time in his life, he was a world record holder. Stumbling from Edie's immediate embrace to his father's proud arms, he battled to stay upright as the jubilant crowd roared and the news of his achievement spread. 'I'm a shade tired,' he told reporters. Elsewhere, there was simply relief. 'For all his outward facade of aggression, there was a vulnerability,' says Peter Bennett. 'We all felt for John. You could see what he'd been through. Well done, John – that was the universal feeling.'

Thirty minutes later, Dave Box crossed the line, utterly drained by his mid-race battle with the winner. In the years ahead, he would never blame his damaged thigh muscle – or the gung-ho Hereford masseuse – for his failure. Adrie simply wouldn't let him. 'You were an absolute idiot that day,' she would always say. 'Absolutely ridiculous. You didn't listen at all.'

'She's right,' Box concedes. 'I was so bad the day after, I had to walk up the stairs backwards.'

Tarrant, meanwhile, still had the energy to walk a lap of honour with Edie alongside him. Every minute here together was precious. Less than eight hours later, his wife would be alone again, and her husband would be at Heathrow being helped up the steps of a plane bound for Durban. It was hard for everyone, but he had a £300 debt outstanding, and he would drive that forklift truck until it was paid, and until he'd left his mark on a race he now felt certain he could win. 'He is indeed a man apart from other men,' wrote Noel Henry in a consoling letter to Edie.

Back in his Hereford bedroom, Roger composed a poem for the father who now seemed more like a ghost than ever:

> So now to Africa Tarrant must fly.
> His wife is heartbroken and has a good cry.
> But for the Comrades he must prepare for next May,
> And then to decide whether to come back home or stay.

Chapter Nine

The Only White Man

1970

During his time in Durban, Tarrant had taken little notice of the city's vast black population. Some of them, however, had become deeply curious about him. Tarrant was intriguing, a misfit and a rebel, a heretic outsider whose sustained one-man trench war against the establishment marked him out. Under apartheid in 1960s South Africa, white men like this were rare. Not only had Tarrant competed in Swaziland, but he'd also run alongside black ghosts in the Comrades, no more welcome in that whites-only extravaganza than they. His life – like his running – had never been constrained by fear, and, although he said very little, his actions seemed entirely devoid of prejudice.

Within Durban's seething political underground, these were qualities which had been quietly noted by a handful of the city's black and Indian activists. In the monosyllabic ghost runner they'd sensed an improbable ally for a controversial plan. During the following year, they hoped to unveil their own alternative to the Comrades: an exultant 55-mile multiracial road race, open to runners of every colour and creed.

There would be risks, but if they could find just one high-profile white man brave enough to run with them – someone who truly knew how to run – the publicity payback would be enormous. At the very least, it would humiliate South Africa's sporting elite. At best, it might even transform black athletics forever. Looking around, only one white man seemed tailor-made for the challenge, and as the boiling summer sun ripened the coconuts over the waterfront, he was running shirtless – and lost in thought – towards his thirteen-hour shift at the Durban waterfront.

In some ways, it felt good to be back in South Africa. In many others, it did not. He'd not forgotten how withering the English winter could be, and it was always hard to be in Hereford without thinking of the years he'd wasted cleaning floors. But there were things in this sun-sweet country which he knew were wrong.

At the Durban railway workers' hostel, his Afrikaner fellow residents referred to its black cleaners as 'monkeys', and he hated it when they did. It wasn't simply that he'd once done that sort of work. Any kind of bullying turned his stomach. He'd been on the wrong end of far too much of it over the years. Not feeling qualified to comment, he'd kept his mouth shut. So far. If he was really honest, he'd heard plenty worse around the army barracks back home.

Other quandaries were disturbing the charmed rhythm of Tarrant's Durban routine. The more he pondered, the more he realised his life had been cleaved into two separate worlds which were different in almost every conceivable way. In one, he had a home, a wife and a teenage son, and he was virtually unemployable. In the other, he lived alone in a quasi-barracks and held down a well-paid, steady job, which he loved. Sooner or later he'd have to choose which world to inhabit permanently. Until then, he'd concentrate on the 1970 Comrades – his third attempt – and finding the money he still owed for his last flight back home. Wheeling around E Shed on Durban docks, he'd calculated that it would be April 1971 before the debt was cleared. Plenty of time before then to decide his long-term future. Still plenty of time for Edie to change her mind.

In only one key aspect of Tarrant's double life was there any symmetry. As 1969 drew to a close, Tarrant was loathed by South Africa's white sporting governors just as much as he'd once been reviled by Jack Crump and his like. Every attempt to isolate him had failed. Every time he'd gone home, he'd come back. And Tarrant had developed an infuriating knack for winning all their races – apart from the Comrades. The whole situation was impossible. The man didn't seem to care that his performances went unacknowledged; ordinary athletes rather seemed to like him; and latterly his attitude towards the country's officials had become disturbingly belligerent.

During his first few months back in the city, he'd applied repeatedly to join the Bluff Athletic Club – just a five-minute run from his friend Dave Box's home – but each time his application had been refused, and patience on both sides was wearing dangerously thin.

'He was a pain in the neck, a hot potato. His name used to come up at every committee meeting I went to,' recalls then club captain Derek Stringer. 'He was always on the agenda. What were we going to do about him? No club would let him join. No one could touch him. It was so bad that when he left England, the British officials got in touch with our guys and reminded us that he was deemed a professional and that that could put us in a very exposed position if we didn't do the right thing.'

A well-orchestrated squeeze on Tarrant was undoubtedly on. Under renewed pressure from Britain, the South African AAA had reminded its elected representatives in Durban that Tarrant was to be afforded no slack. It didn't help his case that, on a personal level, officials like Stringer – and many others –

found him such a difficult character. 'He was arrogant and brash. Selfish. Unpopular. A lot of us couldn't understand how he'd left his family behind. We were a very moral country back then and found it difficult to accept that he'd come to live out here alone just to run a few races.'

It wasn't a universal view. No one found him easy, but everyone in Durban was in awe of his talent, and many rank-and-file runners were deeply sympathetic to his cause. The Bluff AC newsletter had felt sufficiently well disposed towards him to print his son's ode to the 100-mile record, and, unofficially, he was even allowed to run. Every Wednesday night, the club would stage a four-mile timed road trial, and every week Tarrant would win it. Fifty years later – although the route has changed – its challenging gradients have not, and Tarrant's personal best time of nineteen minutes has never been touched.

Today – as then – the time trial is followed by a braai (barbecue), around which the runners cluster to eat flamed steaks, compare times and sink large chilled beers in a convivial, predominantly masculine – and white – ambience from which Tarrant would have felt wholly excluded. 'He never, ever socialised,' says Stringer, 'and the longer I knew him, the more bitter he became. I can remember after one of the time trials he was standing by my car going on and on about his situation until my wife got so bored she went off to find something else to do and he just eventually buggered off.'

By early 1970, Tarrant – never a natural diplomat – was no longer capable of managing this accretion of slights and frustrations. Durban was pleasing, but the past, as always, was proving impossible to leave behind. After so many snubs and calculated silences, it was his publicly expressed view that South Africans were the most 'narrow-minded and insincere' officials in the world. Rumours of his persistent bellicosity were even filtering back to Britain, where a senior figure in the Road Runners Club had written privately to Vic warning him that 'in SA they are a little perturbed by [John]' and that he 'really must learn to trust people and not approach people mentally with his fists up, if you get my meaning'. Informed of the letter's contents, Tarrant let fly a furious broadside replete with all the old battle cries:

> Had I gone to Oxford I would not have been barred in the first place . . . the ghost will be around for some time yet . . . Never ever will I give up my fight for JUSTICE . . . whatever the cost I will fight to the bitter end . . . please excuse my scribble, only I'm writing this on Durban Docks in between working 14 hours a day, seven days a week . . . yes, life is tough for a dirty pro.

Still, at least he had Dave Box. There were never any problems with Box. Every evening, they kept up the 'hell run' back through the thunderous stink of the docks, and at weekends the two men ran up to fifty non-stop miles before plunging into the ocean at Brighton Beach for cooling late-afternoon swims. Tarrant had never known a man with Box's 'boundless energy'. Box had never encountered a man who could talk so much about one thing. Over supper with Dave and Adrie, his sole topic of conversation was the ban. 'He'd come to hate officialdom with a simple venom,' says Box. 'He'd always be saying his situation was diabolical. At this point, it controlled everything he did in his life. It was so awful. So stupid.'

Tarrant's state of mind had never been so friable. Nor had he ever trained with such furious release. During February 1970 – in the broiling steam of summer – Tarrant totalled 501 miles. The following month, he pushed that figure up to 560. By the end of the year, he'd completed 570 training sessions and run

5,033 miles, the highest annual total of his life, almost exactly twice the figure he'd recorded in 1960, aged 28 and dreaming of a British blazer in Rome. Back then, he'd lost out to Brian Kilby in the marathon. Welwyn Garden City. He still remembered every crushing stride.

Ten years on, as the days ticked down to his third Comrades, it was becoming clear that Tarrant's biggest challenger was himself. The failures of 1968 and 1969 had gnawed into the granite of his confidence, and no amount of punishing mileage could restore it. Anxiety overwhelmed him and every time he unfolded his inspirational dog-eared poem – 'If you think you're beaten, you are' – he couldn't shake the 'awful premonition' that he would once again be crushed beneath the weight of his own impossible expectations.

Barely five miles from the start, Tarrant's hopes of winning the 1970 Comrades race began to unravel. Struck a glancing blow by a car, he lost time and rhythm and slipped rapidly down the field. 'The life suddenly just drained out of him,' says Colin Shaw, who had again wheeled out on his motorcycle as Tarrant's second. 'Very early on, he more or less told me he'd lost the will to run and couldn't go on. I remember thinking, how am I going to get him back to the start on my bike? I'm not sure how he did [get back there] in the end. An ambulance, probably.'

After 18 miles, Tarrant's race was over. 'I wasn't in pain . . . I couldn't run fast enough to hurt myself.' Distraught, humiliated and mystified, he fled back to the hostel to contemplate the ruins of his adventure. 'My whole world had collapsed. I just wanted to be alone,' he revealed later. 'The more I thought about it, the less logic there appeared to be in what had happened. Perhaps the occasion had proved too much for me to cope with.'

It was a rare moment of acute self-awareness. Tarrant's preoccupation with the Comrades had passed beyond mere obsession. It had become an illness. Because of it, his family were counting their pennies 6,000 miles away and had spent last Christmas without him. Every stride was hobbled by guilt and the mortifying fear of failure. The harder he tried – and the more important winning became – the less likely it seemed that he would ever succeed. Three attempts, three failures, and this time he'd not even reached the halfway point. Even if he won, the history books would never show it. 'I felt absolutely wretched, not only for myself but for my wife and family who would have to share this crushing disappointment.'

It didn't help that his life already felt plagued by the dripping torture of other small indignities. In January, his 100-mile world record had earned him a prestigious Benrus Citation Award – a gold chronometer watch – and an invitation (which he couldn't afford to accept) to a presentation in New York. By the time the package finally arrived in Durban, the watch had mysteriously gone missing.

Back in Britain, the salacious weekly magazine *Tit-Bits* had run an article headlined 'Broke, Banned and Humiliated', claiming that 'malicious gossips' were 'whispering about Edie Tarrant's marriage'. It didn't add up to much, but it still hurt like hell. 'The gossips think my husband is living it up abroad but the truth is he's on the breadline. I'm the lonely wife of a long-distance runner,' Edie had told a reporter. If she could only see him now, having crashed out of the Comrades, alone, tear-streaked and desperate. Still, at least he had Dave Box.

A few hours after Tarrant's latest Comrades disappointment, his friend called round to the hostel to commiserate. For the second year running, Box had trailed in behind the winner, Dave Bagshaw. Just like Tarrant, Dave Box was running out of chances, and just like Tarrant, he would never win it. Better than anyone, he understood precisely how John felt. Neither man could stay down for long. Both had been blessed with unquenchable optimism, and there was always next year. As Box drove his friend across to The Bluff for tea with Adrie and their daughters, there was also a tantalising new distraction to discuss.

In the minutes before the Comrades had started, leaflets had been clandestinely circulated inviting white runners to run with black, Indian and coloured athletes in a multiracial fifty-mile road race scheduled for three months' time. Dave Box wanted nothing to do with it. Tarrant was intrigued and wrote immediately to the Indian organisers accepting their invitation. Of the 835 white runners who took part in the 1970 Comrades, he was the only one who did.

The way Tarrant saw it, he had nothing left to lose. It would probably never happen anyway.

Five weeks later, he'd moved on from the humiliating debacle of his third attempt at the Comrades. His debt had continued to shrink, he was already fixating on the 1971 race, and a 100-mile track race was being set up to take place in Kings Park Stadium, Durban, in two weeks' time. It would be Tarrant's first chance to defend his world record, and it would give Dave Box the opportunity for revenge. Only the location gave Tarrant any serious cause for concern. Running on a public highway had always guaranteed him a welcome degree of immunity. A controlled event inside a private stadium – especially one on foreign soil – presented him with a legitimate reason to panic.

If the authorities chose to, they could physically restrain him from running. Even if he was allowed to compete, any time he recorded – including a new world best – would be invalidated by his ban. Reluctantly, he reached out to Arthur Gold in London, seeking ritual clarification of the position. Gold's reply was so predictable Tarrant could have penned it himself. 'Although I have great admiration for your enthusiasm we both know the IAAF ruling on your status and there really is nothing further the BAAB can do about it.'

Even after all these years, he could be dumbfounded by this nonsense. To defend his own title, he would be forced to run as a ghost, and his time would never count. It was too absurdly familiar to be destabilising. Reasoning that a world best 'would still be a moral victory', Tarrant ignored Gold's letter and hurled himself into his preparations. Box versus Tarrant over 100 miles. Two great friends; one triumphant winner. He could scarcely wait. It was the race all of Durban wanted to see.

Forgoing overtime, he ran in every free daylight hour – 186 miles in one week alone. Every evening and every Saturday, he'd train with Box. Then, as dusk fell and the air sharpened, he'd pound up and down the Blamey Road, a steep half-mile hill at the back of his hostel. Labouring lorries laden with black workers parped at him as he sprinted up and past them in their spew of exhaust. Hands on haunches and pulse galloping, he'd rest for a moment by the Girls' High School, take in the sleepless industrial sprawl and jog back down. Another ten loops and then maybe he'd stop. It would be dark by then. Only the bats and stray dogs for company. Six hours' kip should see him right. These days, he didn't need any more. At 6 a.m., he'd be up and running to work.

By the summer of 1970, Tarrant had turned out illegally, as a ghost, on more than 100 occasions. At various times, he'd been chased, vilified, abused and ignored, but no one had yet pulled him from a race. As his duel with Dave Box drew closer, it seemed his enemies in South African athletics had run out of patience. For three years, his flagrant disregard for the rules had exposed them to international ridicule. When he was a serial loser in the Comrades, it was bearable. When he was the headline act in a world-record attempt on private South African soil, it wasn't. 'We were trying to keep our noses clean . . . always wanting to be readmitted into the fold,' says one high-placed official. From Britain, Arthur Gold had pointedly restated Tarrant's position. In Durban, the hint had been taken.

Rumours had been circulating for weeks that he would be prevented from defending his 100-mile world record and with two days to go, the whispers were confirmed. 'Tarrant Banned From 100 Miler' declared the *Natal Mercury*. As John had feared, running on a closed circuit brought his activities within the reach of the IAAF. Any athlete found competing alongside him, said the organisers, risked being banned for life. Should Tarrant himself make any attempt to take part, he would be removed from the field. To ensure his absolute compliance, a letter was dispatched to the railway workers' hostel in Clairwood, asking for Tarrant's formal withdrawal from the event.

History was repeating itself. The Doncaster-to-Sheffield Marathon? What had the organisers said to Victor? 'Mr Tarrant of Buxton would not be permitted to run on Easter Monday.' Thirteen years on, different players, same depressing script. Convinced they were bluffing, Tarrant arrived at Kings Park on the morning of 31 July fully expecting to run. Waiting for him there was Stan Foley, the chairman of the organising committee, who reconfirmed the ban face to face. During the heated exchange that followed, Tarrant offered to run in a separate lane or even start a few minutes after the other runners, but Foley could not be shifted.

'I personally had huge sympathy for Tarrant,' says Foley. 'Some of us had tried to help him find work at various times, but he was a very, very pig-headed man at this time.' To be absolutely sure of his position, Foley had even contacted John Jewell at the Road Runners Club in Britain, only to be told that Tarrant could not, and should not, be allowed to compete. Once again, it seemed his so-called friends in the RRC had no time for their errant member's antics, nor the inclination, privately, to cut him any slack.

For the first time ever, the ghost had been stopped, and in the final despairing minutes before the gun, he sought out Dave Box to wish him luck. There were no hard feelings, just the terrible bruise of frustration. 'I wanted John to run,' says Box. 'I wanted to prove I was better than him, and he wanted to do the same. I wanted to run against the best but I couldn't. It was bloody tragic. If he'd been in that race, I'd have run even faster.'

Shortly after midnight – barely 12 hours later – Dave Box had sliced 16 minutes off Tarrant's 100-mile world record. Just like his vanquished 40-mile world record, John's benchmark had been swept away in less than a year. Sportingly, he'd stayed to watch, offering his services as a second to a young Capetown runner who'd arrived alone. But it had been an inadequate distraction. 'In the passing of time we all become ex-world champions,' he wrote ruefully, but behind his genuine happiness for Box, Tarrant was mortified.

Years before, during his domestic fight for reinstatement, his former mentor Joe Lancaster had evoked 'the freedom of action, mind and soul' that running embodied. How could anyone still claim the right to deprive him of that freedom? 'People here look right through me,' he griped to a Durban reporter. 'It's as though I don't exist. It's no joke, I can tell you.'

In a northern suburb of Durban, a young man called Rajendra Chetty had been watching Tarrant's humiliation with rising curiosity. On his desk sat an application from this solitary Englishman to run in his new race. By their actions at Kings Park, the authorities had driven the ghost runner straight into Chetty's arms. 'An historic event was about to happen,' he reflects. 'We couldn't have asked for anyone better.'

For years, Rajendra Chetty had been chipping away at

apartheid. As a young Durban-based journalist with a passion for sport, he'd evolved from critic to activist, becoming ever more radicalised by each government-sponsored indignity. A non-racial table-tennis team had flown secretly out of South Africa to compete in Switzerland. When they returned, their passports were seized. Coloured cricketer Basil D'Oliveira had been driven from South Africa but was refused permission to return when selected as a member of the English touring party in 1968. The tour was abandoned. Everywhere he looked, discrimination was denying thousands of blacks the same 'freedom of action, mind and soul' that John Tarrant craved.

As a sports presenter with the South African Broadcasting Corporation, Chetty himself had resigned in a row over his pursuit of news stories which exposed the rotten unfairness of the prevailing regime. His resistance was proving a lonely, uphill struggle, made harder by what Chetty identified as white liberal hypocrisy. Even those who professed opposition seemed horribly comfortable with the status quo: 'No matter how vociferously they disagreed with the Afrikaner nationalists, they were quite happy to vote them into power to protect their own vested interests.'

In normal life, any integration between the white and black sections of the population had been impossible – by law – for 20 years. The Group Areas Act of 1950 had assigned racial groups to different residential and business sections of the country's cities. Any non-white found living in the 'wrong' area could be forcibly removed. In 1953, the Separate Amenities Act had racially segregated buses, trains, toilets and public areas. Only on the pavements and roads could a black safely share space with a white. Every time Tarrant ran along the ocean shoreline, he passed a chilling sign on the beach: '*Uitgehou vir die uitsluitlike gebruik van lede van die blanke rassegroep*' (Reserved for the sole use of members of the white race group)

– the same '*blanke rassegroep*' which wouldn't allow a 'dirty pro' like him to take part in the Comrades, notwithstanding the acceptably pallid hue of his skin.

In the late 1960s, Chetty had masterminded the non-racial Natal Runners Association, an organisation formed specifically to fight the persistent refusal of the Comrades organisers to allow official black participation in its annual race. Although high principles were at stake, Chetty's campaign had a practical imperative. There were brilliant black runners in South Africa – excluded from white athletic clubs – who were living and dying without a chance.

'We had world-class athletes,' remembers runner and fellow activist V.S. Naidoo. 'If we'd had the opportunity and good training, we'd have been on top, but the whites loved the system as it was. They had all the facilities, all the money. They had everything. They never gave us a thought.'

In early 1970, the fledgling NRA had come up with a novel riposte: an alternative 50-mile road race to be staged that September between Stanger – the historic epicentre of the Zulu nation – and Durban. It would be South Africa's first-ever multiracial road race. Runners of any colour would be welcome, but it would be the participation of high-profile white athletes which would determine its success, and, as Chetty's plans advanced, there seemed little prospect of that happening.

At the Comrades in May, scores of white runners had worn black armbands in support of the black athletes competing alongside them as numberless ghosts. Under pressure from Chetty to turn out for his alternative event, however, their 'support' had melted away. Hundreds of leaflets had been circulated, but none had come back. One former Comrades winner had shown some interest, but an injury two weeks before the deadline had forced him to withdraw.

Only a single serious application remained, the one from the

Englishman the Durban newspapers always referred to as 'the ghost runner', the man whose close-cropped hair made him look like a policeman. It was time for Chetty to take a trip across town to the railway workers' hostel to find out what this John Tarrant fellow was all about.

From the beginning, there was a spark. Tarrant's unpretentious dignity touched Chetty deeply, and Tarrant was lifted by the younger man's conviction. It was a relief for the Englishman – and immensely flattering – to be in the presence of someone who embraced him without conditions. There was something disarming in the cherubic, smiling face of this articulate Indian, and something about his evocation of a dispossessed people fighting back against discrimination which resonated with Tarrant. A month or two before, Tarrant might have walked away, but the recent events in Kings Park had stirred him. It would be refreshing to run officially, in the welcoming company of these people, whatever the risk.

Rajendra Chetty was thrilled. Tarrant was like no Englishman he'd ever met. 'A very private person . . . very dignified . . . with an upbeat spirit and a great deal of positive energy.'

As Chetty carefully spelled out the legal position, Tarrant listened attentively. Providing he got changed before the race in his own dressing-room, there would be no infringement of the Separate Amenities legislation. There were no laws which could prevent him from running down a public highway, and the government ban on mixed sport applied only to contact activities such as wrestling. Furthermore, Chetty's assessment was that any judicial attempt to crush his race would unravel under proper legal scrutiny, and that the government would not want to risk the uncertainty of a test case. Having scrutinised every angle, he felt confident the race would proceed.

'I explained this was tantamount to one of the most historic events in South African sport, a test of the government's apartheid policy . . . intended to expose the fallacy of the state's policy . . . and send a strong statement that certain codes of sport were exempt from the laws of the country. John sat listening all the while. He smiled pleasantly, got up and shook my hand. That told me he was a thorough gentleman and ready for action.'

The following weeks would prove a test of nerve for both men. Potential race sponsors had already turned away. Others simply ignored the organisers' letters and calls. Two specialist agencies which had agreed to provide communications links and first-aid services had pulled out with less than one week to go.

At race headquarters, Chetty became convinced that a dirty-tricks campaign to wreck the event was under way. Worse still, their star man was getting cold feet. 'I think I'm responsible for what's happening,' he told Chetty. 'Maybe they're afraid.' Chetty reassured John that the race was legal but was unable to guarantee that he would not be arrested and imprisoned. The decision to run had to be John's alone. With or without him, 94 black runners would be setting off anyway.

Tarrant was in turmoil. Everything Chetty had said made sense. There was a stink in this country he'd been trying not to notice. Put your head down and keep on running. That's what everyone else did. Back home, he voted Labour, but this wasn't about politics, it was about injustice, and Tarrant had known a bellyful of that. Every fibre of his soul was telling him he should run. Almost every white man he knew in Durban was saying he shouldn't.

As news of Tarrant's alliance with Chetty spread, South Africa's marathon-running community peered into its collective conscience. Publicly, most runners paid lip service to the black cause. Privately, very few of them were prepared to gamble their own futures by taking part. Seeing an outsider like Tarrant make such a valiant – albeit foolhardy – stand was humiliating, but they'd live with it. For the city's other expat British runners – Dave Bagshaw and Dave Box in particular – it was the cause of excruciating discomfort.

Bagshaw had arrived in Durban via Nigeria, Togo, Ghana and the Ivory Coast. In Nigeria, he had done voluntary work, met his wife and married, and then moved on as civil war erupted. He didn't doubt that apartheid was 'odious', but after what he'd seen elsewhere in Africa, he felt the regime had what he terms 'the virtue of stability'. 'People felt it was wrong but didn't seem to know how to change it,' he explains.

The following year, he'd be going for a third successive Comrades win, not slinking in as a ghost like Tarrant but as a validated star. Regretfully, he was not prepared to join Tarrant in this multiracial experiment. 'Yes, there was a lot of soul-searching, but there was also no real clarity about how it might affect our status if we took part,' he explains. 'We had other races, which John couldn't run in, and there was a view around that it was wrong for a white runner to deprive a black runner of his success.'

Dave Box was in a similar quandary. 'What John did was a knock against apartheid, no doubt. But he couldn't lose by running in Chetty's race, because John was already banned. The rest of us could have been barred, and, of course, we weren't like him. We could still run in the Comrades.'

Dave Box's decision not to get involved would mark a cooling in their friendship. Over the coming months, Tarrant would be drawn deeper into his new circle. There was no falling-out and no formal break, but the two men would never be quite so close again. The halcyon days on The Bluff were over. 'He was being used as a political tool,' insists Adrie. 'I think the Indians were well aware of John's power in this regard.'

From Chetty and fellow Durban journalists like Farook Khan, the disappointing reticence of white athletes like Box and

Bagshaw drew contempt. 'A glamour boy' was Khan's withering assessment of Bagshaw. 'People like that sat in their pearly protected kingdoms,' says Chetty. 'If they really cared . . . they would have acted on their conscience, not waited for someone to beg and plead.' From other quarters – white ones – there was sympathy, laced with realism, for the impossible situation athletes like Bagshaw had unwittingly found themselves in. 'If Bagshaw and Box had run that race, they'd have lost their amateur status. Simple as that,' insists Ronnie Borain. 'There's a fine line between determination and stubbornness. Judgement is the thing which separates them.'

As the day of the race – 6 September 1970 – approached, white support appeared to have shrivelled away completely. Three little-known white runners who'd planned to participate had withdrawn twenty-four hours before the start. Only Tarrant remained, impervious to the dire rumblings of career suicide and police reprisals. Thanks to an Indian soft-drinks company, the race had acquired a name – the Goldtop Marathon – and at Stanger Town Hall, a boisterously curious crowd was gathering. 'You've no idea of the excitement this was causing,' remembers Farook Khan. 'Who was this new champion the whites didn't like? How, from such a quagmire, had such a noble human being arrived in our midst?'

Moments before the start, two armed white policemen approached Tarrant, shook his hand and asked for his autograph. It wasn't what he'd expected, but then nothing about this day was normal. It was quite unlike the Comrades. A dishevelled festival air hung over the proceedings. If any traffic lights were on red, all the runners had to stop, and all along the route down the coast, hundreds of blacks and Indians rushed from their homes with cooling ice and drinks.

Black runners he'd never met before clustered around him as he ran, fascinated by his style and his tactics. 'For the first time, they were running with someone who acknowledged their existence . . . feeling humbled and privileged to be rubbing shoulders,' says Chetty. 'They had never had the opportunity of this kind of interaction in their lives.'

Few of them had ever trained before, most had never run further than a few miles and not one had ever competed against a white man while wearing an official number on his shirt. As a test of Tarrant's form, it was a non-event. But that had never been the point. When he reached the finish line at the decrepit Curries Fountain Stadium in Durban, he was 40 minutes ahead of the next man – he'd run 50 miles in a comfortable 5 hours and 43 minutes – and a throng of black South Africans rose to applaud the only white man in sight. 'It was the first time I'd ever seen him smile,' says Khan. 'He was so reluctant and shy, and rather than give a victory speech, he quietly congratulated all the other runners. We'd got our hero.'

Tarrant had never experienced adulation. Since he'd left England, one snub had followed another. Only the previous month, he'd been warned to stay away from the all-white Durban City Marathon. Not that he'd listened. Two bouts of gut trouble and he'd still sauntered home in first place. Unofficially. Now, this one crazy run along the Indian Ocean from Stanger to Durban had changed everything. Out of such unpromising raw material, in the outpouring of goodwill which followed the Goldtop, Tarrant had discovered something new. This was what it felt like to be on the inside.

For Rajendra Chetty, Farook Khan and their fellow campaigners, the ghost runner's presence had transformed the Goldtop from shambles to PR heaven. The man was a gift – a godsend – and they would offer him every consideration that his white hosts denied him. In the weeks that followed, instead of training with Box, Tarrant was collected from his hostel by his Indian friends and chauffeured to the decrepit Curries

Fountain, tucked between the city's lush botanical gardens and a knot of potholed flyovers.

Behind closed doors – on a lumpy track intended exclusively for non-whites – Tarrant would run endless circuits, circling herons as they munched fresh green shoots sprouting from damp puddles of rain. Invariably, trailing in his slipstream would be a posse of runners who couldn't quite believe what was happening. One of them, Ram Sumer, had reached 39 years of age without ever running freely with a white man like this. 'If any whites ever saw him training with us,' he says, 'you could see the way they looked and what they were thinking, but John knew no barriers.'

Back at the hostel, Tarrant made a point of mischievously introducing his new friends to the white Afrikaner workers who filled up its beds. 'He became firmly entrenched in our community,' says Khan. 'We'd pick him up as a matter of course. We felt sure the authorities were keeping an eye on him and we felt concerned that his visa might be revoked. Anti-apartheid feeling was picking up steam in Britain. The unions, the Labour Party – things were changing and John was very much a part of that struggle.'

Just how much Tarrant was aware of this radical undertow is unknown. What is certain is that he wanted no bigger role in it. Tarrant's world-view was a simple one, and he lacked the intellectual machinery to engage in sophisticated debate. His new-found happiness wasn't rooted in deep analysis. It arose from the same instincts which had guided his entire life. Class had always been the issue for John – not colour – and he was comfortable in the company of these beaming underdogs. If Chetty and company could provide him with the opportunity to run and race, then for both parties it would be the perfect marriage. They'd get their 'hero' and he'd get what mattered.

* * *

Throughout the closing months of 1970, this meant only one thing. Ever since Dave Box's unchallenged run in Kings Park, Tarrant had wanted his 100-mile world record back. In Britain, Victor had been pestering the *Daily Mirror* to help his brother find a venue. In Cape Town, one attempt had already been sabotaged. Learning that the city might shortly be staging a 100-mile event, Tarrant had posted his interest, hoping that someone might tell him he was wanted. He wasn't. And, as now seemed to be the norm in South Africa, Tarrant was advised to keep his distance.

Acid was even dripped on his plans from London. In a letter from the dependably lukewarm Road Runners Club, Tarrant was told to stop wasting his own time 'and other people's as well'. 'This will be unpalatable but you might as well face facts,' wrote RRC official John Jewell. Tarrant's old sense of isolation returned, and wearily he turned to Chetty for help. Together, the two new allies picked 5 December for a stab at the fifty-mile world record, the summer days already being too hot for a realistic crack at Box's incendiary time over the longer distance. Chetty would organise, and Tarrant would be the star billing. No other white runners were expected to take part.

As with the recent Goldtop, there was a demoralisingly makeshift quality to the planning. Curries Fountain was crumbling, uncomfortable and small. To run a mile would require five laps of the track, not the usual four. To run 50 miles would require 250 laps and not 200. Not only was the running surface pitted and poor, but, with two days to go, the special police turned up demanding evidence that Tarrant would not be getting changed in the same room as blacks. Pointing to a flimsy nearby tent, Chetty reassured them that no contamination would occur. 'The white man will not be privileged to use our luxury facilities,' he promised.

The moment passed – and Chetty's heavy sarcasm went

unpunished – but it was a stark reminder to Tarrant of the peculiar place he'd reached. Whatever had gone before, his open embrace of black athletes now put him way beyond any prospect of rehabilitation. Of this time, he would later write, 'I had no hope of competing in a race organised by any white governing body.' Fittingly enough, the race would take place under a cloudburst.

In the end, seven non-white runners turned up on the night, and after thirty miles every one of them had dropped out. Only a bare-chested Tarrant was left out under the track's watery lights, watched by a bemused crowd as the skies opened and hailstones the size of pigeons' eggs smashed down on his naked back. Within minutes, the standing water was up to his ankles. A half-hour later, it was up to his knees in places. Undeterred, a local band, appropriately called the Naked Truth, kept on playing throughout.

With so little action to distract them, a vicious fight broke out between two rival Durban gangs. As John circled obliviously in the downpour – periodically illuminated by flashes of lightning – a man armed with a cane knife jumped on a spectator, who lashed back fiercely with a walking stick. Another man, bleeding heavily, rolled out of the melee and sprawled in a daze across the saturated outside lanes. By the time Tarrant had waded back round, the brawl was over. 'He had seen nothing,' remembers V.S. Naidoo, 'but at that time I was still in the race – just – and thought they were after me . . . It was the only thing that made me run faster.'

Ten years before, once all prospect of a meaningful result had vanished Tarrant would have stormed from the track, but for 6 hours and 18 minutes he'd struggled gamely on to the end. 'It was the least I could do,' he explained, too polite to acknowledge that the event had descended into black farce, a distant sideshow of so little sporting significance that one local newspaper merged its truncated race report with the story of a dog killed in the storm by a falling tree.

John had found a welcome place to run, and he was fiercely proud of his contribution to Chetty's cause, but that support had dragged him deeper into the sporting wilderness. It was time to go home.

Edie had never once faltered. For all its shortcomings, she had adapted to her life in Hereford, impervious to her husband's siren letters about the sunshine and the money. Now, as she'd always hoped, he was letting go of his plans to emigrate. 'I had come across couples where things had not worked out well,' he admitted. 'The husband had usually settled down, but the wife was dissatisfied because of the lack of television . . . Edith is a big television fan.' It was an ungracious aside which reflected poorly on Tarrant, but it wasn't the only reason why Tarrant was finally ready to return to his council flat.

Indiscernibly, the childhood years of his son had trickled away. School had never suited him, and in October 1970 – with his father still in Durban – Roger had left home to join the Royal Navy. He was 16 years old, and for most of his adolescence the father he idolised had lived on another continent. Touchingly, the two had established a regular written correspondence, marked by Tarrant's recurrent warnings about the perils of alcohol and nicotine – 'your life will be much richer if you avoid either of these bad habits' – but letters couldn't provide a son with a father any more than John's written plea for Roger to 'take care of Mum' could ease his wife's loneliness.

Roger's departure to join HMS *Raleigh* in Cornwall (where he'd be tempted with 300 subsidised cigarettes a month) meant that Edie could add an absent son to her invisible husband. It didn't come easily, but even a man as relentlessly self-centred as Tarrant could see where his responsibilities lay. 'Under the circumstances,' he recalled ruefully, 'I decided that my future was to be living in England.' He'd been away for more than a year. The gruelling shifts on the docks had sorted out his finances – there were even a few hundred quid in the bank – and by mid-December Tarrant had run out of excuses to stay. Even for him, another Christmas away would be pushing it.

Invited to a farewell party at Rajendra Chetty's flat, he was reduced to tears by the gathering's sadness at his going. 'You are made in the mettle of great men,' Chetty wrote to him. 'Maybe someday, sometime, we will meet again under different circumstances.' It would be sooner than either man thought. Thanking him for his courage, Chetty presented Tarrant with two wristwatches – one for him, one for Edie. 'We pray that the day will dawn when . . . you take your rightful place in the world of athletics.'

'In so many ways, he was conservative – the most unlikely of flower-power children,' explains Farook Khan. 'We hated his short back and sides. He was soft-spoken, didn't drink, didn't smoke, turned down invitations to dance at functions, and yet people who saw him always crowded him, shook his hand and asked for his autograph.

'In some ways, John had enjoyed the future South Africa long before its time. He certainly gave us our first taste of what it could be, and for that we would always be grateful to him.'

Charlton Avenue in Hereford looks much the same today as it did when John Tarrant arrived home in 1970 with just four days to go before Christmas. Now, as then, it's a council estate of unfashionable virtues. On a winter's afternoon, an elderly lady in a floral blouse leans heavily against her three-wheeled shopping trolley. A pensioner cycles uncertainly back from his allotment, clutching soil-smudged vegetables wrapped in yesterday's *Daily Express*. For both of them, momentum is everything.

Although prefab concrete slabs are the norm, the houses have been afforded breadth and light, and the best of them face south. As yet, not every wall sports a satellite dish, and most certainly not that of Edie Tarrant, who still lives there today and whose first-floor flat would always be gleaming, whether her husband was coming home or not.

She'd arranged a tea party – Victor was there, of course – and Roger had secured leave from the navy to be reunited, albeit briefly, with his father. In the living room at the top of the stairs, a glittering shrine of trophies covered an entire wall, from floor to ceiling, and as Edie fussed with pots of tea and mince pies, her travel-weary husband was dragged out into the frosty night for a two-mile run with his son. 'He had improved a great deal,' remarked Tarrant, who must have been impressed to see Roger in full uniform, looking so very different from the lonely child who'd once lamented his father's departure in rhyming couplets.

But the euphoria of John's homecoming would not last. Tarrant had never enjoyed the winter, and this one was no different. If anything, it was worse. After so long in Durban, his surroundings seemed claustrophobic and dank, and Hereford a city devoid of colour. Edie had taken seasonal work at Woolworths on the Christmas card counter. Without a job of his own – or any apparent interest in one – her husband's time drifted during the day, and for the first time he was struggling to find the will to train, choosing instead to stare out lazily from his spotless kitchen across back yards and weak, icy skies.

'There were nearly three-quarters of a million unemployed,' he lamented, 'and I made one extra.' The money he'd saved soon disappeared on household expenses, and by late January the Tarrants were broke, John was depressed and Edie was staring at the inevitable: her husband wanted to go back to South Africa.

Indeed, since the turn of the year, he'd been campaigning openly for funds. In letters to Durban – between rants about 'snow and strikes' – Tarrant had pleaded for money from Rajendra Chetty and his supporters, a request which was met with vibrant enthusiasm. 'A pity you are unemployed,' Chetty bubbled. 'However, have faith and things will shine fairly bright one day. I went to see Mr Kara today about the fund. You can expect 100 rand from him for a start.' In another letter, he added with concern, 'I hope your coming here will not rob them [Edie and Roger] of the bare essentials of life.'

Back in Hereford, Tarrant's torpor had vanished. For the fourth time, he prevailed upon the generosity of Ned Waring, and the funds for another one-way ticket looked well within reach. By any standards, the Hereford businessman's philanthropy had already been a remarkable act of faith. Without Waring's cash, Tarrant could never have left the country, and yet with it he'd won nothing, and he remained hell-bent on one more attempt at a race in which his recent performances had fallen off a cliff.

This time, he assured Waring, it would be different. There were omens, after all. His first London-to-Brighton victory hadn't come until his fourth attempt, and this would be his fourth bid for Comrades glory. But Waring really wasn't that bothered. Since that first Poughkeepsie trip, his support had never been conditional upon results, and Victor had paid all of the recent loans back. There remained this sorrowful, stoical air about Tarrant which moved him, and while there was fight left in the runner's bones, he'd continue to help, no strings or expectations attached.

By Easter, confident that he could afford the £225 airfare, Tarrant's self-belief was fully reinflated and his zest for competition had returned. In April, he won a 50-mile track race, finishing in 5 hours and 43 minutes, well outside world-record pace but still 11 minutes clear of the next man in. Of fourteen starters, only four had finished, in freezing conditions. Even his old rival Lynn Hughes – the man he'd once waded up sand-dunes with – had been blown away, staggering exhausted from the track after 42 blistering miles. 'The cinders had been laid on an old rubbish dump, and after 20 miles I had glass sticking out of my toe,' remembers one of the day's competitors, Phil Hampton. 'It was a terrible day, but they were hard guys – shove you in a ditch as soon as look at you.'

A few weeks later, Tarrant suffered one of his puzzling slumps during the Exeter-to-Plymouth road race but shook off the disappointment as a freak. Whatever they were, the stomach problems seemed stable. In his 39th year, Tarrant reassured himself that he was still a winner. It was true what his peers said: ultra-distance runners got better with age. This year, the Comrades would be his.

It was time to go. He'd been home just five months, and Edie loyally accompanied her partner to Hereford railway station and waved him on his way. They never talked about emigration any more – she knew he'd be back eventually. Last time, he'd been away for more than a year. This time, she'd simply no idea. Six months? Maybe more? He'd need to find work out there to pay off his debts again, so it wouldn't be quick. No doubt for her there'd be a cleaning job somewhere, and when John was ready he'd fly home. Sooner or later, he'd run out of steam and slow down, although what he'd do then was anyone's guess.

By the end of May, Tarrant was back in Durban, but there was to be no fairytale finish in the Comrades Marathon, and his time in South Africa would rapidly tumble from disappointment to nightmare. At the start, everything had been comfortingly familiar. He'd been met at the airport by Colin Shaw and welcomed into his friend's home for the days before the race. Shaw's wife had stitched a Union Jack onto his running vest in place of the official number Tarrant was still denied. The newspapers seemed delighted he was back and were speculating furiously about his chances of spoiling Dave Bagshaw's bid for a third successive victory in a record field of more than 1,200 athletes.

Waiting damply at the start in Pietermaritzburg, Tarrant had every reason to believe he could win. Three years before, he'd been an innocent. Today, he knew every fold of the route which lay between him and the outskirts of Durban. For once, he'd slept well, waking to find a cold, comforting rain falling. Feeling exultant in such familiar Pennine-like damp, Tarrant ran strongly from the start, comfortably snug alongside the leading bunch of six. Eighteen miles later, he was forced into the bushes to defecate. After 20 miles, the same, and at 21 miles the same again.

It was hopeless. Nothing the bewildered Shaw could do or say seemed to help. Dehydrated and drained, Tarrant drifted further and further down the field, his situation worsened by an injury to his left thigh. 'I didn't even see him finish. He just suddenly disappeared off the road,' says Shaw. At around 33 miles, unseen by his second, Tarrant had flagged down a lift in a passing camper van and fled from the race. It was to be his last, and most ignominious, exit from a race he'd fantasised about winning for ten years. 'I just wanted to go away from everyone, but there was no hiding place for me to go.'

Bagshaw had claimed his hat-trick and was the toast of world athletics. Tarrant was inconsolable, penniless and fast becoming the forgotten man of his sport. Journalists wanted controversy, officials only feared him in victory, and Tarrant could no longer guarantee either. Something wasn't right. Much older men than him had won the Comrades. His levels of fitness remained high, and between races he felt no sign of the dreadful stabbing pains which turned his bowels to slush and sent him stumbling from the road, wiping up the mess with his fingers, waiting for the stink and the gut cramp to subside before it all came surging back through him again.

Whatever was wrong with him was soon forgotten. Nervous stress, some people said, but Tarrant wasn't convinced. It had been a long time since he'd fretted about running without a number, and his debts were the only thing that kept him from sleep. To help him out, Rajendra Chetty had provided him with a sofa at his flat in Carlisle Street, but Tarrant couldn't settle. His staying with Chetty might get his friend in deep trouble. He needed to move on and the South African Railways came to his rescue. Merchant traffic at the docks was heavy, and Tarrant's much improved skills as a forklift driver were in demand. With the old job came a new bed at the Clairwood hostel, and Tarrant's life settled down again as quickly as his stomach.

It was as if he'd never been away. Durban's athletics officials still shunned him, and the rank-and-file athletes were just as pleased to have him back. To some of them, however, he seemed more pitiful than on previous visits, turning up on training nights with a scrapbook full of his newspaper cuttings, and on one occasion wearing a long coat and flat cap over his kit.

Despite his sadly diminishing powers, Tarrant had attained a grizzled, almost legendary status throughout the city: an elusive man who was there one day and gone the next; a man who, providing you could endure the prevailing bitterness, spoke with the forthright single-mindedness of a martyred saint. For a 15-year-old South African called Dave Upfold, in these final months of Tarrant's time in South Africa, the ghost runner's unique brand of charisma was to prove life-changing.

Upfold was a precocious, gifted runner with a rebel streak. In 1969, still too young to compete officially, he'd run in the Comrades without a number. He'd been just 13 years old. Two years later, he could run five miles in twenty-six minutes, and on midweek evenings, when he trained above the ocean with the Bluff Athletic Club, his prowess had drawn him to the side of the dark-browed man who seemed to talk about only one thing.

It was a fleeting companionship with every reason to blossom. The two men had been chipped from the same rock. Like Tarrant, Upfold was an outspoken rocker of boats with a fiercely independent streak. He was also close to Roger Tarrant's age, and in the arm which the older man threw around the teenage prodigy it was possible to discern the sad surrogacy of regret. Whatever the source of their chemistry, a strong bond had quickly formed. Throughout the spring of 1971, Tarrant and Upfold trained together constantly, racing buses up the steep hill behind his hostel or running halfway across the city to take part in time trials, before jogging back joyously after dark.

'We ran everywhere then,' remembers Upfold, who 40 years later is working as a stage hypnotist in New Zealand. 'I'd say to him, "Where shall we meet?", then we'd meet and we'd be off. I remember the Natal Cross-Country Marathon in 1971. I ran nine miles to the start, ran it, came fifth and then ran all the way back again. John wasn't saying to me, "You're too young, bugger off," like the South African runners were. He genuinely wanted me along and we'd talk while we ran – on the downhill stretches – but always about running.'

As July approached, Upfold and Tarrant talked about one race in particular. Undeterred by visits from the Security Police

– 'they are waiting for a slip-up but there won't be one' – Rajendra Chetty was pressing ahead with plans for a second multiracial Goldtop 50-mile marathon between Durban and Stanger. 'I believe in integration and nothing is going to shake me,' he told Tarrant, whose cast-iron promise to take part had re-energised the fledgling project. Dave Box was already a certain absentee – 'These guys are full of excuses,' lamented Chetty in a letter to John – but at least one other white runner had shown serious interest: a 15-year-old called Dave Upfold.

Tarrant was not surprised. During their evening training, he and the teenager often ran with black or Indian athletes. 'They knew they could [run with us] and they knew they'd be welcomed,' says Upfold. 'A lot of the white athletes would never have done that. It was just not the done thing to do. But I was already refereeing black football matches, and that too was unheard of. I just did it because I felt like it.' Provided Upfold's parents gave their blessing – which they did – Tarrant had no doubts that his student could complete 50 miles, notwithstanding his tender years. Whatever happened, now there would be two white runners in the field – twice as many as in 1970.

On 11 July, the pair arrived at the start at Curries Fountain in the back of Chetty's car. 'It was all a bit loose,' recalls Upfold. 'The start was shambolic. Someone muttered, "Everyone ready? You sure? OK, let's go," and we were off.' Apart from a handful of students who walked the course in protest against apartheid, no other white athletes turned up. Despite the promise of support from white universities, only the renegades Upfold and Tarrant had found the courage to run. 'Perhaps they were warned against it,' wondered Tarrant, who endured two bad attacks of diarrhoea to win the race comfortably in 5 hours and 40 minutes.

'We used to laugh at him a bit in those races, but the Indians loved him to bits,' says one white runner who stayed away. 'They weren't very well organised and they used to cheat like hell. Two runners – same vest – swapping from one to the other at the halfway point. John won anyway. That's why they loved him. They'd accepted him. For John, it was uncomplicated for once.'

Unlike the previous year, Tarrant's triumph gave him little pleasure. It had been 'a crushing disappointment' to see such a feeble white contingent, and he'd been incensed to learn that Upfold (whom he'd beaten by 75 minutes) had subsequently been banned for a month for competing with coloured runners while wearing his club's official vest. 'Those responsible were not fit to lace Dave's running shoes,' sniffed Tarrant. But there was something else – something about the fitful behaviour of his body – which had seriously troubled him. The years of denial were almost over. 'Somehow I'd never felt really well in the race,' he was to write later, knowing by then that worse was to come, and with appallingly swift consequence.

As the South African summer began, Tarrant was planning his return home. Three more months on the docks and his finances would be in order. In late October, another 100-mile world record attempt was being organised in England, and, unless it was this persistent 'stomach trouble', nothing would keep him away. However, on that score, there were alarming signs. Four weeks after the Goldtop, Tarrant had come apart trying to defend his unofficial title in Durban's annual City Marathon. A fortnight later – on the evening of 21 August – he'd 'sat out' a time trial on The Bluff, feeling uncharacteristically out of sorts and lacking the energy to compete.

At the hostel that night, he'd set his clock for 5.30 a.m., planning a 20-mile dawn run before meeting Rajendra Chetty for an official photograph with the Goldtop trophy. A good night's sleep had settled him down before, he reasoned. He'd be fine in the morning. At 11 p.m., Tarrant awoke suddenly and rushed to the bathroom vomiting blood. Barely able to stand, he slumped to the toilet seat, where he discovered that blood was seeping from his rectum. Attempting to return to his bedroom, he collapsed in the corridor before dragging himself to his feet using the door frame and inching dizzily into his bed.

For the next ten hours, Tarrant slept deeply, rising at 9.30 a.m. 'feeling better but terribly weak . . . I felt as though I could go to bed and sleep forever.' After a shower to clean off the dried blood, Tarrant took stock of his situation. He had no appetite, no thirst and no strength. He was also unable to stand for more than a few seconds. At no time had he summoned a doctor, and, despite his shocking condition, Tarrant remained determined not to let Chetty down. 'It took me an age to prepare for the photograph . . . I looked in the mirror and it was most frightening. I thought I had seen a ghost.'

Remarkably, the photographs that were taken a few hours later show scant signs of what Tarrant had just been through. Looking lean and wearing a dark suit, he seems to be clutching the trophy for support, and a tired smile has popped a deep dimple into his gaunt cheeks. Tarrant's skin, however, appears bloodless and pale, and the weathered tan of previous summers is entirely gone. The following day, a doctor told him he'd suffered a haemorrhage and was almost certainly nursing a stomach ulcer. A few days after that, Tarrant felt sufficiently recovered to run ten miles in seventy-five minutes, before dropping in after breakfast to see his GP for the results of his tests.

It was not what Tarrant wanted to hear. During his bleed, he'd lost four pints of blood, and he was suffering from acute anaemia. Although they'd found no signs of anything more sinister, he'd be required to spend time in hospital undergoing X-rays and tests. Training was forbidden, and when he arrived on the ward carrying his running kit, the nursing staff threatened to send him home. 'I was tempted to go but was anxious to know the cause of my trouble,' he wrote. Locked in the hospital bathroom, he consoled himself by secretly jogging up and down on the spot. There were just two months to go before that 100-mile track race, and no doctor on earth would keep him away.

Everyone – friends and medical staff – was astonished at how quickly Tarrant bounced back and how soon the sense of panic dissipated. 'I'd been to see him and he was concerned but not scared,' remembers Dave Box. 'I ran ten years and did seven Comrades and periodically I pissed blood, but when they looked into it they couldn't find anything. Those things happened in athletics. The doctor seemed to think he'd torn something in his stomach and it didn't come on again – not then, anyway.'

After three days, Tarrant was discharged. His blood count remained low, but the various tests had revealed no underlying menace, and a regime of iron tablets and rest was prescribed for his recovery. Satisfied that he had nothing more than an ulcer, Tarrant's spirits soared, and within three weeks of the bleed he was back at work on his forklift. Shortly after that, he was running 150 miles a week, confident that those terrifying hours alone in his hostel room would never be repeated.

By the end of September, Tarrant – for once – was ready to go. He almost certainly knew he would never be coming back. Travelling out to the airport past verges ablaze with hibiscus, he was leaving South Africa with the dream which had drawn him there unfulfilled. For so long, the Comrades had been the beginning, middle and end of everything, and he had fallen short four times. He'd miss Dave Box, and the docks and the weather, but next year he'd be 40, and the cloud of illness had brought a belated sense of perspective. A few weeks before, he'd written movingly to Edie, his words haunted by a sentimental mixture of pride and regret:

> In my travels around the world, I have not met anyone who compares with you. Neither am I interested in doing so. I am quite happy with my lot. A wife who is faithful, honest and true. Yes, a wife in millions . . . My trips to South Africa have not been in vain . . . perhaps I did not win the Comrades, but many black people are grateful to me [and] it must never be forgotten that the organisers of this race [the Goldtop] are the only body of people outside the United Kingdom to have the moral fibre to accept my entry officially . . . Black people striving for justice for a white man. It makes one think. Thank you darling once again for all you have done for me over the years.

On 7 October 1971, Tarrant boarded the plane for London Heathrow. In his own modest and unspectacular way, he was leaving people he'd helped change forever. 'Thanks to John's early endeavours, bit by bit, inch by inch, we moved towards transformation,' claims Rajendra Chetty.

'I idolised him,' says Dave Upfold. 'He got up and he made things happen. Whatever the odds against him, he still took things on. He taught me these things. If there are obstacles in the road, don't throw in the towel. Maybe it was subconscious with John, but it stuck. "You can do it," he said, and I did.'

Five minutes after take-off, the plane tilted over the city, the ocean blinked and Durban was gone.

Chapter Ten

The Greatest Race

1971

As a boy at the Lamorbey children's home, Tarrant had once fallen from a tree and impaled his hand on a spiked iron railing. Rather than cry out and risk a beating, he'd kept silent for weeks while the wound slowly healed. 'Always the unlucky one,' says Victor ruefully. In the days which followed his return to England, Tarrant was once again stifling the ominous signals which his body was sending him. It was an act of self-denial which would prove impossible to sustain. Only Edie and Vic had been told about his traumatic collapse in Durban. Soon it would be publicly apparent to everyone that something was seriously wrong.

Since the haemorrhage, Tarrant's superhuman resilience had stood him in good stead. Being naturally hostile to morbid thinking, Tarrant presumed himself fully recovered and hurled himself into training for the 100-mile track race, which was now just two weeks away. Nothing had ever mattered quite so much. No indignity had ever hurt more than the South African ban which had allowed Dave Box to snatch Tarrant's world record unimpeded. But even though Box would not be travelling from Durban to defend his crown, Tarrant was gripped by doubt. During training, he felt lacklustre and lethargic, as if a gear was missing or a spark had been extinguished. Characteristically, he brushed it away. 'I was sure things would work out on the day,' he wrote. 'I did not let it worry me unduly.'

For the first time in years, the old gang were going into action together. Victor drove. Edie and John and Roger squeezed into the car. Travelling down by train from Buxton came Jack and Maysie, and by first light, alongside the Uxbridge Sports Centre track, a shivering crowd had gathered to watch the proceedings. With less than a minute to go, however, there was no sign of John Tarrant. Locked in the stadium's public toilet, he was undergoing a crisis of confidence of such magnitude that it seemed unlikely he would run. In his memoir, he recalled:

> In the toilet I tried to instil in myself the importance of the race . . . why I had more incentive than any other runner to win . . . I thought of my family . . . They would be there to support me for 12 hours and longer if necessary . . . I promised to myself to give my all . . . and made my way to the start with only seconds to go.

John had kept his secret well. After ten miles out on the track, he could no longer hide it. The trademark front-running had disappeared. The perpetually pumping, rolling gait which for two decades had ground down all forms of human resistance had gone. Tarrant wasn't running, he was wallowing like a stricken ship, and after twenty miles he'd fallen six minutes behind the leading pack.

Ahead of him he could see Ron Bentley – stocky like Box in his hooped vest – running alongside his older brother Gordon. Side by side, as always, the notorious Bentley brothers, two hard-living, hard-running Midlanders who'd recently taken long-distance running by storm. Their father had been a professional road-runner, and his bedtime yarns about the sport had persuaded both to follow in his footsteps. Together, they'd turned the Tipton Harriers into the Manchester United of the asphalt, without ever surrendering their working man's sense of perspective. Alcohol had always been, and remained, an integral part of their training. 'It's what you did,' explains Ron. 'The night before I won the Exeter-to-Plymouth, I had three pints of Whitbread and steak and chips at a Berni Inn.' The night before this latest excursion, the two brothers had done the same.

It wasn't the first time Tarrant had found himself circling a track with Ron Bentley. Exactly two years before, when Tarrant had set his 100-mile world record, the straight-talking Tipton Harrier had been 'press-ganged' into making up the numbers. 'I'd never run more than 30 miles before. I was saving up to buy a house, working hard, and I hadn't been training properly,' he says.

Ron hadn't made it to the end that day – 'my feet had gone' – but his brother Gordon had somehow kept on going, finishing in fourth place two shattering hours after Tarrant, who had by then rested, showered and changed. It had been a lesson from a master the brothers wouldn't forget. 'I wasn't ready for that first 100-mile run,' admits Ron, 'but I was ready for the second one.'

For months, he'd been clocking up 120 miles a week, running four hours solid on Saturdays and five hours the morning after. If the Tipton Harriers clubhouse was locked when he got back, four pints of beer (and three bottles of lemonade) would be waiting for him in a bucket by the back door.

Plodding along in their slipstream, Tarrant must have sniffed the Bentley brothers' renewed sense of purpose. Never had he felt so disinclined to respond. After 30 miles of 'sheer hell', every lap had become a torture, and but for the constant exhortations of Victor and Edie, he'd have slid away and vanished. 'I kept saying one more mile and if I don't improve I'll drop out . . . I was flogging my body unmercifully to get on terms.' During the 59th mile, he'd had enough. His previous four laps had taken eighteen excruciating minutes. The weary trudge turned into a walk and finally he slumped to a complete standstill.

As Victor and Jack pummelled his legs and argued fiercely that he should continue, Tarrant lashed back bitterly – 'A mental lapse,' he admitted. 'I lost control of myself.' After 11 furiously tense minutes – and a quinine sulphate tablet from the track doctor – Victor's remonstrations broke through. 'He was raging at himself, not us,' he says.

All around John, others were struggling too. If he could somehow gather himself, he could still win the race. Restored to the track, his first lap took almost three minutes – barely walking speed – but the next one was down to two. Tarrant was beginning to feel better. The 17 minutes between him and Ron Bentley was a daunting gap, but there were still 40 miles to run. Yard by yard, lap by tedious lap, Tarrant pulled himself together and the race was on.

'I'd seen him leave the track,' says Bentley, 'but when he came back, he was flying. I just couldn't believe the way he was running. One minute he'd been dying and the next he was lapping me and I was starting to lose my confidence.' After seventy miles Tarrant was up to second place and the gap was down to fourteen minutes. Ten miles later, Bentley's advantage had shrunk to thirteen minutes. At ninety mind-numbing miles, it had shrivelled to six. Finally, at around ninety-five miles, Tarrant had hauled himself to within two laps of the leader. From dawn to dusk – for eleven appalling hours – he'd floundered hopelessly behind the metronomic Ron Bentley. At last, as darkness hunched around them, he'd run his rival down.

Everyone left inside the stadium pressed to the edge of the track, hypnotised by what they were witnessing. Timekeepers, stewards, family members, journalists – even the ladies of the Uxbridge Athletics Club whose '100 Miler' fruitcake was awaiting the eventual winner – everyone still awake had been sucked towards the final moments of the duel.

'It was Tarrant's greatest race,' reckons race organiser Eddie Gutteridge, who stood hoarse-voiced, on the point of tears, as the two men battled towards the finish. 'He was in absolute bits. Mortally ill, as we now know. God knows how he did it. Christ, it moved you to be there, because he was not physically capable and yet his mental approach was magnificent. I was yelling, "You can do it! You can do it!" But he couldn't. And yet the effort he poured in. Extraordinary.'

Tarrant's defiant last-gasp heroics wouldn't quite be enough. Inspired by the sulphurous proximity of the ghost, Bentley had summoned one last prodigious kick and broken his charge. Utterly spent, and incapable of response, John could only watch as Bentley flew away. Tarrant knew what he'd be feeling. Victory was the ultimate anaesthetic. Defeat could age a man where he stood. When he finally hobbled across the line in second place, Bentley's winning margin had swollen back up to 14 minutes, but his time of 12 hours and 51 minutes left Tarrant's UK record intact. It was a mercy but only a very small one.

Even in his pomp, Tarrant's wretched condition after a race could shock people. Bernard Gomersall remembers seeing him with blue lips and froth around his mouth. 'He'd always give 110 per cent. You'd never have been surprised to see him carted off in an ambulance.' Now, as Ron Bentley and third-placed Gordon headed for the pub, Tarrant sat swaddled in blankets, scarcely capable of speech.

'I knew he was very ill, but there was nothing we could do,' says Ron.

'He was in one hell of a state,' remembers Eddie Gutteridge.

Slowly, as people drifted away, Victor helped John to his car, and the Tarrants began their silent journey home.

For two weeks, John was too crippled to run. Never had his recovery rate been so depressingly slow. By the New Year, his ordeal forgotten, he was training hard and looking forward to racing as a veteran. On 4 February 1972, he would be 40, and the prospect of new competitive horizons lifted his jaded spirits. Two weeks after his birthday, he'd helped his old club Salford Harriers win the national veterans' cross-country title. At Cannock Chase, over 21 miles, he'd finished 19th – 2 minutes ahead of Ron Bentley – claiming the prize for the fastest runner over 40.

Suddenly, he was dreaming again. Perhaps the international ban might not apply now he was a veteran. Perhaps as a veteran the ghost runner might yet turn out for England. By April, he was running 100 miles a week and brimming with the old confidence, quietly certain that his health issues were behind him. During the Easter weekend, however, two races in two days would bring him crashing down to earth. In a ten-mile race at Newport, he fared disastrously – a lifetime worst at the distance – and on Easter Monday in Pencoed he was barely able to complete what should have been a four-mile stroll. More puzzled than scared, Tarrant eased back on his miles, expecting the storm to soon pass.

In the middle of the night on 7 April, as Edie slept, Tarrant staggered to the bathroom of his council flat and suffered his second massive haemorrhage.

As in Durban, Tarrant threw up horrifying quantities of blood. Trying to get back to his bedroom, he collapsed and disturbed

Edie, who wanted to summon a doctor immediately. It was typical of her husband that he should say no. Doctors needed their sleep too. He'd lived through this alone in South Africa, he insisted. He could survive for a few more hours now without causing a fuss.

The following morning, Tarrant's condition had not improved. Refusing a stretcher, he stumbled weakly to an ambulance, and at the local hospital – despite his initial protestations – he was given an emergency four-pint transfusion of blood. It was clearly serious, but, not for the first time, no one seemed sure what was wrong. After a week of tests, including X-rays and barium meals, Tarrant was discharged under the '99 per cent certain' impression that the problem was still an ulcer. Pleased with that diagnosis, he resumed training the same day – to Edie's disgust – and two weeks later he was back up to his constitutional bare minimum of 100 miles per week.

Being in hospital had been insufferable, but Tarrant had not been entirely idle. For several months, he'd been painstakingly jotting down an account of his life. From his hospital bed, he wrote to his old ally at the *Daily Mirror*, Peter Wilson, asking for advice. Wilson replied warmly:

> I'm quite sure there's a book in your career, but without trying to teach you your business I wonder if you should think of slowing down a bit now. You have proved your point. You are one of the greatest super-long-distance runners of our time [but] I'm afraid you will never be accepted as long as the "old guard" hold sway.

It was the sort of flattery Tarrant loved to hear, but Wilson couldn't help. He too had health issues, and he was hoping to retire to Majorca. The ghost would have to manage without a ghostwriter.

It's interesting to speculate as to why Tarrant decided to write his memoir at this time. He and Edie had never discussed how serious his illness might be, and his remarkable capacity to bounce back seemed to confirm what he badly needed to believe: that nothing serious was amiss. Privately, however, Tarrant had grave doubts which he would never openly disclose. Much later – in a letter to Dave Box – he talked about 'subconsciously knowing' his situation was 'a serious one'. If he didn't write it down himself now, his version of events might never be recorded. Being penniless wasn't an insignificant factor either, and nor was his vanity.

For some years, Tarrant's letters had often referred to himself in the third person; as 'the ghost runner' and not simply as 'I'. ('I can assure you, Reg, the ghost runner will be around for some time yet.') The previous year, from Durban, he'd written to Victor asking him to contact the organisers of a 33-mile race in Rhodesia. 'Tell them about the "Ghost Runner". I think this will set the stage for me,' he'd said. 'Enclose a sheet with my record on it, and write on your special notepaper.'

The way he saw it, the ghost runner wasn't simply a person. He – John Tarrant – was the living embodiment of a cause. The ghost was his alter ego, his weapon and his disguise. In Durban, everyone had groaned when he produced his faded cuttings. Yesterday's news. Just like all of his records. But Tarrant passionately believed that the ghost should never be forgotten and that his story wouldn't be simply the record of a life but a morality tale which every other sportsperson should heed.

For 20 years, he'd been kicking against the double standards of a sport which had always kicked him harder. Even with nothing left to gain, that was still a cause worth fighting for. What had happened to him should never happen again, and no one should ever flinch from the truth of it. To let it drop was inconceivable, and yet already he knew the myth was fading. Yesterday's news. No one was watching him any more.

Fleet Street had lost interest and the Alf Tupper generation was hanging up its running shoes. Gomersall, Keily, the lot of them. All fading away. Only a book would fill that gap – protect his legend, assuage his brittle ego and ensure that the ghost runner was around 'for some time yet'. He'd always loved to write. Someone would surely want to publish it. With a bit of luck, it might even make a bob or two. And while he had his pen out, he'd drop a line to Arthur Gold at the BAAB. Maybe as a veteran he could finally run overseas with a number on his vest. Nothing was ever lost for the price of a stamp.

As summer ripened the Herefordshire countryside, Tarrant battled gamely on, rarely winning races but never losing hope. Although he always performed creditably, the old habit of winning appeared lost. Mostly these days he'd trot in second or third, blaming the heat or the unfamiliarity of the shorter distances – never the pains in his stomach or the tablets he was taking to counteract a suspected bleeding ulcer.

Three months after leaving hospital, he even felt well enough to put his name down for the London-to-Brighton race in the autumn. It was important to be busy. It helped stave off regrets, and there were still plenty of those. Arthur Gold had quickly squashed his hope of running in international veterans' meetings. 'Nice to hear from you,' he'd written. 'Reinstated domestic amateurs are not eligible to compete.' Another door closed.

From Durban, he'd recently heard that one of his few remaining records had fallen. An 18-year-old Indian boy had won the third Goldtop, lopping five minutes off Tarrant's best time. 'Because of you, there's no stopping us,' Chetty wrote to his friend. 'We have discovered several outstanding [non-white] athletes . . . I only hope it would be possible to have you back with us.'

That would not be happening. In late August, Tarrant was called back into hospital for more tests. Never the easiest of patients, he was plainly furious to have had his training plans disrupted less than two weeks before his comeback in the London-to-Brighton. As doctors subjected him to another barrage of probes, Tarrant and his brother concocted a ruse to subvert his enforced horizontal idleness. During evening visiting hour, while the nursing staff were distracted, Tarrant ghosted out of the building wearing his running kit under a dressing gown.

Waiting for him at the wheel of his car – its engine already running – was Victor, and together they'd run five miles in a local park before the patient slipped back onto the ward undetected. It was like the glory days all over again; the old double act was back in business. John remembered:

> On one occasion I'd been back a few minutes when the nurse called to take my pulse. She was very concerned that it was registering 85 beats to the minute instead of my normal 45 to 50. I assured her that my visitors had excited me a great deal.

Tarrant's frustrations were understandable. After four days of intense scrutiny, the diagnosis had progressed no further than an ulcer, and, seen through a lens, his stomach appeared to be healing. There seemed no possible reason to keep him in bed. But Tarrant's apparent insouciance was not shared by that of his medical team, who remained puzzled by the mismatch between cause and effect. The catastrophic symptoms he'd experienced seemed at odds with what they were seeing, and Tarrant was urged to undergo an immediate exploratory operation to end the mystery surrounding his condition.

It was a delicate moment. Surgery would give him the answers – but it would also rule him out of competitive running for weeks. Pressing his specialist on the consequences of delay, Tarrant was reassured that there wouldn't be any. A month or two's wait for a bed wouldn't be a problem. 'The specialist's parting words were, "I am certain you have not got cancer; if I thought you had I would not hesitate to go straight ahead with the operation." I breathed a sigh of relief.'

In the event, it would be 15 months before Tarrant finally went under the knife, and by then it was too late. His special pleading had secured him the time to run. It may also have cost him his life.

Tarrant's 'sigh of relief' was revealing. Slipped in among the medical platitudes, the C-word had been uttered for the first time. He wasn't stupid. Cancer was something he'd always feared. Now every step he took would be a step away from that possibility. Only in motion had Tarrant ever felt fully alive, and even in full health he had absolutely nothing in his life without running. Release from the prospect of surgery – and the knowledge of what it might find – brought a sudden, fresh and tragic intensity to his time, as if to stop once might be to stop forever.

The day after postponing his operation, he ran 26 miles, feeling a 'power and strength I'd seldom experienced before'. A week later, he joined the start of the London-to-Brighton at Westminster Bridge, running purposefully in warm sunshine until his 'wretched trouble' drove him from the road four times before he dropped out completely, twelve miles short of Brighton.

For the next few months, his form – and his spirits – swerved violently between hope and despair. One moment he was winning a 10,000-metre track event and the next he was crawling to a finish in a 50-mile race, 12 lb lighter than when he'd started. For a man with a supposedly healing ulcer, it was mystifying. No pattern seemed discernible. And yet by spring 1973, after a string of low-key victories, local journalists had begun to twitter about the ghost runner's 'amazing' comeback. Suddenly, he was openly plotting a bash at the epic 24-hour track record in November. If he could somehow run 160 miles in 24 hours, the record would be his. Even now, he felt sure he could do it. But it was not to be. On 30 September, in Cardiff, he took the veterans' prize in a 15-mile road race with a sparkling average of 5.5 minutes per mile. It was the last competitive race the ghost ever ran.

Hidden behind his resistance, Tarrant's health was in freefall. Privately, he almost certainly knew why. Surely there had never been such a recalcitrant ulcer. Since the summer, he'd lost almost 18 lb in body weight. Despite his exertions, both his appetite and his thirst seemed to be tailing away. There were frequent pains in his stomach and violent spells of vomiting, and when he could summon the energy to run, he could cover 30 miles without breaking sweat. 'Strange things were now happening to me,' he wrote. Whatever hyperbole the papers gushed, Tarrant was acutely aware that his recent successes had come at shorter and shorter distances and that his world was fast closing in. With scarcely a week to go, he withdrew his entry from the 24-hour race and resigned himself to the revelations of surgery. Almost immediately, his condition worsened.

On 11 November – Armistice Day – Tarrant was admitted to Hereford County Hospital. The same day, he wrote warmly to his father, ruefully pointing out that Ron Bentley had just beaten the 24-hour record in the event he'd pulled out of, running 161 miles and 545 yards. 'Perhaps my turn will come in the future,' he pondered, adding, 'I never have any luck on the football pools. Do you still do them, dad? It's the working man's only hope of making a fortune. Edie won a couple of quid at bingo the other night . . . All our love.'

There was no mention in the letter of his deteriorating condition or of the fact that 48 hours later he'd be operated on. 'We are all OK here in Hereford and hope the same goes for you in Buxton.' It wouldn't do to worry his old dad too much until he had all the answers. 'He was always looking ahead,' remembers Victor. 'That's what got him through just about everything.'

Another five agonising days would pass before Tarrant's specialist shared his findings – or some of them – with his patient. They had found no ulcer. Instead, they had discovered a stomach ravaged beyond the point of repair by chronic gastritis. Tarrant's only hope was to permit the complete removal of his stomach, followed by the construction of a new digestive tract using sections of healthy bowel. 'You could run again,' he was told, 'although I doubt you could reach your former ability.' The word 'cancer' was not mentioned.

It was a devastating diagnosis, but Tarrant was unconvinced. Immediately looking up gastritis in a 'health book', he found nothing which necessitated such draconian remedies, and when Edie and Vic visited that evening, he insisted that a change of diet – or a cocktail of alternative remedies – would eliminate his problem.

Ever since his days as a council plumber, when he'd rejected Maysie's formidable packed lunches, Tarrant had taken care of his body. He didn't smoke, he didn't drink, he preferred his food grilled not fried and white bread had been eschewed in favour of brown. Besides, his recent performances surely couldn't have been possible if things were as bad as the doctors were saying. Forcefully, he told his wife and brother that he would not permit his stomach to be removed. With equal insistence, they told him that it should. 'At least I have one thing to be grateful for,' John told Edie as visiting time ended. 'I've not got cancer.'

'"Of course not, John," she said without a bat of an eyelid,' as John remembered.

By the following night, Tarrant's intransigence had soured into anger. He was right. The specialists were wrong. There were natural alternatives he would try before anyone carved him open. When Vic and Edie arrived to see him, his bags were packed and he demanded that they drive him home to Charlton Avenue immediately. Once again, Edie held strong to her position. 'It's your only hope,' she told him, ominously, but in the furious row which broke out between the three of them, Tarrant could still not be shifted. Either they took him home or he would walk out of the hospital in his dressing gown.

For 40 years, Victor had been his brother's rock. Big Tarrant. Little Tarrant. Always ready with a lift or a couple of quid when money was tight. Forever ago, he'd ridden his motorbike at stewards to keep John in a race; he'd made and sold chocolate eggs to get him to South Africa; he'd written countless letters begging for John to be reinstated; and he'd counted the seconds during the long, dreary nights of those world records. 'I had never married and if anything our friendship had deepened over the years,' says Victor. Now it would fall to the younger brother to tell Big Tarrant why he wouldn't be going home that night. It wasn't gastritis the surgeons wanted to exorcise; it was cancer.

Vic broke the news to me ever so gently in the way that only Vic could be capable of doing. I know of no one who

could be more kind or sympathetic at a time like this . . .
For a moment I sat there in shocked silence, and then I just
broke down and cried. Edith sat down beside me on the
bed and she was also in tears. To give us privacy, Vic drew
the curtains around the bed and left us to it . . . [they] had
known for more than a week.

'I wouldn't have told him, but he was ready to get his kit on
and go running,' explains Vic. 'He said it was only a slight pain
but that was all. So I had to tell him. It was a terrible thing,
because he knew that was the end of his running.'

'When he heard what it was, he seemed to immediately lose
something,' thinks Edie. 'He hated that word "cancer". But
inside he always knew, I think. He was many things, but daft
wasn't one of them.'

Tarrant had often thought himself forgotten. As word of his
illness spread, he discovered how wrong he had been. Letters
were arriving every day on the Nell Gwyn ward, and every
day Tarrant's handwritten replies flowed back out. From South
Africa and the United States came words of encouragement
from people he knew and others he scarcely remembered.
Complete strangers who'd followed his battles for years wanted
him to know how his resistance had inspired them.

A contingent of Fleet Street's finest sportswriters put their
signatures to a letter urging a speedy recovery, among them
Roy Moor, the first true champion he'd ever had. The father of
Olympic medallist Lillian Board – who'd died suddenly two
years before – had a message of encouragement. From the
Durban YMCA, where he'd briefly holed up before his
Comrades debut, came words of unequivocal admiration:

We have unfortunately too many cowards and opportunists

> . . . men without honour . . . and it is in this regard that I
> would like to say that you stand head and shoulders above
> most of your fellow human beings and peers as a veritable
> Mars at Perihelion.

As the letters poured in – and as he worked furiously on his memoir – Tarrant seems to have adjusted quickly to his situation. 'It didn't bother me so much now that I knew what was wrong [but] I did so much want to live.'

He'd never dwelled for long on his defeats before. The next race had always been the most important one. Somehow, this illness felt the same. Every day, there were visits from Edie and Vic to look forward to, and Ned Waring, his steadfast benefactor, was a regular bedside companion. 'If only I could change places with you, John, I would,' he apparently told his ailing friend.

On 28 November – the day before an operation he'd been warned carried a high risk – Tarrant wrote movingly to Edie, Victor and Roger. To his wife, he said: 'When I feel like giving up the fight I will think of Darling Edie, the greatest prize in life I ever won. Honestly.' To Roger: 'Take care of Mum until I get home . . . take care of yourself and good running in the future.' And to Victor, the most emotionally raw tribute of them all: 'You are almost too good for this world but thank God you are my brother . . . Thank you for all your generous actions. The rest is up to me.'

That evening, Vic and Edie joined him at the hospital, but John mentioned nothing about the letters he'd posted. They watched *Some Mothers Do 'Ave 'Em* ('really funny,' wrote John, 'Michael Crawford had us all in stitches') until it was time for them to go. After declining the nurse's offer of a sedative, Tarrant 'slept like a log' until 9 a.m., when he was wheeled into theatre to have his stomach removed.

As the surgeons worked, his letter reached Edie, and she in

turn penned a reply to be read by her husband when he came round later that afternoon:

> If only I could go through the operation for you I would so gladly do so . . . I have prayed day and night for you my darling . . . you will pull through because you have the fighting spirit in you . . . you are indeed a very plucky man . . . all our devoted love always – love from Edie, Vic and Roger.

Later that afternoon, Tarrant was told that the five-hour operation had gone well – and that his astounding physical condition had played a part in his reaction. 'Your heart and lungs are in magnificent shape,' he was told by his surgeon. 'My job would be a lot easier if everyone took the care of their body that you have obviously done.'

Writing to Dave Box in South Africa, Edie revealed, 'The doctors are amazed at his recovery rate . . . he is being very plucky and fighting hard.' But Tarrant's body was literally no longer what it was. In place of his stomach, he had a surgically reconstituted stretch of his own gut, held together by 200 stitches. After a month in hospital, he was painfully delicate and – to the friends who poured in to see him – almost unrecognisably drawn.

Ron Bentley was among the first visitors – fresh from his triumph in the 24-hour race Tarrant had so desperately wanted to run. 'As soon as he saw me on the ward,' he says, 'he started cheering and telling everyone around him that I was a world-beater. He looked terrible, though, skeletal and thin, and although he never once mentioned the illness, one of the nurses told me he was refusing to take painkillers. This was the last time I ever saw him.'

Just as they had before the operation, letters continued to

stream in to Tarrant's ward, letters which reached deep into his past. From Tom Osler – who'd loaned him a woolly hat on that freezing New York morning – came speculation that 'God has selected this setback in order to spur you on to greater challenges'. From Alan Phillips – his great rival over 40 miles – the touching revelation that the ghost's 'invincible spirit' had been a lifelong inspiration.

And from Rajendra Chetty in Durban – wretched that his friend was so ill – came news that lifted the ailing runner's heart: 'Things are slowly beginning to change for the good in South Africa. It looks like non-racial sport will soon be here.'

Sixteen days after his operation – just in time for Christmas – Tarrant was allowed home. Refusing a wheelchair, he walked from the ambulance to his front door, tightly gripping the banister to inch step by step up to the sanctuary of the council flat above. Over the coming days, he adjusted slowly to the indignity of his newly foreshortened horizons. Instead of three main meals, his tiny stomach now required feeding every couple of hours.

Eating, not exercise, became the governing priority of his days. Too much food, or too little, would cause intense discomfort and pain. 'It is not necessary (thank God) to take any drugs,' he told Dave Box, in a long and revealing letter. 'On the night before my operation I got on my hands and knees and said a prayer. I felt a right hypocrite . . . however, Dave, I am sure it helped. I got a feeling of confidence it would be all right.' Thanking Box for a card signed by dozens of Durban athletes, he added, 'I honestly never realised so many people were concerned about "the ghost runner" and it makes me feel very humble indeed.'

Tarrant's health wasn't the only thing weighing on his mind. Since returning from South Africa, he'd earned very little money. For a few months – thanks to Victor – he'd worked as a labourer on a local army base, but his sick pay had run out, and there was no prospect of his doing hard physical labour ever again. With no savings, and with Edie needing to nurse her sick husband, the couple were broke.

Tarrant's desperate efforts to sell his life story to a national newspaper had fallen on deaf ears. 'Not enough sex or scandal to interest the general public,' he complained to a friend. When he felt strong enough, he battled on with his handwritten memoir, but with no publisher in sight, it seemed unlikely that his story would ever see the light of day. Up till now – again, thanks to Victor – he and Edie had survived countless financial crises, but this one seemed hopeless. And they would not escape it without help.

At first glance, Chris Brasher seemed an unlikely saviour. Educated at Rugby School and Cambridge, Brasher (with other Oxbridge graduates) had helped pace Roger Bannister to the first four-minute mile in 1954. He'd won gold at the 1956 Melbourne Olympics and seemed born of that same gilded stock as Crump, Gold, Abrahams and all the others who'd thwarted Tarrant's life whilst living charmed ones of their own. But Brasher was different. Brasher's was a restless, maverick soul driven by gargantuan self-belief and what his obituary in *The Times* would call 'a near-fanatical devotion to the outdoor life'.

After his running career was over, he'd emerged as one of Britain's finest sportswriters, distinguishing *The Observer* with columns of shrewd wit and campaigning humanity. For some years, he'd been exchanging infrequent – but heartfelt – letters with Tarrant, a man whose story had genuinely angered and moved him. In 1969, when John had been contemplating a sponsored coast-to-coast run across the United States, it had been Brasher who had warned Tarrant against the lure of easy money: 'It must be tempting for someone unemployed like yourself but . . . you might come out with a few hundred pounds . . . in exchange for entirely losing your amateur status.'

On Brasher's advice, Tarrant had shelved those plans, but the landscape was sadly different now. After five years of decline, he no longer gave a damn about his amateur status. Money was what Tarrant needed, and the only commodity he could trade was his life story. Once again, he turned to his new ally in Fleet Street for help. Unaided, he'd got nowhere, but Brasher knew people. Brasher had leverage. Before leaving the Nell Gwyn ward, Tarrant had called him up and explained the predicament he was in. A few days later, Brasher rang back saying he'd secured a £400 fee from the *Sunday People* for an exclusive on the saga of the ghost runner. It was the largest sum of money Tarrant had ever seen in his life.

> The money helped settle some hire purchase debts on my furniture and put a few quid aside for a rainy day. Life can be rather a struggle when you have only the State to depend on for a living. My total income for Edith and I to live on is little more than £20 [a week]. It's a good job neither of us smokes or drinks.

Shortly after leaving hospital, Tarrant contacted Brasher again. The manuscript he'd been patching together was making progress, but he badly needed an outsider's honest appraisal. Everyone who'd been to his bedside knew he'd been writing it. His old friend from the TA running team Derek Davies had turned up at Charlton Avenue to find 'John's bedspread covered with stuff for the book and *Athletics Weekly* results on the brain'. One of his cousins had been drafted in to turn his notes into a presentable, typewritten document. Unless Brasher could help, Tarrant hadn't a clue what he'd do with it. In early June, he got his reply. His new mentor was effusive.

'I read it through at one sitting and very much enjoyed it,' enthused Brasher, adding the caveat that Tarrant needed to reveal more of his inner self. 'A straight story about who won a race in what time is not nearly so interesting as a story about your feelings and emotions as an athlete and a family man.' It was a big ask. Until his illness, Tarrant had rarely indulged in prolonged introspection and felt awkward putting his deepest thoughts into words. The early loss of his mother had rocked him badly, but he couldn't explain why and felt certain no one would be interested. Victor was better at all that stuff.

The story he wanted to tell – and which he hoped would earn him some money – concerned the ghost runner and his lifetime of humiliations. What he needed from Brasher was an outlet for his clumsy literary endeavours, however deficient they might be in emotional intelligence. 'A publisher?' said Brasher. 'I am pretty convinced that I can find you a publisher . . . Let's talk again when you have got further . . . very, very glad to hear that your health continues to improve. Don't overdo the training.'

Brasher's parting advice was well judged. Tarrant had proved incapable of sitting still. Watching the Commonwealth Games on Victor's colour telly was fine, but not for long. Less than two months after his operation, he saw his specialist and secured medical clearance to start light training for a sponsored ten-mile run. That night, he set to work on Edie with the same persuasive tenacity which had overcome her resistance to his first illegal marathon almost two decades before.

Ten minutes later, under cover of darkness, he was slipping out onto Charlton Avenue in his tracksuit to totter through the excruciating pain of a mile run in eleven long minutes, his muscles jellied from months of idleness, his ribs still raw from the gravity of the surgery he'd endured. 'It was a wonderful feeling inside to be running again,' he wrote. But it would still be three days before he felt strong enough to give it another try.

For three weeks, he persevered, adding an extra half-mile at every outing, the effort so profound that he chose to run at night under the street lights, hoping no one would see how frail he'd become. Nothing he ate seemed to build up his weight. If anything, it was still falling away. And yet within a month he was running 10 miles in 90 minutes and felt sufficiently confident to announce that the ghost runner was back – albeit a shadow of his former self – and hoping to raise money for the hospital which had extended his life, not in a race or a record attempt but in a charity run before Hereford FC kicked off their last home game of the season in April. If Tarrant could hold it together, he'd complete ten miles around the perimeter of the pitch. Everyone close to him knew it might be the last time he ever ran in public. Everyone in the ground that day would remain haunted by what they saw.

As the crowd trickled in and the terraces began to fill, Tarrant started his run, wearing a long-sleeved Salford Harriers vest and with his hands gloved against poor circulation. Never before had he looked so mortal, his deep-set eyes black with concentration and his colourless face furrowed by illness. To begin with, as if propelled by memory, his pitifully thin frame moved cautiously around the touchline of the heavy Hereford pitch. But slowly, some chemically stupefied, dormant instinct stirred.

At home, he'd been spending hours climbing the 14 steps to his flat – sometimes 300 times a day. Anything to protect himself from humiliation. Now, as the spectators swelled, and as Victor encouraged him on, shards of the old John Tarrant began to bleed through, the pace swiftening, the strides lengthening and those insistent, trusty lines bouncing around inside his head. 'If you think you're beaten, you are.'

Alongside him on the run, even Tarrant's son Roger was astounded by what he was seeing. 'You can see me in the photographs struggling to keep up,' he says. 'Despite everything, he was really running hard and well.' After an hour, and with just a few laps to go, the crowd had risen to 7,000 and even those who knew nothing of Tarrant's story felt moved enough to join the rising ovation. By the end, he'd run the 10 miles in 75 minutes – 15 minutes faster than he'd hoped. There was life in the ghost runner yet, but it was ebbing away fast.

'I now know I can never run again,' he told the local paper. 'It is a bitter pill to swallow.'

For almost 20 years, John had been fuelled by anger. Inevitably, in the final months of his life, the furies were abating. So long as he could run, there had always been a chance of official redemption, but throughout the second half of 1974, Tarrant's condition slowly worsened – a decline he mostly bore with his familiar stoical forbearance. If it seemed terribly unfair that a life of abstinence should have left his body so shattered, then Tarrant rarely said so. 'I am going through a bad patch at the moment,' he confessed to Dave Box in a letter to Durban, 'losing a lot of weight and vomiting after eating.'

By September, Tarrant weighed just 8 st. 7 lb and had gone weeks without running. Confined to bed or slumped in an easy chair, he consoled himself by corresponding with the many friends who clamoured for better news. 'I can virtually feel my body degenerating,' he told his son Roger. 'How I hate being unfit.'

On television, he watched Ali fight Foreman ('an anti-climax'), and in his search for a reprieve he developed a distracting obsession with the properties of natural foods. Vegetarians, he explained to sceptical visitors, seldom contract cancer. Encouraged by the story of a man who'd earned remission after eating 5lb of grapes a day, Tarrant had experimented with a grapes-only diet but struggled to meet the target, writing to Roger:

> I am barely eating 1lb a day. That's 28lb per month compared with 130lb the man in Africa was getting through. For this reason I will soon be coming off the 'cure' because I might be endangering my health by not eating enough.

Using his cash from the *Sunday People*, he was also paying £8 a time for futile 'herbal injections' administered by a local 'doctor'. 'More than worth it if I can sit down to eat a meal without being sick,' he explained.

There were other reasons for Tarrant's belated quest for salvation through natural remedies. As winter loomed – always his least favourite season – and his health deteriorated, relations between the patient and the proponents of conventional medicine were becoming strained. His diary had already noted, with carefully suppressed irritation, the two years in which cancer had been misdiagnosed as an ulcer, and by October the ongoing shroud of medical silence was clearly straining his patience. 'Everyone at the hospital treated me with great reverence and respect . . . it's a much better atmosphere than being at one another's throats,' he told Roger, adding the fatherly postscript 'Please buy a raincoat'.

Precisely what had provoked his ire is unknown, but by this time Tarrant's spartan resilience was at breaking point. A blockage in his 'stomach' was preventing digestion, causing acid to back up into his throat and mouth. Living on a diet of raw eggs and soup (fortified by melted cheese), Tarrant could still boast a pulse rate of 50 beats per minute – and his X-rays showed no apparent cancer – but at night, he told Roger, he lay 'dreaming about food' and the ongoing bafflement of his doctors was infuriating.

In mid-October, Victor gave him a lift to Cardiff to hand out the winners' trophies after a 15-mile road race. He was capable of little more. Two weeks later, he was a patient on Ward West 3 at the Queen Elizabeth Hospital in Birmingham. 'Down to 8.5 stone,' he wrote to Box. 'It is a grim situation and I will be glad when I know something positive.'

By December, Tarrant had resigned himself to spending Christmas in a hospital bed attached to a drip. As his weight dropped towards seven stone, letter-writing had become virtually impossible and work on his memoir had ground to a halt. Latterly, it had become more of a goodbye letter anyway, fitfully illuminated by weak glimpses of his old optimism. 'I often wonder what the future holds in store for me,' ran its final sentences. 'In spite of extensive tests my "new" stomach is rejecting all food . . . This has stopped me running for the moment, but I still nurse an ambition to be reasonably fit again . . .' Of his final excursion to present trophies, he added, 'It's nice to know that the athletic world has not forgotten the "ghost" runner.'

Fearful of the worst, Roger had been given a compassionate posting at the navy careers office in nearby Worcester, and four times a week two other people made the 112-mile round trip together from Hereford to be at Tarrant's bedside. Almost every night, Victor and Edie would battle to keep John alert, planning their next adventures, just as they had always done. The old triumvirate. Dreaming up schemes and headlines. A charity run from John O'Groats to Land's End was mooted. Wouldn't that be a story and a comeback to top them all? The legendary ghost runner – acclaimed and acknowledged at last – pounding the roads of Britain, with his brother and son striding out alongside him.

While Tarrant dozed, Edie chattered, sharing running news and opening the get-well letters which still came through their letter box almost every day. A day or two before Christmas, a recorded package arrived from Dave Box in Durban. It was always good to hear from Box. As Tarrant opened it, a medal fell out and with it a brief letter from the friend he'd grown to love. 'Dear John, ever since I received this I have felt by rights it should have been yours. You earned it John and I'm proud to be able to send it to its rightful owner.'

It was the gold medal Box had been given for finishing fourth in the 1968 Comrades. It was the gold medal Tarrant should have won. Box hadn't finished fourth, Tarrant had. Box had been promoted to fourth after the South African organisers wiped the ghost from their official results. Box had been fifth and Tarrant had been a nuisance. An outlaw. A non-person. Not even worth announcing over the tannoy as he crossed the line. Who were all those people?

Now, simply holding it in his feeble fingers brought it all swimming back. Only the good, though. None of the bad. Too late for that now. Too late to put any of it right. Instead he saw the 'Valley of a Thousand Hills' and heard the roar of the ocean surf, and the laughter of Dave and Adrie's children. And just maybe the beery rumble of a crowd hunched around a boxing ring in Buxton. Such incredible times.

Rolling the medal over – with tears streaming – he found his name freshly engraved on the back. Finally, his own Comrades medal. He'd never known a sporting gesture like it, but then he'd never known anyone quite like Box. 'Edie had told me he was not going to last much longer,' Box says, 'so I had my name erased and replaced with his, and if that was all I could do then that was what had to be done.'

Tarrant replied warmly the same day: 'A fine sporting gesture by a great sportsman. I appreciate the sacrifice you have made on my part. Excuse me for being brief but it's hard to concentrate for too long.'

By early New Year, it was clear that Tarrant's once inexhaustible appetite for a fight had reached its limit. The cancer had returned and there was to be no miraculous surge from the back. On Saturday, 18 January, Edie, Victor and Roger gathered by his hospital bed for one last time together. 'He had great difficulty talking, even whispering,' says Edie, 'but we could grasp some of what he was saying.' Once John's brother and son had returned home, Edie stayed on alone, maintaining her vigil through the night as her husband slipped in and out of wakefulness.

At around 9 a.m. the next day, she took a phone call. It was from Chris Brasher. He had good tidings. A publisher had been found for John's life story, and he prayed it wasn't too late for Tarrant to be told. He was just in time. John was slipping fast, and Edie rushed to his side with the news.

'The nurse said he could hear me but could not give any response or signal. I would love to think and know that he did understand.' Barely an hour after Brasher called, Tarrant gave up the race. He was 42 years old.

No one could catch him now.

Afterword

Writing for *The Observer* two weeks after Tarrant's death, Chris Brasher wrote, 'There are in this world very few utterly honest men. John Tarrant was one of them.' Brasher went on to help found the London Marathon, which in 2010 saw around 37,000 runners complete the course. In Tarrant's first Liverpool Marathon in 1956, fewer than 70 runners were involved.

Just a few months after Tarrant died, the Comrades became a multiracial event, welcoming black South Africans for the first time. In 2010, 13,000 runners took part.

Four years after his death, Tarrant's book was finally published by *Athletics Weekly*.

In 1981, the IAAF conceded that the age of amateurism was over and trust funds were permitted for the first time.

Four years later, Zola Budd – a white South African-born teenager running in a British vest – ran a showpiece long-distance event in London for a reputed sum of £90,000.

In 2006, the IAAF allowed Dwain Chambers – a proven drugs cheat – to return to the international athletics circuit.

In 2008, Rafael Nadal, a multimillionaire tennis professional, won Olympic gold in his sport. By this time, only one Olympic sport remained truly amateur. Ironically, it was boxing.

John's brother Vic went on to become one of Herefordshire county's most successful athletics coaches. He never weakened in his aversion to the married state.

Some 35 years after his death, Edie still lived in the same first-floor council flat she'd shared with her husband. She never remarried.

John Tarrant's Career Highlights

World Records

At 40 miles in 1966 (4 hours, 3 minutes and 28 seconds)
At 100 miles in 1969 (12 hours, 31 minutes and 10 seconds)

Race Wins

Salford Harriers 10-mile race (every year between 1958 and
    1966)
Liverpool Marathon (1960)
Isle of Wight Marathon (1960, 1961, 1962)
RRC Marathon (1962)
Liverpool-to-Blackpool 48-mile race (1965, 1967, 1968)
Exeter-to-Plymouth 44-mile race (1965, 1966, 1967, 1968, 1969)
Isle of Man 40-mile race (1965, 1966, 1967)
London-to-Brighton 54-mile race (1967, 1968)
Epsom 40-mile race (1967)
Durban City Marathon (1969, 1970)
Swaziland Marathon (1969)
Goldtop non-racial 50-mile race, South Africa (1970, 1971)
50-mile race at Alexandra Track, Portsmouth (1971)
Races at various distances in Newport, Roath, Hereford,

Oxford, Southend, Radcliffe, Halesowen, Tipton and London between 1960 and 1970

Around 51 other road races – unofficially – from 4 miles to 50 miles in South Africa